CONDUCT AND CHARACTER
Readings in Moral Theory
THIRD EDITION

Mark Timmons
University of Memphis

Wadsworth Publishing Company
I(T)P® An International Thomson Publishing Company

Belmont, CA • Albany, NY • Boston • Cincinnati • Johannesburg • London • Madrid • Melbourne
Mexico City • New York • Pacific Grove, CA • Scottsdale, AZ • Singapore • Tokyo • Toronto

Philosophy Editor: Peter Adams
Assistant Editor: Kerri Abdinoor
Editorial Assistant: Kelly Bush
Marketing Manager: Dave Garrison
Print Buyer: Stacey Weinberger
Production Coordinator: Merrill Peterson, Matrix Productions Inc.
Permissions Editor: Robert Kauser
Copy Editor: Jan McDearmon
Compositor: Eisner/Martin Typographics
Printer: Transcontinental

Printed in Canada
1 2 3 4 5 6 7 8 9 10

For more information, contact Wadsworth Publishing Company, 10 Davis Drive, Belmont, CA
94002, or electronically at http://www.thomson.com/wadsworth.html

International Thomson Publishing
    Europe
Berkshire House 168-173
High Holborn
London, WC1V 7AA, England

Thomas Nelson Australia
102 Dodds Street
South Melbourne 3205
Victoria, Australia

Nelson Canada
1120 Birchmount Road
Scarborough, Ontario
Canada M1K 5G4

International Thomson Publishing
    GmbH
Konigswinterer Strasse 418
53227 Bonn, Germany

International Thomson Editorés
Campos Eliseos 385, Piso 7
Col. Polanco
11560 México D.F. México

International Thomson Publishing Asia
60 Albert Street
#15-01 Albert Complex
Singapore 189969

International Thomson Publishing Japan
Hirakawacho Kyowa Building, 3F
2-2-1 Hirakawacho
Chiyoda-ku, Tokyo 102, Japan

International Thomson Publishing
    Southern Africa
Building 18, Constantia Park
240 Old Pretoria Road
Halfway House, 1685 South Africa

Library of Congress Cataloging-in-Publication Data
Conduct and character : readings in moral theory / [edited by]
    Mark Timmons. — 3rd ed.
      p.   cm.
    ISBN 0-534-55205-6
    1. Ethics.   I. Timmons, Mark,   .
  BJ1012.C63   1998
171—dc21   98-14695

Contents

Preface   v

Chapter 1   Introduction to Moral Theory: The Aims, Structure, and
Evaluation of Moral Theories   1
The Aims of Moral Theory   2
The Structure of a Moral Theory   6
The Evaluation of a Moral Theory   14

Chapter 2   Egoism   23
Plato / *The Myth of Gyges*   23
Ayn Rand / *The Virtue of Selfishness*   26
James Rachels / *Egoism and Moral Skepticism*   32
Peter Singer / *Egoism, Altruism, and Sociobiology*   42

Chapter 3   Ethics by Authority: The Divine Command Theory
and Relativism   50
Robert C. Mortimer / *Morality is Based on God's
Commands*   50
John Arthur / *Morality Without God*   54
Ruth Benedict / *A Defense of Ethical Relativism*   62
James Rachels / *The Challenge of Cultural Relativism*   69

Chapter 4   The Natural Law Theory   76
St. Thomas Aquinas / *Treatise on Law*   76
C. E. Harris / *The Ethics of Natural Law*   85
Philippa Foot / *The Doctrine of Double Effect*   98
Emmett Barcalow / *Problems for Natural Law Theory*   103

Chapter 5   Utilitarianism   108
Jeremy Bentham / *The Principle of Utility*   108
J. S. Mill / *In Defense of Utilitarianism*   114

Kai Nielsen / *Against Moral Conservatism*   122
John Rawls / *Two Concepts of Rules*   132
J. L. Mackie / *The Ethics of Fantasy*   142

Chapter 6   **Kantian Ethical Theory   154**
Immanuel Kant / *The Moral Law and Autonomy
    of the Will*   154
Robert L. Holmes / *Kantianism*   162
Onora O'Neill / *Kant on Treating People as Ends
    in Themselves*   175
Fred Feldman / *On Treating People as Ends in Themselves:
    A Critique of Kant*   180

Chapter 7   **The Ethics of Care   188**
Carol Gilligan / *Moral Orientation and Moral
    Development*   188
Nel Noddings / *An Ethic of Caring*   197
Claudia Card / *Caring and Evil*   209

Chapter 8   **Pluralism and Particularism   215**
Jean-Paul Sartre / *Moral Choice Without Principles*   215
W. D. Ross / *What Makes Right Acts Right?*   218
David McNaughton / *Principles or Particularism?*   224

Chapter 9   **Virtue and the Ethics of Perfectionism   233**
Aristotle / *Virtue and Character*   233
Bernard Mayo / *Virtue and Moral Theory*   244
Edmund L. Pincoffs / *A Defense of Perfectionism*   249
Robert B. Louden / *On Some Vices of Virtue Ethics*   259

Preface

This third edition of *Conduct and Character* includes a balance of classical and contemporary writings on moral theory designed to introduce students to the study of ethics. The book is organized according to type of moral theory, and is preceded by an introduction, which provides the needed conceptual framework for studying ethics.

This collection is suitable for ethics courses that focus on theory, and it can serve as a supplementary text for "applied" ethics courses. It also can serve as readings for the ethics component of an introductory philosophy course.

Prompted by comments of those who reviewed the second edition of this book, I have added a few selections from Ayn Rand, Philippa Foot, Robert L. Holmes, and Claudia Card.

Since every chapter is self-contained, they can be taught in any order one chooses. The order I have chosen reflects the fact that in my experience with teaching ethics, students often begin with questions like: "Why not just do whatever you think will benefit yourself?" "Isn't morality just a matter of what some authority like God or society says?" So the readings begin with chapters on egoism, the divine command theory and ethical relativism. The next three chapters on natural law theory, utilitarianism, and Kant's ethics represent moral theories that are standard in teaching ethics. The last three chapters on the ethics of care, pluralism and particularism, and virtue-based ethics represent, in different ways, challenges to the standard views.

I especially wish to thank Linda Sadler for her help in preparing this edition. I also wish to thank Kelly Bush and my editor, Peter Adams, for their support and help in bringing out this new edition of *Conduct and Character.*

Finally, I thank the following reviewers who made many useful suggestions for improving the third edition: Michael Gorr, Illinois State University; Ronald Koshoshek, University of Wisconsin, Eau Claire; Judith A. Little, State University of New York, Potsdam; Scott Lowe, Bloomsburg University; Mark van Roojen, University of Nebraska, Lincoln.

CHAPTER 1

Introduction to Moral Theory

THE AIMS, STRUCTURE, AND
EVALUATION OF MORAL THEORIES

> The two main concepts of ethics are those of the right and the good;
> . . . The structure of an ethical theory is, then, largely determined by
> how it defines and connects these two basic notions.
>
> —JOHN RAWLS

The area of philosophical inquiry called ethics is primarily concerned with moral theory. But what is moral theory? And why is it important? This introduction addresses these questions, which are likely to occur to individuals unfamiliar with the philosophical study of ethics. As we shall see, a moral theory is a construction intended to answer questions about right and wrong action, about what goals are worth pursuing in life, and about what sorts of things are valuable or good. In short, moral theory purports to answer very general questions about what to *do* and how to *be*.

In order to clarify the nature of moral theorizing—to explain what it is and why it is important—we must do three things. First, we must specify the main *aims* of moral theory, in order to establish what moral theorizing is intended to accomplish. Second, since the notions of the right and the good are central in moral theory, we must clarify these and related notions. Clarifying and explaining connections among such notions involve inquiring into what philosophers call the *structure* of a moral theory. Finally since philosophers have developed a number of competing moral theories, we must consider the issue of how to *evaluate* their relative merits and deficiencies.

So let us begin our study of moral theory by clarifying its central aims. We can best focus our attention on this matter if we pause to consider the sorts of situations that might lead someone to ask questions that are of interest to the moral theorist.

The Aims of Moral Theory

People normally take an interest in what to do and how to be, and they think that on occasion their decisions and actions have great significance for their own lives and for the lives of others. One source of this interest is people's recognition of certain demands that prescribe how they *should* decide and act. Such demands may have various sources: the laws enforced in society, the rules governing membership in a club, the table manners parents teach children. In addition, certain felt demands, often formulated as rules, make up what we ordinarily refer to as *moral demands*. In fact, the moral demands that a person acknowledges often strike the person as being more demanding than rules of etiquette or rules governing club membership, and perhaps even more demanding than any of society's legal rules. This is frequently the view asserted by people who engage in civil disobedience: they publicly break some law on the grounds that doing so is required by morality.

Because we take moral demands seriously, and because we often face personal decisions in which moral considerations come into play, it is particularly distressing that we should encounter so much conflict and uncertainty about what we should do and about what sort of person we should be. Consider the following cases.[1]

A. John and Linda, both in their early 40s, have been happily married for ten years and have two children, Eric, who is 8, and Amanda, who is 5. For a number of years now Linda has looked forward to resuming her career as a nutritionist, which she put on hold after she and John agreed that she would be a full-time mother until their younger child began school. In order to prevent any further pregnancies, Linda was fitted with an IUD, but now finds that she is two months pregnant. John is delighted at the news: he had all along wanted another child, but hadn't made his feelings known to Linda, because he knew how much she wanted to rejoin the workforce. Linda does not want another child and insists on an immediate abortion. To John, however, abortion is out of the question, even though both he and Linda agree that at the two-month stage the fetus is not a full-fledged person, but only a potential person. John insists that having an abortion, even in the early months of pregnancy, is morally wrong and that Linda, in putting her career ahead of her family, is being selfish. Linda strongly disagrees. She feels that she has every right to have an abortion since the pregnancy was unplanned, since she acted responsibly in trying to avoid getting pregnant, and since, anyway, the fetus is not a person. Moreover, she disagrees that she is being selfish; she has, after all, been a devoted mother to Eric and Amanda.

B. Mary and Pat, now seniors in college, have known each other since they were roommates their freshman year; although they are by no means best friends, they like each other and occasionally do things together. Pat, recently married, lives with her husband in a small apartment near campus. Mary, who shares an apartment with two other women, has been engaged to Tom for several months. Tom, also a senior, has a job lined up with an advertising agency, which he'll begin after graduating in May. Mary isn't sure about her career plans, but the couple has set an August date for getting married, by which time Tom will be settled into his new job. Recently, Pat found out through one of her friends that, a week or so ago, Tom had slept with this friend's sister, who was visiting for a weekend. The news greatly distresses Pat. In thinking about what, if anything, she should do, she finds herself caught in a dilemma. On the one hand, she knows that, if she were in Mary's place, she would want to be told about her fiancé's one-night stand, despite the hurt it would cause. Furthermore, she feels that it would be disloyal to withhold the information from her friend. On the other hand, she worries that revealing all to Mary might well result in the breakup of the couple, perhaps making things worse for everyone involved. Besides, many women in Mary's situation might prefer not to know, and anyway she doesn't want to be a meddlesome busybody. So maybe she shouldn't tell Mary after all.

C. Jim and Gail, both in their mid-30s, have been married for eight years, for the past five of which Gail has tried to become pregnant. The couple very much wants a child, and Gail has felt somehow inadequate as a result of not having been able to conceive. After years of frustration, the couple finally decided to go to a nearby fertility clinic, where tests revealed that Gail is infertile due to an obstruction of her fallopian tubes. The attending physician suggested that they consider an *in vitro* (literally, "in glass") fertilization, in which an ovum is taken from the women's body, fertilized under laboratory conditions, and then implanted into the woman's uterus where the normal process of gestation can occur. Initially, Jim and Gail were quite relieved that something could be done to help them and, of course, excited about the prospect of finally being able to have children. Their initial excitement was dampened, however, shortly after finding out about *in vitro* and other means of artificial reproduction, when they saw a television special about reproductive technology in which critics voiced certain moral objections to such medical procedures. Although neither Jim nor Gail had originally thought of it this way, the critics claimed that, since such procedures break the connection between reproduction and sexual intercourse, they are unnatural and hence morally wrong. While not entirely convinced by this argument, both Jim and Gail now wonder about the morality of what they were planning to do. Furthermore, the couple does not want to be in any way reckless or negligent in making such an important decision; and in light of the moral controversy surrounding these types of medical procedures, they feel especially hesitant in going ahead with such a procedure. At this point, they aren't sure what to do.

The sorts of phenomena illustrated in these stories—*interpersonal conflict* in the first, *intrapersonal conflict* in the second, and *uncertainty* in the third—seem to be pervasive features of everyday thought and discussion about morality. From time to time, we find that our own moral beliefs conflict with one another or with the moral beliefs of other people, and often we are simply uncertain about what moral beliefs to hold. Resolving such conflicts and uncertainty in a rational manner often requires an investigation into both *factual* and *conceptual* matters. Would Mary want to know about her fiancé's sexual encounter? This is a factual issue. What does it mean to say that an action is "unnatural"? This is a conceptual issue about the meaning of a word. But most important, reflecting on these situations naturally leads a person to ask: "What makes an action morally right or morally wrong?" "What sorts of things are worth pursuing in life?" "What sort of person should I strive to become?" Such questions are obviously relevant because, if we could determine what particular features make actions wrong, we could use this information to help dispose of the kind of uncertainty and conflict illustrated in the preceding cases.

Take, for example, the case of John and Linda. If Linda's act of having an abortion involves the various features that make an action wrong, we could conclude that it would be wrong for her to go through with the abortion. Otherwise, we could conclude that it would not be wrong for her to do so. The same holds for the other two cases. Thus, if we could answer the general moral question, "What features of an action make it right or wrong?" we could then formulate a standard or principle that would help us evaluate the morality of actions. And, with that principle in hand, we could readily assess the sorts of cases described earlier and judge whether the actions in question were right or wrong.

PRINCIPLES OF RIGHT CONDUCT AND VALUE

Some philosophers have argued that only the *consequences* of an action determine whether it is right or wrong. Their view is that an action is wrong if it might bring about worse consequences than would have resulted from some alternative action that could have been performed instead. Corresponding to this theory about what makes an action wrong is the following moral principle:

An action is forbidden if and only if its consequences are more undesirable than the consequences of some alternative action one could do instead.

Referring again to the case of John and Linda, imagine that we somehow determined that, of the various actions open to Linda, having an abortion would produce effects more undesirable than the effects of some alternative action. This information, together with the moral principle, would yield the result that her having the abortion would be morally wrong. The general idea, then, is that, if we could formulate moral principles that specify the conditions under which an action is right or wrong, we could use them to help settle cases of conflict and uncertainty in moral belief. And since the decisions we make and the actions we perform are guided by our thinking—by what we believe—such principles would be of great practical importance in helping us decide what to do.

Similar points can be made about moral questions having to do with how one should *be*—that is, with what sorts of character traits are worth developing. In each of the preceding cases, the people involved not only worry about what to do, they also worry about how to be a certain kind of person: unselfish, loyal, responsible, and so forth. Such worries raise general moral questions about the worth or value of certain character traits in particular, and of people in general. One aim of moral theory is to provide principles or standards for determining what is and what is not of value, in order to help resolve conflict and uncertainty about what sort of person to be.

Moral theorizing, then, aims at providing general principles: *principles of right conduct* that specify the conditions under which an action is right or wrong, and *principles of value* that specify under what conditions something is good or bad (has value or disvalue). But while we want to be able to use these principles in reaching decisions about what to do and how to be, we are aware that not just any principles will do. We want to make *reasonable* decisions, and we want to be *confident* of the principles we accept. Consequently, we want the principles that we believe to be *well supported*—principles that are not arbitrarily made up, but ones that can be shown to be reasonable.

The Central Aim.   Bringing together the points just discussed, we can as a first approximation express the central aim of a moral theory as follows:

CA: The central aim of moral theory is to provide well-supported principles of right conduct and value that are useful in guiding the thought and action of individuals and groups.

Although not all philosophers would agree with this characterization, it does capture a dominant view about the aim of moral theorizing. Our formulation of the central aim mentions *well-supported* and *useful* moral principles, about which more will be said later. As we shall see, evaluating a moral theory involves determining whether (and to what extent) the principles of the theory are useful and well supported. Just what is involved in such an evaluation can only be explained after we have considered more fully some of the ingredients that go into moral theories. To this subject we now turn.

The Structure of a Moral Theory

Moral theory attempts to provide moral principles for guiding and evaluating conduct and character. As we have seen, the two main sorts of moral principles are principles of right conduct, which have to do with the morality of actions, and principles of value, which are related to the morality of character. In fact, corresponding to these two sorts of principles are two main branches of moral theory: the theory of right conduct, and the theory of value.

To deepen our understanding of moral theory, we must explore the ordering and structure that theories of right conduct and theories of value tend to exhibit. Doing so requires us to focus on the meanings and interrelations of certain moral categories—categories referred to by such terms as *right, wrong, obligation, permission, good, bad, virtuous,* and *vicious.* Since moral philosophers have typically expended most of their efforts on the theory of right conduct, let's begin there.

THE THEORY OF RIGHT CONDUCT

The central aim of any theory of right conduct can be extracted from our previous statement of the central aim of moral theory:

CA': The central aim of a theory of right conduct is to provide well-supported principles of right conduct that are useful in guiding the thought and action of individuals and groups.

In order to clarify this branch of moral theory further, we need to consider three topics: the subject matter of the theory of right conduct, namely, actions; the relationships among the various moral categories involved in an assessment of the morality of actions; and the application of moral principles of right conduct in an assessment of the morality of actions.

Actions.   Sometimes, in speaking of actions, we have in mind *types* of actions: eating, running, reading, writing, studying, and so forth. An action type is something that is repeatable; both you and I can read the newspaper, and in doing so we perform actions of the same general type. However, *my* reading the newspaper at some particular time differs from *your* reading the newspaper at some particular time. Furthermore, my reading of the paper is something done by me at some particular time, and *that very act* of reading cannot be repeated by me. Of course, after I've read the Sunday *New York Times* editorial page, I can later reread that page, but this rereading is still a different reading from the first.

We can call specific, nonrepeatable doings *concrete actions.* Every concrete action—something done by a particular person at a particular time and place—is an instance of some general type. In fact, concrete actions are always instances of many different action types. Suppose that a police commissioner lies to a murder suspect in order to extract a confession. The concrete act of the police commissioner is an instance of each of the following action types: uttering words, lying, lying to a murder suspect, and breaking the law, to mention just a few.

Moral Categories of Right Action.   In providing principles of right conduct, we are interested in evaluating the morality of action types and of concrete actions. But what sort of evaluation are we concerned with here? In English, the terms *right, wrong, forbidden, obligatory, permissible, optional, ought,* and *should* are typically used in judging the morality of actions. Of course, these terms can be used for purposes other than moral evaluation, as in the statements "You took the wrong turn" and "Brown shoes should not be worn with a tuxedo." However, in moral contexts, these terms refer to particular moral categories into which an action may fall. The basic categories used in the moral evaluation of actions—both of action types and of concrete actions—are as follows:

1. The category of the *obligatory:* the category of actions that, from the point of view of morality, are mandatory; actions that one should or must do.

2. The category of the *forbidden:* the category of actions that, from the point of view of morality, it is mandatory not to do; actions that one should not or must not do.

3. The category of the *optional:* the category of actions that are neither obligatory (it is not mandatory that one do them) nor forbidden (it is not mandatory that one not do them).

Now it should be clear that some of the moral terms just mentioned refer to the same moral category as, for example, *wrong, forbidden,* and *impermissible.* Some of the terms refer to overlapping categories. For example, the category of the right or permissible overlaps the categories of the obligatory and the optional. The relationships among these categories are represented in Figure 1.

Because the three basic moral categories are of primary interest, a philosopher setting forth a theory of right conduct will typically formulate principles for determining whether an action is obligatory, optional, or forbidden. A moral principle states the conditions under which an action belongs to one of the moral categories. An example from our earlier discussion is this:

An action is forbidden if and only if its consequences are more undesirable than the consequences of some alternative action one could do instead.

In presenting a theory of right conduct, a philosopher rarely explicitly formulates separate principles, one for each moral category. Instead, philosophers usually propose a single principle. But since the notions central to the theory of right conduct are *interdefinable,* an author need only present a single principle, after which other principles can be derived by definition.

To understand this more clearly, notice that we can begin with the category of the forbidden and then express the idea that some action is obligatory in terms of what is forbidden. For example, if my failing to repay a debt by a specific date would be forbidden or wrong (because of a promise I made), then we could alternatively express this same moral evaluation by saying that my repaying the debt on time is obligatory. So, taking the notion of the forbidden as basic, we can define the notion of the obligatory as follows (letting "=df" be our sign for definition):

An action A is obligatory (=df) failing to perform A is forbidden.

FIGURE 1   Moral categories of right action.

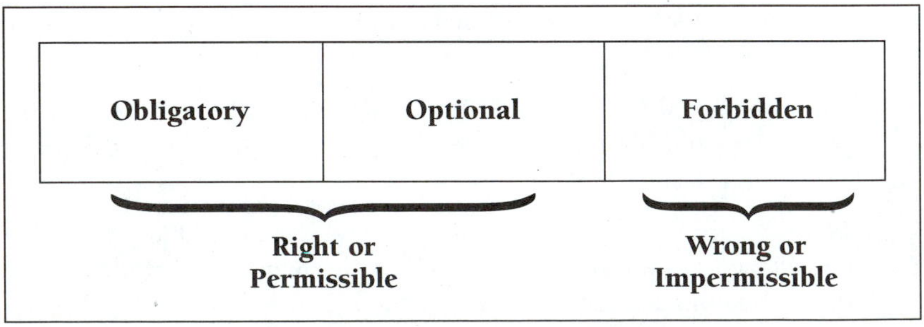

We can do the same with the notion of the optional. If my going to a film this evening is morally optional, then we may alternatively express this judgment (though somewhat awkwardly) by saying that my going to the film is not forbidden, but my not going to the film is also not forbidden (the actions of my going and failing to go are not forbidden). So, again, taking the notion of the forbidden as basic, we can define the notion of the optional as follows:

An action A is optional (=df) performing A is not forbidden and not performing A is not forbidden.

I have been taking the category of the forbidden as basic, but one could begin with the category of the obligatory and then proceed to define the notions of the forbidden and the optional.

Now suppose a philosopher proposes the following as a principle of right conduct:

An action A is forbidden if and only if performing A would conflict with human nature.

This principle tells us explicitly only what makes an action forbidden. But given what we have just learned about the interdefinability of the basic moral categories of right action, we can determine fairly easily what implications the above moral principle has when it comes to actions being either obligatory or optional. For example, putting the above definition of an obligatory action together with our moral principle, we arrive at the following principle:

An action A is obligatory if and only if failing to perform A would conflict with human nature.

The same sort of reasoning could be used to formulate a principle for determining when actions are optional. The important point here is that many philosophers present their theory of right conduct in the form of a single principle, and different authors differ in their choice of the moral category to use in enunciating that principle. But given the interdefinability of the moral categories, these differences do not matter.

Applying Moral Principles. Given that our aim in moral theorizing is to provide principles that we can then *use* to guide thought and action, it is reasonable to ask how we are supposed to use them for this purpose. Suppose that someone presents us with principles of right action—principles concerning the conditions under which actions are obligatory, optional, and forbidden. If we now want to use them, how do we proceed? From what has been said so far, the answer should be pretty obvious. We take the moral principles in question, plus any relevant factual information about the action we wish to evaluate, and derive a moral conclusion about the action. Consider, for example, how to use the following principle:

An action is forbidden if and only if it would involve treating some person merely as a means to one's own ends.

Assuming that we can determine whether or not a contemplated action involves treating a person merely as a means, we simply take the principle, plus factual information about whether or not the action would involve such treatment, and draw a conclusion about the morality of the act. The basic argument scheme, together with an example, is contained in Table 1.

Summing up, a theory of right conduct attempts to provide principles of right conduct—principles that set forth conditions under which actions (both concrete actions and action types) belong in one or another of the basic moral categories. Such principles, together with relevant factual information, can then be applied to specific situations in order to make judgments about the morality of actions performed in those situations.

THE THEORY OF VALUE

The central notions involved in the theory of value include *good, bad, virtuous, vicious, praiseworthy, blameworthy, honest,* and *courageous.* Since moral theory[2] generally involves questions about what to do and how to be, and since (as we have seen) the theory of right conduct focuses exclusively on what to do, the theory of value focuses on questions of how to be—on

TABLE I

Argument Component	Argument Scheme	Example Argument
Premise	1. Moral principle	1'. An action is forbidden if and only if it would involve treating some person merely as a means to one's own ends.
Premise	2. Relevant factual information	2'. James's act of lying to Brenda involved treating Brenda merely as a means to James's own ends.
Conclusion	3. Conclusion about the morality of an action	3'. James's act of lying to Brenda was forbidden.

questions of character. In addition, however, we also judge the value (or the goodness and badness) of physical objects, experiences, and certain states of affairs. For example, the following items are often called good: money, fast cars (physical objects); pleasure, contentment, happiness (experiences); peace on Earth, economic prosperity, health (states of affairs). We say of such things that they have nonmoral value, and we say of people (or certain features of them) that they have or fail to have moral value. Judgments of nonmoral value are important for the moral evaluation of actions and persons and so must be included in our discussion. Consequently, the theory of value divides into the theory of moral value and the theory of nonmoral value.

Nonmoral Value.   Why should we bother with issues having to do with nonmoral value when our concern is with moral theory? According to some theories of right conduct, the morality of an action depends on the nonmoral value that would result if the action were performed. For example, according to a classical version of utilitarianism, whether an action is right or wrong depends solely on the balance of good versus bad that would result from the action, were it performed. Here, talk of good and bad refers to nonmoral value. Similarly, according to the natural law theory, the morality of an action depends on whether or not it would interfere with certain valuable states of affairs such as human life, procreation, and knowledge. So according to some theories of right conduct, judging the morality of an action requires us to judge the nonmoral value brought about by actions. Thus, the study of nonmoral value must be included in our investigation of the theory of value.

To understand further the theory of nonmoral value, we must distinguish between *intrinsic* and *instrumental* value. An object, experience, or state of affairs is intrinsically valuable if it is good simply because of what it is. By contrast, something is instrumentally good if it serves as a means to what is intrinsically good.

This latest distinction between two types of value is reflected in ordinary thought. Were I to ask you what things you find valuable in life, you might respond with a list that includes such items as wealth, power, playing softball, eating pizza, and so forth. If I then were to ask you why, for example, you find money valuable, you might reply by saying that it is useful for obtaining all sorts of things you want (like a big house with a swimming pool), thus indicating that you consider money to be instrumentally good. If I were to press on and ask why you value this second array of things, you might well say that having such things is part of what makes (or would make) you happy, and that your own happiness is something you find valuable *as such* and not for any other thing it might bring about. This would indicate that you value happiness intrinsically—simply because of the sort of thing it is—and that you value the other things (money, big houses, and so forth) instrumentally—as a means to happiness.

Since whatever is instrumentally good or valuable depends for its value on what is intrinsically good or valuable, the latter notion is the more important one. Therefore, in theorizing about nonmoral value, philosophers have sought to provide principles of intrinsic value—principles specifying what is intrinsically good and intrinsically bad.

Two general views about intrinsic value have been proposed. According to *hedonism*, pleasure and pleasure alone is intrinsically good; pain and pain alone is intrinsically bad. All other things have value or disvalue only as a result of being a means to what has intrinsic value or disvalue. Opposed to this view is *nonhedonism*. A nonhedonist, while perhaps agreeing that pleasure is intrinsically good (and that pain is intrinsically bad), flatly denies that *only* such things have intrinsic value. In defending this view, some philosophers have argued that such things as life, knowledge, self-expression, friendship, and creativity (to mention a few) are intrinsically good.

Moral Value.   Moral value, as has already been noted, depends on features of people such as their motives, intentions, and character traits. The primary aim of this part of the theory of value is to identify the particular features of people that have moral value and as a result of which a person can be said to be morally good. Two sorts of views are typically discussed. According to an extreme view held by the Stoic philosophers and by the German philosopher Immanuel Kant, acting out of a sense of duty is the only thing that has moral value. A morally good person is one who is disposed to act on that sort of motive. Less exacting theories grant that other features of people have moral worth—for example, such motives as brotherly love and compassion, and such character traits as honesty and benevolence.

Summarizing, the theory of value can be divided into theories of nonmoral value and of moral value. The central aim of the theory of value generally can be put this way:

CA″: The central aim of the theory of value is to provide well-supported principles of moral and nonmoral value that are useful in guiding the thought and action of individuals and groups.

TYPES OF MORAL THEORY

Teleological and Deontological Theories.   Moral theories are typically classified according to how the theory connects the notion of right conduct to the notion of value. According to *teleological* theories (from the Greek word *telos*, which means end or goal), the good is prior to the right in the sense that what is good or valuable is defined or specified independently of what counts as right conduct; and then the notion of right conduct is defined in terms of producing good consequences. For example, according to one sort of teleological theory, *utilitarianism,* the morality of an action depends on the nature of its contribution to such valuable ends as human happiness.

By contrast, *deontological* moral theories (from the Greek work *deon,* meaning duty) reject the idea that the good is prior to the right. Rather, these theories propose that certain actions are wrong just because of the kinds of actions they are. For example, the act of killing an innocent person, even in circumstances in which doing so would produce good consequences, is nevertheless wrong according to the deontologist. The moral theories of Immanuel Kant (see Chapter 6) and W. D. Ross (see Chapter 8) are deontological.[3]

In recent years, many philosophers have preferred the terms *consequentialist* and *nonconsequentialist* to classify moral theories. A consequentialist theory is one according to which the morality of an action depends entirely on the value of its consequences; all other theories are nonconsequentialist.[4]

Monism, Pluralism, and Particularism.   In addition to distinguishing between teleological and deontological moral theories, we can also classify moral theories according to whether they are *monistic* or *pluralistic.* Monistic theories set forth a single moral principle of right conduct from which we are supposed to derive (together with relevant factual information) more specific moral rules and judgments. In essence, a monistic theory tells us that there is some single characteristic of actions in virtue of which they are right or wrong. According to utilitarianism, all wrong actions are wrong in virtue of failing to maximize utility. According to Kant's moral theory, all wrong actions are based on maxims (personal policies of action) that the agent could not will that everyone adopt. These theories are monistic.

Pluralistic theories reject the monistic idea that there is some single characteristic in virtue of which right actions are right and wrong actions are wrong, and instead insist that there is a plurality of characteristics in virtue of which an action might be right or wrong. So, for the pluralist there is no single moral principle that encapsulates the nature of right and wrong action; instead the pluralist claims that we must make do with a plurality of moral principles, no one of which is more basic than any of the others. So, for example, Ross's moral theory, according to which there are seven basic types of duties, is a version of ethical pluralism.

Recently, some moral philosophers have been skeptical of the importance and use of moral principles in our moral thinking. Their idea is that often enough we are confronted with highly complex situations calling for moral decision where moral principles and rules are not helpful. How, then, without the aid of principles are we to make reasoned moral choices? The particularist claims that trained moral perception (whereby we are sensitive to the complexity of a situation) can result in reasonable moral decisions. Because the particularist is skeptical about the importance and use of moral principles in guiding thought and behavior, one might be inclined to deny that the particularist is offering a moral theory at all. After all, as I have already explained, a moral theory is typically understood as providing a set of principles for guiding thought and behavior. The particularist breaks from this tradition. But whether or not one wishes to count the particularist as providing a moral theory is not as important as the view the particularist has about morality. The particularist outlook is represented in Chapter 8.

The Evaluation of a Moral Theory

Since theories are constructed with certain aims in mind, it makes sense to ask how well a theory helps us accomplish those aims. The better the theory does in this regard, the better or more adequate the theory is. The first part of this chapter presented a very general formulation of the central aim, CA, of a moral theory. Since a moral theory has two parts—a theory of right conduct and a theory of value—we made CA more precise by formulating the central aims of each: CA' for the theory of right conduct, and CA" for the theory of value. Now, in evaluating a moral theory, we need to examine both parts.

This section briefly explains some criteria philosophers use in trying to determine the adequacy of a moral theory in relation to its aims. Since (as was noted earlier) philosophers have devoted more attention to the theory of right conduct than to the theory of value, we will focus on criteria for evaluating it, too. In fact, however, most such criteria can easily be adapted for evaluating theories of value.

CRITERIA FOR EVALUATION

Recall the central aim of the theory of right conduct:

CA': The central aim of a theory of right conduct is to provide well-supported principles of right conduct that are useful in guiding the thought and action of individuals and groups.

Notice that, in constructing a theory of right conduct, we are not satisfied with any random set of principles; we want *well-supported* principles that will be *useful* in guiding thought and action. In judging the usefulness and support of moral principles, philosophers have employed six criteria: consistency, determinacy, livability, publicity, coherence, and external support. Let us briefly consider each of these in turn.

Consistency.   The principles of a theory of right conduct are inconsistent if they classify a particular action as belonging in one moral category (obligatory, optional, forbidden, permitted) *and* they classify the very same action as belonging in an opposing moral category. For example, if a moral principle, when applied to some situation, implies that some concrete action—say, someone killing in self-defense—is both obligatory and forbidden (hence, *not* obligatory), the principles has inconsistent implications. And, of course, any theory whose principles lead to such a result is unacceptable and must either be revised or rejected.

We should be careful here. If a theory leads to the conclusion that some *concrete* action both is and is not obligatory (for example), it is guilty of inconsistency. Similarly, if a theory leads to the conclusion that some action *type* both is and is not forbidden (for example), it is again inconsistent. But it is not inconsistent for a theory to yield the result that *in general* lying (as an action type) is forbidden and at the same time to yield the result that *in some specific case* a concrete act of telling a lie is not forbidden. There need be no inconsistency here, because from the outset the claim that lying is forbidden has been limited by the implicit modifier *in general,* implying that the normal rule may, in special circumstances, have exceptions.

The rationale for consistency relates to the aim of providing useful moral principles. Quite simply, principles asserting that some action both is and is not forbidden, or both is and is not obligatory, are useless for guiding action.[5]

Determinacy.   Part of the aim of any theory of right conduct is to provide principles that can be used by individuals and groups as guides to desirable thought and action. This aim requires that the principles of a theory be *determinate*—that they can be used to draw conclusions about the morality of actions. A moral principle yields a determinate conclusion when the principle, together with relevant factual information, implies that the action belongs in one of the moral categories. A moral principle is indeterminate when, together with relevant factual information, it fails to classify the action. Imagine, for example, a theory having the following basic principle:

An action is forbidden if and only if performing that action is degrading to humanity.

The problem with this principle is that its application in a great many cases would yield no determinate conclusion about the morality of the action under scrutiny, since talk of what is *degrading to humanity* is extremely vague. Of course, as part of an overall theory of right conduct, one might attempt to specify just what is degrading to humanity; but unless that is done, the principle (and therefore the theory, too) lacks determinacy. Obviously, the determinacy of a moral principle or a set of moral principles is a matter of degree, since a principle can be more or less determinate in its implications. The criterion of *determinacy*, then, can be put this way: for any two competing moral theories, if the principles of the first are more determinate than those of the second, then the first is (in this respect) more satisfactory than the second.

Livability.   Two other criteria, *livability* and *publicity*, also relate to the usefulness of a theory. Some philosophers have complained that the principles of right conduct of some theories are not livable or, to use J. L. Mackie's term, "practicable." Acting morally involves constraining one's behavior in ways that frequently conflict with what one would otherwise like to do. But for most people conformity to the demands of a system of morality is possible. If one were to propose principles for right conduct that required so great a personal sacrifice that most people would find themselves unable to comply with them voluntarily, then those principles would not be livable or practicable. Since part of the aim of a theory of right conduct for human beings is to set forth usable (as well as useful) principles, a moral theory is inadequate if its principles cannot serve this function.

The *livability* criterion can be expressed this way: of two competing theories, if the first is more livable than the second, then the first is (with regard to livability) the more satisfactory of the two.

Publicity.   If a set of moral principles is to help guide people's behavior, it must be taught and communicated to them. Imagine that, according to some set of moral principles, it is morally forbidden to teach or publicize the very principles in question. According to ethical egoism, for example, we are each obligated to do whatever will best serve our own self-interest. If you were an ethical egoist, then—since it would not be in your self-interest to make your theory public (because other people would react negatively toward you)—you would be morally forbidden to teach or publicize the principles of your theory. Thus it would appear that ethical egoism is at odds with the aim of providing useful moral principles—since to be useful to people, they must be transmitted to them somehow. Therefore, according to the criterion of *publicity*, if the principles of a theory of right conduct forbid the teaching of those principles, then the theory is (in this regard) inadequate.

Coherence.   The final two criteria—*coherence* and *external support*—involve types of support that philosophers have marshaled in defending various principles of right conduct. Of course, considerations of consistency, determinacy, livability, and publicity are important in determining the adequacy of a set of moral principles as a guide to choice and action. But philosophers championing moral theories have also sought to produce arguments that show the correctness of some set of moral principles. One measure of correctness involves determining whether or not the principles of a theory cohere with people's "core moral beliefs." The idea behind this criterion can be explained as follows.

We all have firm moral convictions about the morality of certain actions. For instance, we believe that the concrete action of intentionally torturing another person for fun is forbidden. Furthermore, we agree that certain types of action (lying, theft, kidnapping, murder) are generally forbidden. In fact, widespread agreement exists among people about what actions are right and wrong, although this fact is obscured because we tend to focus on cases over which there is disagreement in moral belief. Let us call the set of more-or-less agreed-upon beliefs *core moral beliefs*—beliefs about the morality of actions that we all tend to share and that we hold with some high degree of conviction.

The criterion of coherence invites us to evaluate a theory by checking the implications of its principles against our set of core moral beliefs. For example, it is safe to say that, exceptional circumstances excluded, torture is forbidden. Were the principles of a theory to imply that an act of torture is not forbidden, the principles would fail to "fit" or cohere with one of our core moral beliefs. In such a situation, we would have to choose between (1) accepting the theory and revising our belief about the action in question and (2) holding onto our belief and rejecting the theory. In many cases—since most of us, upon reflection, are more certain of our core moral beliefs than we are of some moral theory—we take the lack of coherence as a mark against the correctness of the principles. The *coherence* criterion, then, can be put this way: for any two competing theories, if the principles of the first cohere better with our core moral beliefs than do those of the second, then the first theory is (in this regard) more satisfactory than the second.

Two comments about this criterion are in order. First, the coherence criterion should not be confused with the consistency criterion described earlier. Both have to do with the implications of moral principles, but the consistency criterion does not appeal to core moral beliefs; rather, it focuses on whether a principle or set of principles is consistent in what it implies about the morality of actions.

Second, the coherence criterion helps us determine whether a moral principle is well supported by urging us to seek some kind of unity among our core moral beliefs. If we were to make a list of the various core moral beliefs we have about forbidden actions, the list would include beliefs about many different action types (such as torture, lying, fraud, and forgery) as well as beliefs about many concrete actions. Given the great variety of actions classified as forbidden, we might wonder whether any underlying principle could explain why they were forbidden and hence provide insight into the nature of forbidden action. We might be able to formulate a moral principle of the form, "An action is forbidden if and only if *C*" (where *C* stands for some feature(s) of an action), that coheres well with the core beliefs in question. Presumably the coherence would be due to the fact that the principle expresses some common feature shared by all forbidden actions—for example, interfering with human well-being. Knowing what this common feature is would help us explain why forbidden actions are forbidden and would disclose to us an underlying unity that we might not previously have recognized. The ability to explain and unify surely counts in favor of a moral principle, and for this reason coherence has some bearing on their correctness.

External Support.   The criterion of coherence might be described as having to do with the degree of *internal* support a moral principle receives—that is, support from within the realm of moral considerations. The criterion of *external support* involves the degree to which moral principles receive support from nonmoral assumptions and theories. As J. L. Mackie puts it: "Moral principles and ethical theories do not stand alone: they affect and are affected by beliefs and assumptions which belong to other fields, and not least to psychology, metaphysics, and religion."[6] Not every moral philosopher thinks that such external support is possible or even needed; some do. The issues underlying the controversy between those who do and those who don't are extremely complex and extend well beyond the scope of this introduction. But since a central part of any moral theory consists of providing reasons or support for accepting the principles of that theory, and since many theorists have sought such support by appealing to nonmoral considerations, some discussion of these matters is important.

Philosophers who claim that moral principles need no external support have typically argued that certain moral principles are correct either as a result of the *meanings* of the moral terms mentioned in the principles or because such principles are *self-evident.* For example, some supporters of the divine command theory of right conduct, according to which (roughly) the morality of an action depends on whether or not God commands it, appeal directly to the meanings of such terms as *forbidden* and *obligatory.* They claim that describing an action as forbidden merely acknowledges that God commands us not to do that action. They then argue that the principle, "An action is forbidden if and only if God commands us not to do that action," is correct in virtue of the meaning of the word *forbidden.*

Other philosophers claim that, upon reflection, anyone of reasonable intelligence can grasp the correctness of certain moral principles—that the principles are, in a sense, self-supported or self-evident. Defenders of such a view usually compare moral principles to certain mathematical principles. In Euclidean geometry, for example, such self-evident principles as, "If equals be added to equals, the wholes are equal," and "Things that coincide with one another are equal to one another," are not susceptible to proof, but even so they are accepted and are not thought to need such support. Some philosophers have claimed that basic moral principles are like such mathematical axioms and postulates in this regard: they are in no need of support from other considerations but can immediately be understood to be correct.

For reasons we need not go into here, most contemporary philosophers are suspicious of such appeals to meaning and self-evidence, and they regard external support for moral principles as both possible and important. Theorists who have attempted to find external support for certain moral principles have typically offered arguments premised on perceived facts about the nature of human beings and society. Immanuel Kant, for example, argued that only a certain principle of right conduct, which he called the "categorical imperative," was consistent with our nature as free agents. In his view, the fact that we are free—a deep-going fact about the nature of human beings—supported a certain moral principle. Similarly, J. S. Mill sought to defend a utilitarian moral principle by invoking what he deemed to be universal facts about human motivation—facts having to do with what people desire. Kant and Mill, then, attempted to offer positive external support for the moral principle each sought to defend. Other philosophers have *criticized* moral principles for *failing* to fit with certain facts about human beings. John Rawls, for example, claims that classical utilitarian moral principles conflict with the idea that each human being is, in some interesting sense, separate from all others.

We can formulate the criterion of *external support* in this way: if the principles of one theory fit better with certain nonmoral considerations than do those of another theory, then the first theory is (in this respect) more satisfactory than the second.

EVALUATING THE CRITERIA

We now have six criteria for evaluating theories of right conduct. Consistency, determinacy, livability, and publicity help us judge the *usefulness* of moral principles, and coherence and external support help us judge their *correctness*.

In closing, a few remarks about these criteria are in order. First, it is fairly obvious that the criteria of consistency, determinacy, coherence, and external support are useful for judging theories of value. For example, some people have argued that a hedonistic principle of nonmoral value, according to which states of pleasure alone are intrinsically good, fails to cohere with our firm convictions about the goodness of such things as beauty, knowledge, liberty, and self-expression. Therefore, a separate discussion of the evaluation of theories of value is not necessary for our purposes.

Second, it is worth noticing that most of the criteria are *comparative;* that is, they are formulated in terms of one theory's being more satisfactory than another in some respect.[7] This reflects the fact that, in the end, judging the overall adequacy of a moral theory is a matter of comparing it with its competitors. We select the theory that is best overall—that beats out the competition. But exactly how are we to judge the *overall* adequacy of a moral theory? Do we take the six criteria to be of equal importance, so that in comparing two theories we simply determine which one does better in relation to a majority of the criteria? If not, can we rank the criteria in order of importance, assign some numerical value to each of them, and then use a point system to decide which theory is most satisfactory?

This question about overall adequacy is important and unfortunately quite difficult. Part of the difficulty stems from the fact that not all philosophers would agree about the relative importance of the six criteria. In fact, not all philosophers would agree that the six criteria listed here are the proper ones to use. Some theorists, for example, do not think that livability and publicity are appropriate measures for determining the adequacy of a moral theory.[8] Which criteria one thinks are relevant for evaluating a moral theory and how one ranks those criteria depend largely on one's conception of the aims of moral theorizing; and philosophers do disagree about just what goals or aims moral theorizing is intended to accomplish. Such issues— issues about moral theorizing itself—constitute too broad a subject for this introduction.

There is no decisive answer to the question of how we are to judge the overall adequacy of a moral theory. Obviously, if one theory outperforms a competitor with regard to each of the criteria, it is the more satisfactory theory of the two. But in other cases, where some of the criteria favor one theory and some of them favor a competing theory, judging overall superiority is not so easy. Although this may be disconcerting to someone just beginning the study of moral theory, it might be of some comfort to know that the same sort of problem arises in connection with evaluating scientific theories. Scientists disagree about the specific aims of scientific theorizing, and consequently they have disputes over the evaluative criteria to be used in theory selection and over the relative importance of the criteria they do agree on. But such disputes do not undermine the validity or worth of scientific theorizing, and neither should they be thought to undermine the validity or worth of moral theorizing.[9]

Notes

1. The first and third cases are adapted from cases presented in John E. Thomas and Wilfrid J. Waluchow, *Well and Good* (Lewiston, N.J.: Broadview Press, 1987). Reprinted by permission of Broadview Press.

2. The terms *good* and *bad* require special comment. Ordinary speakers of English use these terms in evaluating people, actions, and states of affairs generally. However, philosophers typically restrict their application of the terms *good* and *bad* to certain features of people (motives, intentions, character traits) and to various states of affairs that might be brought about through a person's actions. Thus, were we to characterize someone's action as morally good or bad, we would be making a statement about either the motives, intentions, or character of the person responsible for the action, or about the effects of the action.

3. Two comments are in order here. First, versions of the divine command theory and ethical relativism might be either teleological or deontological theories, depending on how they are worked out. For example, one might hold that what is intrinsically valuable depends on what God approves, and then define notions belonging to the theory of right conduct in terms of what is valuable. The result would be a teleological theory. Alternatively, one might hold that right and wrong action is determined by what God commands, and then define value notions in terms of right and wrong. Or again, one might hold that right and wrong are determined by God's commands, that value is determined by what God approves, and that there is no conceptual connection between the notions of right conduct and value. The latter two ways of working out the divine command theory would be classified as deontological views.

    Second, I said earlier that moral theory is concerned with questions about what to do and how to be—that is, with questions about actions and agents. I also said that moral philosophers have characteristically focused most of their attention on questions about what to do—on the theory of right conduct. Recently, however, some moral philosophers have insisted that the emphasis on right conduct is misplaced and that questions about agents—their character— should occupy center stage in moral theorizing. As a result, one sometimes finds the teleological/deontological distinction used only in connection with moral theories whose primary focus is on right conduct. The term *virtue-based ethics* is then reserved for moral theories that make questions about agents central in moral theorizing. See, for example, "On Some Vices of Virtue Ethics," by Robert B. Louden in Chapter 9 of this book.

4. However, some philosophers use this terminology in a more restrictive way. Samuel Scheffler, for example, defines consequentialism as follows: "Consequentialism in its purest form is a moral doctrine which says that the right act in any given situation is the one that will produce the best overall outcome, as judged from an impartial standpoint which gives equal weight to the interests of everyone" (Samuel Scheffler, ed., *Consequentialism and Its Critics* (New York: Oxford University Press, 1988), p. 1). By this definition, ethical egoism (for example) is classed as a nonconsequentialist view.

5. Strictly speaking, the consistency criterion can be defended by appealing to the aim of providing well-supported principles, as well as by appealing to the aim of providing useful principles. We are interested in well-supported principles because we want some assurance that they are correct. One might well assert that, in order for any principle to be correct, it must be consistent in its implications.

6. J. L. Mackie, *Ethics: Inventing Right and Wrong* (Harmondsworth, Middlesex, England: Penguin Books, 1977), p. 203.

7. I formulated the consistency and publicity criteria in a noncomparative way simply because, in evaluating a moral theory, moral philosophers seem inclined to reject out of hand any theory that leads to inconsistency or fails to satisfy the publicity criterion.

8. See, for example, Derek Parfit, *Reasons and Persons* (New York: Oxford University Press, 1984), Ch. 1, §§9, 12, 17.

9. I wish to thank Michael Gorr for his comments on an earlier draft of this essay. In writing the essay I benefited from William Frankena's *Ethics,* 2d ed. (Englewood Cliffs, N.J.: Prentice-Hall, 1973) and Fred Feldman's *Introductory Ethics* (Englewood Cliffs, N.J.: Prentice-Hall, 1978).

CHAPTER 2

Egoism

THE MYTH OF GYGES
Plato

Plato (428–348 B.C.E.) was a student of Socrates and a teacher of Aristotle. In a famous passage from The Republic, *Glaucon (one of the characters in the dialogue) argues to Socrates that, by nature, human beings are egoists strongly inclined to pursue their own self-interest. Thus "those who practice justice do so against their will because they lack the power to do wrong." To illustrate his point, Glaucon recounts the story of Gyges.*

So, if you agree, I will do the following: I will renew the argument of Thrasymachus; I will first state what people consider the nature and origin of justice; secondly, that all who practise it do so unwillingly as being something necessary but not good; thirdly, that they have good reason to do so, for, according to what people say, the life of the unjust man is much better than that of the just. . . .

Splendid, he said, then listen while I deal with the first subject I mentioned: the nature and origin of justice.

They say that to do wrong is naturally good, to be wronged is bad, but the suffering of injury so far exceeds in badness the good of inflicting it that when men have done wrong to each other and suffered it, and have had a taste of both, those who are unable to avoid the latter and practise the former decide that it is profitable to come to an agreement with each other neither to inflict injury nor to suffer it. As a result they begin to make laws and covenants, and the law's command they call lawful and just. This, they say, is the origin and essence of justice; it stands between the best and the worst, the best being to do wrong without paying the penalty and the worst to be wronged without

From G. M. A. Grube, trans., *Plato's Republic* (Indianapolis, 1974), by permission of Hackett Publishing Co., Inc., Indianapolis and Cambridge.

the power of revenge. The just then is a mean between two extremes; it is welcomed and honoured because of men's lack of the power to do wrong. The man who has that power, the real man, would not make a compact with anyone not to inflict injury or suffer it. For him that would be madness. This then, Socrates, is, according to their argument, the nature and origin of justice.

Even those who practise justice do so against their will because they lack the power to do wrong. This we could realize very clearly if we imagined ourselves granting to both the just and the unjust the freedom to do whatever they liked. We could then follow both of them and observe where their desires led them, and we would catch the just man redhanded travelling the same road as the unjust. The reason is the desire for undue gain which every organism by nature pursues as a good, but the law forcibly sidetracks him to honour equality. The freedom I just mentioned would most easily occur if these men had the power which they say the ancestor of the Lydian Gyges possessed. The story is that he was a shepherd in the service of the ruler of Lydia. There was a violent rainstorm and an earthquake which broke open the ground and created a chasm at the place where he was tending sheep. Seeing this and marvelling, he went down into it. He saw, besides many other wonders of which we are told, a hollow bronze horse. There were window-like openings in it; he climbed through them and caught sight of a corpse which seemed of more than human stature, wearing nothing but a ring of gold on its finger. This ring the shepherd put on and came out. He arrived at the usual monthly meeting which reported to the king on the state of the flocks, wearing the ring. As he was sitting among the others he happened to twist the hoop of the ring towards himself, to the inside of his hand, and as he did this he became invisible to those sitting near him and they went on talking as if he had gone. He marvelled at this and, fingering the ring, he turned the hoop outward again and became visible. Perceiving this he tested whether the ring had this power and so it happened: if he turned the hoop inwards he became invisible, but was visible when he turned it outwards. When he realized this, he at once arranged to become one of the messengers to the king. He went, committed adultery with the king's wife, attacked the king with her help, killed him, and took over the kingdom.

Now if there were two such rings, one worn by the just man, the other by the unjust, no one, as these people think, would be so incorruptible that he would stay on the path of justice or bring himself to keep away from other people's property and not touch it, when he could with impunity take whatever he wanted from the market, go into houses and have sexual relations with anyone he wanted, kill anyone, free all those he wished from prison, and do the other things which would make him like a god among men. His actions would be in no way different from those of the other and they would both follow the same path. This, some would say, is a great proof that no one is just willingly but under compulsion, so that justice is not one's private good, since wherever either thought he could do wrong with impunity he would do so. Every man believes that injustice is much more profitable to himself than justice, and any exponent of this argument will say that he is right. The man who did not wish to do wrong with that opportunity, and did not touch other people's property, would be thought by those who knew it to be very foolish and miserable. They would praise him in public, thus deceiving one another, for fear of being wronged. So much for my second topic.

As for the choice between the lives we are discussing, we shall be able to make a correct judgment about it only if we put the most just man and the most unjust man face to face; otherwise we cannot do so. By face to face I mean this: let us grant to the unjust the fullest degree of injustice and to the just the fullest justice, each being perfect in his own pursuit. First, the unjust man will act as clever craftsmen do—a top navigator for example or physician distinguishes what his craft can do and what it cannot; the former he will undertake, the latter he will pass by, and when he slips he can put things right. So the unjust man's correct attempts at wrongdoing must remain secret; the one who is caught must be considered a poor performer, for the extreme of injustice is to have a reputation for justice, and our perfectly unjust man must be granted perfection in injustice. We must not take this from him, but we must allow that, while committing the greatest crimes, he has provided himself with the greatest reputation for justice; if he makes a slip he must be able to put it right; he must be a sufficiently persuasive speaker if some wrongdoing of his is made public; he must be able to use force, where force is needed, with the help of his courage, his strength, and the friends and wealth with which he has provided himself.

Having described such a man, let us now in our argument put beside him the just man, simple as he is and noble, who, as Aeschylus put it, does not wish to appear just but to be so. We must take away his reputation, for a reputation for justice would bring him honour and rewards, and it would then not be clear whether he is what he is for justice's sake or for the sake of rewards and honour. We must strip him of everything except justice and make him the complete opposite of the other. Though he does no wrong, he must have the greatest reputation for wrongdoing so that he may be tested for justice by not weakening under ill repute and its consequences. Let him go his incorruptible way until death with a reputation for injustice throughout his life, just though he is, so that our two men reach the extremes, one of justice, the other of injustice, and let them be judged as to which of the two is the happier. . . .

THE VIRTUE OF SELFISHNESS
Ayn Rand

Ayn Rand (1905–1982) was author of such novels as Fountainhead *(1943) and* Atlas Shrugged *(1957), as well as many books of nonfiction in which she developed a philosophical view she called "Objectivism." Her nonfiction works include* Capitalism: The Unknown Ideal *(1966),* For the New Intellectual *(1961), and* The Virtue of Selfishness *(1961). Rand is critical of what she calls "the ethics of altruism," which condemns the pursuit of one's own interests and leads, she claims, to injustice and immoral double standards. Rand's own view, which she calls "Objectivist ethics," advocates the rational pursuit of self-interest. In the second part of the article, Rand explains how her view differs from the ethics of altruism in what it implies about one's duties to others.*

I

The meaning ascribed in popular usage to the word "selfishness" is not merely wrong: it represents a devastating intellectual "package-deal," which is responsible, more than any other single factor, for the arrested moral development of mankind.

In popular usage, the word "selfishness" is a synonym of evil; the image it conjures is of a murderous brute who tramples over piles of corpses to achieve his own ends, who cares for no living being and pursues nothing but the gratification of the mindless whims of any immediate moment.

Yet the exact meaning and dictionary definition of the word "selfishness" is: *concern with one's own interests.*

This concept does *not* include a moral evaluation; it does not tell us whether concern with one's own interests is good or evil; nor does it tell us what constitutes man's actual interests. It is the task of ethics to answer such questions.

The ethics of altruism has created the image of the brute, as its answer, in order to make men accept two inhuman tenets: (a) that any concern with one's own interests is evil, regardless of what these interests might be, and (b) that the brute's activities are *in fact* to one's own interest (which altruism enjoins man to renounce for the sake of his neighbors).

For a view of the nature of altruism, its consequences and the enormity of the moral corruption it perpetrates, I shall refer you to *Atlas Shrugged*— or to any of today's newspaper headlines. What concerns us here is altruism's *default* in the field of ethical theory.

From *The Virtue of Selfishness* (Signet, 1964). Reprinted by permission of the Estate of Ayn Rand.

There are two moral questions which altruism lumps together into one "package-deal": (1) What are values? (2) Who should be the beneficiary of values? Altruism substitutes the second for the first; it evades the task of defining a code of moral values, thus leaving man, in fact, without moral guidance.

Altruism declares that any action taken for the benefit of others is good, and any action taken for one's own benefit is evil. Thus the *beneficiary* of an action is the only criterion of moral value—and so long as that beneficiary is anybody other than oneself, anything goes.

Hence the appalling immorality, the chronic injustice, the grotesque double standards, the insoluble conflicts and contradictions that have characterized human relationships and human societies throughout history, under all the variants of the altruist ethics.

Observe the indecency of what passes for moral judgments today. An industrialist who produces a fortune, and a gangster who robs a bank are regarded as equally immoral, since they both sought wealth for their own "selfish" benefit. A young man who gives up his career in order to support his parents and never rises beyond the rank of grocery clerk is regarded as morally superior to the young man who endures an excruciating struggle and achieves his personal ambition. A dictator is regarded as moral, since the unspeakable atrocities he committed were intended to benefit "the people," not himself.

Observe what this beneficiary-criterion of morality does to a man's life. The first thing he learns is that morality is his enemy; he has nothing to gain from it, he can only lose; self-inflicted loss, self-inflicted pain and the gray, debilitating pall of an incomprehensible duty is all that he can expect. He may hope that others might occasionally sacrifice themselves for his benefit, as he grudgingly sacrifices himself for theirs, but he knows that the relationship will bring mutual resentment, not pleasure—and that, morally, their pursuit of values will be like an exchange of unwanted, unchosen Christmas presents, which neither is morally permitted to buy for himself. Apart from such times as he manages to perform some act of self-sacrifice, he possesses no moral significance: morality takes no cognizance of him and has nothing to say to him for guidance in the crucial issues of his life; it is only his own personal, private, "selfish" life and, as such, it is regarded either as evil or, at best, *amoral*.

Since nature does not provide man with an automatic form of survival, since he has to support his life by his own effort, the doctrine that concern with one's own interests is evil means that man's desire to live is evil—that man's life, as such, is evil. No doctrine could be more evil than that.

Yet that is the meaning of altruism, implicit in such examples as the equation of an industrialist with a robber. There is a fundamental moral difference between a man who sees his self-interest in production and a man who sees it in robbery. The evil of a robber does *not* lie in the fact that he pursues his own interests, but in *what* he regards as to his own interest; *not* in the fact that he pursues his values, but in *what* he chose to value; not in the fact that he wants to live, but in the fact that he wants to live on a subhuman level.

If it is true that what I mean by "selfishness" is not what is meant conventionally, then *this* is one of the worst indictments of altruism: it means that altruism *permits no concept* of a self-respecting, self-supporting man— a man who supports his life by his own effort and neither sacrifices himself nor others. It means that altruism permits no view of men except as sacrificial animals and profiteers-on-sacrifice, as victims and parasites—that it permits no concept of a benevolent co-existence among men—that it permits no concept of *justice.*

If you wonder about the reasons behind the ugly mixture of cynicism and guilt in which most men spend their lives, these are the reasons: cynicism, because they neither practice nor accept the altruist morality—guilt, because they dare not reject it.

To rebel against so devastating an evil, one has to rebel against its basic premise. To redeem both man and morality, it is the concept of "*selfishness*" that one has to redeem.

The first step is to assert *man's right to a moral existence*—that is: to recognize his need of a moral code to guide the course and the fulfillment of his own life.

The reasons why man needs a moral code will tell you that the purpose of morality is to define man's proper values and interests, that *concern with his own interests* is the essence of a moral existence, and that *man must be the beneficiary of his own moral actions.*

Since all values have to be gained and/or kept by men's actions, any breach between actor and beneficiary necessitates an injustice: the sacrifice of some men to others, of the actors to the nonactors, of the moral to the immoral. Nothing could ever justify such a breach, and no one ever has.

The choice of the beneficiary of moral values is merely a preliminary or introductory issue in the field of morality. It is not a substitute for morality nor a criterion of moral value, as altruism has made it. Neither is it a moral *primary*: it has to be derived from and validated by the fundamental premises of a moral system.

The Objectivist ethics holds that the actor must always be the beneficiary of his action and that man must act for his own *rational* self-interest. But his right to do so is derived from his nature as man and from the function of moral values in human life—and, therefore, is applicable *only* in the context of a rational, objectively demonstrated and validated code of moral principles which define and determine his actual self-interest. It is not a license "to do as he pleases" and it is not applicable to the altruists' image of a "selfish" brute nor to any man motivated by irrational emotions, feelings, urges, wishes or whims.

This is said as a warning against the kind of "Nietzschean egoists" who, in fact, are a product of the altruist morality and represent the other side of the altruist coin: the men who believe that any action, regardless of its nature, is good if it is intended for one's own benefit. Just as the satisfaction of the irrational desires of others is *not* a criterion of moral values, neither is the satisfaction of one's own irrational desires. Morality is not a contest of whims.

II

On the question of why man is not a sacrificial animal and why help to others is not his moral duty, I refer you to *Atlas Shrugged*. This present discussion is concerned with the principles by which one identifies and evaluates the instances involving a man's *nonsacrificial* help to others.

"Sacrifice" is the surrender of a greater value for the sake of a lesser one or of a nonvalue. Thus, altruism gauges a man's virtue by the degree to which he surrenders, renounces or betrays his values (since help to a stranger or an enemy is regarded as more virtuous, less "selfish," than help to those one loves). The rational principle of conduct is the exact opposite: always act in accordance with the hierarchy of your values, and never sacrifice a greater value to a lesser one.

This applies to all choices, including one's actions toward other men. It requires that one possess a defined hierarchy of *rational* values (values chosen and validated by a rational standard). Without such a hierarchy, neither rational conduct nor considered value judgments nor moral choices are possible.

Love and friendship are profoundly personal, selfish values: love is an expression and assertion of self-esteem, a response to one's own values in the person of another. One gains a profoundly personal, selfish joy from the mere existence of the person one loves. It is one's own personal, selfish happiness that one seeks, earns and derives from love.

A "selfless," "disinterested" love is a contradiction in terms: it means that one is indifferent to that which one values.

Concern for the welfare of those one loves is a rational part of one's selfish interests. If a man who is passionately in love with his wife spends a fortune to cure her of a dangerous illness, it would be absurd to claim that he does it as a "sacrifice" for *her* sake, not his own, and that it makes no difference to *him*, personally and selfishly, whether she lives or dies.

Any action that a man undertakes for the benefit of those he loves is *not a sacrifice* if, in the hierarchy of his values, in the total context of the choices open to him, it achieves that which is of greatest *personal* (and rational) importance to *him*. In the above example, his wife's survival is of greater value to the husband than anything else that his money could buy, it is of greatest importance to his own happiness and, therefore, his action is *not* a sacrifice.

But suppose he let her die in order to spend his money on saving the lives of ten other women, none of whom meant anything to him—as the ethics of altruism would require. *That* would be a sacrifice. Here the difference between Objectivism and altruism can be seen most clearly: if sacrifice is the moral principle of action, then that husband *should* sacrifice his wife for the sake of ten other women. What distinguishes the wife from the ten others? Nothing but her value to the husband who has to make the choice—nothing but the fact that *his* happiness requires her survival.

The Objectivist ethics would tell him: your highest moral purpose is the achievement of your own happiness, your money is yours, use it to save your wife, *that* is your moral right and your rational, moral choice.

Consider the soul of the altruistic moralist who would be prepared to tell that husband the opposite. (And then ask yourself whether altruism is motivated by benevolence.)

The proper method of judging when or whether one should help another person is by reference to one's own rational self-interest and one's own hierarchy of values: the time, money or effort one gives or the risk one takes should be proportionate to the value of the person in relation to one's own happiness.

To illustrate this on the altruists' favorite example: the issue of saving a drowning person. If the person to be saved is a stranger, it is morally proper to save him only when the danger to one's own life is minimal; when the danger is great, it would be immoral to attempt it: only a lack of self-esteem could permit one to value one's life no higher than that of any random stranger. (And, conversely, if one is drowning, one cannot expect a stranger to risk his life for one's sake, remembering that one's life cannot be as valuable to him as his own.)

If the person to be saved is not a stranger, then the risk one should be willing to take is greater in proportion to the greatness of that person's value to oneself. If it is the man or woman one loves, then one can be willing to give one's own life to save him or her—for the selfish reason that life without the loved person could be unbearable.

Conversely, if a man is able to swim and to save his drowning wife, but becomes panicky, gives in to an unjustified, irrational fear and lets her drown, then spends his life in loneliness and misery—one would not call him "selfish"; one would condemn him morally for his treason to himself and to his own values, that is: his failure to fight for the preservation of the value crucial to his own happiness. Remember that values are that which one acts to gain and/or keep, and that one's own happiness has to be achieved by one's own effort. Since one's own happiness is the moral purpose of one's life, the man who fails to achieve it because of his own default, because of his failure to fight for it, is morally guilty.

The virtue involved in helping those one loves is not "selflessness" or "sacrifice," but *integrity*. Integrity is loyalty to one's convictions and values; it is the policy of acting in accordance with one's values, of expressing, upholding and translating them into practical reality. If a man professes to love a woman, yet his actions are indifferent, inimical or damaging to her, it is his lack of integrity that makes him immoral.

The same principle applies to relationships among friends. If one's friend is in trouble, one should act to help him by whatever nonsacrificial means are appropriate. For instance, if one's friend is starving, it is not a sacrifice, but an act of integrity to give him money for food rather than buy some insignificant gadget for oneself, because his welfare is important in the scale of one's personal values. If the gadget means more than the friend's suffering, one had no business pretending to be his friend.

The practical implementation of friendship, affection and love consists of incorporating the welfare (the *rational* welfare) of the person involved into one's own hierarchy of values, then acting accordingly.

But this is a reward which men have to earn by means of their virtues and which one cannot grant to mere acquaintances or strangers.

What, then, should one properly grant to strangers? The generalized respect and good will which one should grant to a human being in the name of the potential value he represents—until and unless he forfeits it.

A rational man does not forget that *life* is the source of all values and, as such, a common bond among living beings (as against inanimate matter), that other men are potentially able to achieve the same virtues as his own and thus be of enormous value to him. This does not mean that he regards human lives as interchangeable with his own. He recognizes the fact that his own life is the *source*, not only of all his values, but of *his capacity to value*. Therefore, the value he grants to others is only a consequence, an extension, a secondary protection of the primary value which is himself. . . .

EGOISM AND MORAL SKEPTICISM
James Rachels

James Rachels is University Professor of Philosophy at the University of Alabama and author of several books, including The End of Life: Euthanasia and Morality *(1986) and* The Elements of Moral Philosophy, *2d Ed. (1993). Rachels distinguishes between* psychological egoism *and* ethical egoism *and criticizes them both. Psychological egoism is the view that all human motivation is selfish, that the underlying motive of everything we do is the promotion of our own self-interest. Against this doctrine, Rachels argues that not only are there obvious exceptions to the psychological egoist's sweeping claim about all human motivation, but that specific arguments used to defend this view are fallacious. Ethical egoism represents a normative theory according to which everyone's most fundamental obligation is to promote his or her own self-interest. Although Rachels does not think it possible to "refute" the egoist, he argues that we can respond by explaining the considerations of care for others can be a legitimate basis of moral concern.*

I

Our ordinary thinking about morality is full of assumptions that we almost never question. We assume, for example, that we have an obligation to consider the welfare of other people when we decide what actions to perform or what rules to obey; we think that we must refrain from acting in ways harmful to others, and that we must respect their rights and interests as well as our own. We also assume that people are in fact capable of being motivated by such considerations, that is, that people are not wholly selfish and that they do sometimes act in the interests of others.

Both of these assumptions have come under attack by moral sceptics as long ago as by Glaucon in Book II of Plato's *Republic*. Glaucon recalls the legend of Gyges, a shepherd who was said to have found a magic ring in a fissure opened by an earthquake. The ring would make its wearer invisible and thus would enable him to go anywhere and do anything undetected. Gyges used the power of the ring to gain entry to the Royal Palace where he seduced the Queen, murdered the King, and subsequently seized the throne. Now Glaucon asks us to imagine that there are two such rings, one given to a man of virtue and one given to a rogue. The rogue, of course, will use his

Reprinted from *A New Introduction to Philosophy* by Steven M. Cahn (New York: Harper & Row, 1971), by permission of James Rachels.

ring unscrupulously and do anything necessary to increase his own wealth and power. He will recognize no moral constraints on his conduct, and, since the cloak of invisibility will protect him from discovery, he can do anything he pleases without fear of reprisal. So, there will be no end to the mischief he will do. But how will the so-called virtuous man behave? Glaucon suggests that he will behave no better than the rogue: "No one, it is commonly believed, would have such iron strength of mind as to stand fast in doing right or keep his hands off other men's goods, when he could go to the marketplace and fearlessly help himself to anything he wanted, enter houses and sleep with any woman he chose, set prisoners free and kill men at his pleasure, and in a word go about among men with the powers of a god. He would behave no better than the other; both would take the same course."[1] Moreover, why shouldn't he? Once he is freed from the fear of reprisal, why shouldn't a man simply do what he pleases, or what he thinks is best for himself? What reason is there for him to continue being "moral" when it is clearly not to his own advantage to do so?

These sceptical views suggested by Glaucon have come to be known as *psychological egoism* and *ethical egoism* respectively. Psychological egoism is the view that all men are selfish in everything that they do, that is, that the only motive from which anyone ever acts is self-interest. On this view, even when men are acting in ways apparently calculated to benefit others, they are actually motivated by the belief that acting in this way is to their own advantage, and if they did not believe this, they would not be doing that action. Ethical egoism is, by contrast, a normative view about how men *ought* to act. It is the view that, regardless of how men do in fact behave, they have no obligation to do anything except what is in their own interests. According to the ethical egoist, a person is always justified in doing whatever is in his own interests, regardless of the effect on others.

Clearly, if either of these views is correct, then "the moral institution of life" (to use Butler's well-turned phrase) is very different than what we normally think. The majority of mankind is grossly deceived about what is, or ought to be, the case, where morals are concerned.

II

Psychological egoism seems to fly in the face of the facts. We are tempted to say: "Of course people act unselfishly all the time. For example, Smith gives up a trip to the country, which he would have enjoyed very much, in order to stay behind and help a friend with his studies, which is a miserable way to pass the time. This is a perfectly clear case of unselfish behavior, and if the psychological egoist thinks that such cases do not occur, then he is just mistaken." Given such obvious instances of "unselfish behavior," what reply can the egoist make? There are two general arguments by which he might try to show that all actions, including those such as the one just outlined, are in fact motivated by self-interest. Let us examine these in turn:

A. The first argument goes as follows. If we describe one person's action as selfish, and another person's action as unselfish, we are overlooking the crucial fact that in both cases, assuming that the action is done voluntarily, _the agent is merely doing what he most wants to do_. If Smith stays behind to help his friend, that only shows that he wanted to help his friend more than he wanted to go to the country. And why should he be praised for his "unselfishness" when he is only doing what he most wants to do? So, since Smith is only doing what he wants to do, he cannot be said to be acting unselfishly.

This argument is so bad that it would not deserve to be taken seriously except for the fact that so many otherwise intelligent people have been taken in by it. First, the argument rests on the premise that people never voluntarily do anything except what they want to do. But this is patently false; there are at least two classes of actions that are exceptions to this generalization. One is the set of actions which we may not want to do, but which we do anyway as a means to an end which we want to achieve; for example, going to the dentist in order to stop a toothache, or going to work every day in order to be able to draw our pay at the end of the month. These cases may be regarded as consistent with the spirit of the egoist argument, however, since the ends mentioned are wanted by the agent. But the other set of actions are those which we do, not because we want to, nor even because there is an end which we want to achieve, but because we feel ourselves _under an obligation_ to do them. For example, someone may do something because he has promised to do it, and thus feels obligated, even though he does not want to do it. It is sometimes suggested that in such cases we do the action because, after all, we want to keep our promises; so, even here, we are doing what we want. However, this dodge will not work: if I have promised to do something, and if I do not want to do it, then it is simply false to say that I want to keep my promise. In such cases we feel conflict precisely because we do _not_ want to do what we feel obligated to do. It is reasonable to think that Smith's action falls roughly into this second category: he might stay behind, not because he wants to, but because he feels that his friend needs help.

But suppose we were to concede, for the sake of the argument, that all voluntary action is motivated by the agent's wants, or at least that Smith is so motivated. Even if this were granted, it would not follow that Smith is acting selfishly or from self-interest. For if Smith wants to do something that will help his friend, even when it means forgoing his own enjoyments, that is precisely what makes him _un_selfish. What else could unselfishness be, if not wanting to help others? Another way to put the same point is to say that it is the *object* of a want that determines whether it is selfish or not. The mere fact that I am acting on *my* wants does not mean that I am acting selfishly; that depends on *what it is* that I want. If I want only my own good, and care nothing for others, then I am selfish; but if I also want other people to be well-off and happy, and if I act on *that* desire, then my action is not selfish. So much for this argument.

B. The second argument for psychological egoism is this. Since so-called unselfish actions always produce a sense of self-satisfaction in the agent,[2] and since this sense of satisfaction is a pleasant state of consciousness, it follows that the point of the action is really to achieve a pleasant state of consciousness, rather than to bring about any good for others. Therefore, the action is "unselfish" only at a superficial level of analysis. Smith will feel much better with himself for having stayed to help his friend—if he had gone to the country, he would have felt terrible about it—and that is the real point of the action. According to a well-known story, this argument was once expressed by Abraham Lincoln:

Mr. Lincoln once remarked to a fellow-passenger on an old-time mud-coach that all men were prompted by selfishness in doing good. His fellow-passenger was antagonizing this position when they were passing over a corduroy bridge that spanned a slough. As they crossed this bridge they espied an old razor-backed sow on the bank making a terrible noise because her pigs had got into the slough and were in danger of drowning. As the old coach began to climb the hill, Mr. Lincoln called out, "Driver, can't you stop just a moment?" Then Mr. Lincoln jumped out, ran back and lifted the little pigs out of the mud and water and placed them on the bank. When he returned, his companion remarked: "Now, Abe, where does selfishness come in on this little episode?" "Why, bless your soul, Ed, that was the very essence of selfishness. I should have had no peace of mind all day had I gone on and left that suffering old sow worrying over those pigs. I did it to get peace of mind, don't you see?"[3]

This argument suffers from defects similar to the previous one. Why should we think that merely because someone derives satisfaction from helping others this makes him selfish? Isn't the unselfish man precisely the one who *does* derive satisfaction from helping others, while the selfish man does not? If Lincoln "got peace of mind" from rescuing the piglets, does this show him to be selfish, or, on the contrary, doesn't it show him to be compassionate and good-hearted? (If a man were truly selfish, why should it bother his conscience that *others* suffer—much less pigs?) Similarly, it is nothing more than shabby sophistry to say, because Smith takes satisfaction in helping his friend, that he is behaving selfishly. If we say this rapidly, while thinking about something else, perhaps it will sound all right; but if we speak slowly, and pay attention to what we are saying, it sounds plain silly.

Moreover, suppose we ask *why* Smith derives satisfaction from helping his friend. The answer will be, it is because Smith cares for him and wants him to succeed. If Smith did not have these concerns, then he would take no pleasure in assisting him; and these concerns, as we have already seen, are the marks of unselfishness, not selfishness. To put the point more generally: if we have a positive attitude toward the attainment of some goal, then we may derive satisfaction from attaining that goal. But the *object* of our attitude is *the attainment of that goal*; and we must want to attain the goal *before* we can find any satisfaction in it. We do not, in other words, desire some sort of "pleasurable consciousness" and then try to figure out how to achieve it; rather, we desire all sorts of different things—money, a new fishing-boat, to be a better chess player, to get a promotion in our work, etc.—and because we desire these things, we derive satisfaction from attaining them. And so, if someone desires the welfare and happiness of another person, he will derive satisfaction from that; but this does not mean that this satisfaction is the object of his desire, or that he is in any way selfish on account of it.

It is a measure of the weakness of psychological egoism that these insupportable arguments are the ones most often advanced in its favor. Why, then, should anyone ever have thought it a true view? Perhaps because of a desire for theoretical simplicity: In thinking about human conduct, it would be nice if there were some simple formula that would unite the diverse phenomena of human behavior under a single explanatory principle, just as simple formulae in physics bring together a great many apparently different phenomena. And since it is obvious that self-regard is an overwhelmingly important factor in motivation, it is only natural to wonder whether all motivation might not be explained in these terms. But the answer is clearly No; while a great many human actions are motivated entirely or in part by self-interest, only by a deliberate distortion of the facts can we say that all conduct is so motivated. This will be clear, I think, if we correct three confusions which are commonplace. The exposure of these confusions will remove the last traces of plausibility from the psychological egoist thesis.

The first is the confusion of selfishness with self-interest. The two are clearly not the same. If I see a physician when I am feeling poorly, I am acting in my own interest but no one would think of calling me "selfish" on account of it. Similarly, brushing my teeth, working hard at my job, and obeying the law are all in my self-interest but none of these are examples of selfish conduct. This is because selfish behavior is behavior that ignores the interest of others, in circumstances in which their interests ought not to be ignored. This concept has a definite evaluative flavor; to call someone "selfish" is not just to describe his action but to condemn it. Thus, you would not call me selfish for eating a normal meal in normal circumstances (although it may surely be in my self-interest); but you would call me selfish for hoarding food while others about are starving.

The second confusion is the assumption that every action is done *either* from self-interest or from other-regarding motives. Thus, the egoist concludes that if there is no such thing as genuine altruism then all actions must be done from self-interest. But this is certainly a false dichotomy. The man who continues to smoke cigarettes, even after learning about the connection between smoking and cancer, is surely not acting from self-interest, not even by his own standards—self-interest would dictate that he quit smoking—and he is not acting altruistically either. He *is*, no doubt, smoking for the pleasure of it, but all that this shows is that undisciplined pleasure-seeking and acting from self-interest are very different. This is what led Butler to remark that "The thing to be lamented is, not that men have so great regard to their own good or interest in the present world, for they have not enough."[4]

The last two paragraphs show (*a*) that it is false that all actions are selfish, and (*b*) that it is false that all actions are done out of self-interest. And it should be noted that these two points can be made, and were, without any appeal to putative examples of altruism.

The third confusion is the common but false assumption that a concern for one's own welfare is incompatible with any genuine concern for the welfare of others. Thus, since it is obvious that everyone (or very nearly everyone) does desire his own well-being, it might be thought that no one can really be concerned with others. But again, this is false. There is no inconsistency in desiring that everyone, including oneself *and* others, be well-off and happy. To be sure, it may happen on occasion that our own interests conflict with the interests of others, and in these cases we will have to make hard choices. But even in these cases we might sometimes opt for the interests of others, especially when the others involved are our family or friends. But more importantly, not all cases are like this: sometimes we are able to promote the welfare of others when our own interests are not involved at all. In these cases not even the strongest self-regard need prevent us from acting considerately toward others.

Once these confusions are cleared away, it seems to me obvious enough that there is no reason whatever to accept psychological egoism. On the contrary, if we simply observe people's behavior with an open mind, we may find that a great deal of it is motivated by self-regard, but by no means all of it; and that there is no reason to deny that "the moral institution of life" can include a place for the virtue of beneficence.[5]

III

The ethical egoist would say at this point, "Of course it is possible for people to act altruistically, and perhaps many people do act that way—but there is no reason why they *should* do so. A person is under no obligation to do anything except what is in his own interests.[6] This is really quite a radical doctrine. Suppose I have an urge to set fire to some public building (say, a department store) just for the fascination of watching the spectacular blaze: according to this view, the fact that several people might be burned to death provides no reason whatever why I should not do it. After all, this only concerns *their* welfare, not my own, and according to the ethical egoist the only person I need think of is myself.

Some might deny that ethical egoism has any such monstrous consequences. They would point out that it is really to my own advantage not to set the fire—for, if I do that I may be caught and put into prison (unlike Gyges, I have no magic ring for protection). Moreover, even if I could avoid being caught it is still to my advantage to respect the rights and interests of others, for it is to my advantage to live in a society in which people's rights and interests are respected. Only in such a society can I live a happy and secure life; so, in acting kindly toward others, I would merely be doing my part to create and maintain the sort of society which it is to my advantage to have.[7] Therefore, it is said, the egoist would not be such a bad man; he would be as kindly and considerate as anyone else, because he would see that it is to his own advantage to be kindly and considerate.

This is a seductive line of thought, but it seems to me mistaken. Certainly it is to everyone's advantage (including the egoist's) to preserve a stable society where people's interests are generally protected. But there is no reason for the egoist to think that merely because *he* will not honor the rules of the social game, decent society will collapse. For the vast majority of people are not egoists, and there is no reason to think that they will be converted by his example—especially if he is discreet and does not unduly flaunt his style of life. What this line of reasoning shows is not that the egoist himself must act benevolently, but that he must encourage *others* to do so. He must take care to conceal from public view his own self-centered method of decision-making, and urge others to act on precepts very different from those on which he is willing to act.

The rational egoist, then, cannot advocate that egoism be universally adopted by everyone. For he wants a world in which his own interests are maximized; and if other people adopted the egoistic policy of pursuing their own interests to the exclusion of his interests, as he pursues his interests to the exclusion of theirs, then such a world would be impossible. So he himself will be an egoist, but he will want others to be altruists.

This brings us to what is perhaps the most popular "refutation" of ethical egoism current among philosophical writers—the argument that ethical egoism is at bottom inconsistent because it cannot be universalized.[8] The argument goes like this:

To say that any action or policy of action is *right* (or that it *ought* to be adopted) entails that it is right for *anyone* in the same sort of circumstances.

I cannot, for example, say that it is right for me to lie to you, and yet object when you lie to me (provided, of course, that the circumstances are the same). I cannot hold that it is all right for me to drink your beer and then complain when you drink mine. This is just the requirement that we be consistent in our evaluations: it is a requirement of logic. Now it is said that ethical egoism cannot meet this requirement because, as we have already seen, the egoist would not want others to act in the same way that he acts. Moreover, suppose he *did* advocate the universal adoption of egoistic policies: he would be saying to Peter, "You ought to pursue your own interests even if it means destroying Paul"; and he would be saying to Paul, "You ought to pursue your own interests even if it means destroying Peter." The attitudes expressed in these two recommendations seem clearly inconsistent—he is urging the advancement of Peter's interests at one moment, and countenancing their defeat at the next. Therefore, the argument goes, there is no way to maintain the doctrine of ethical egoism as a consistent view about how we ought to act. We will fall into inconsistency whenever we try.

What are we to make of this argument? Are we to conclude that ethical egoism has been refuted? Such a conclusion, I think, would be unwarranted; for I think that we can show, contrary to this argument, how ethical egoism can be maintained consistently. We need only to interpret the egoist's position in a sympathetic way: we should say that he has in mind a certain kind of world which he would prefer over all others; it would be a world in which his own interests were maximized, regardless of the effects on other people. The egoist's primary policy of action, then, would be to act in such a way as to bring about, as nearly as possible, this sort of world. Regardless of however morally reprehensible we might find it, there is nothing *inconsistent* in someone's adopting this as his ideal and acting in a way calculated to bring it about. And if someone did adopt this as his ideal, then he would not advocate universal egoism; as we have already seen, he would want other people to be altruists. So, if he advocates any principles of conduct for the general public, they will be altruistic principles. This would not be inconsistent; on the contrary, it would be perfectly consistent with his goal of creating a world in which his own interests are maximized. To be sure, he would have to be deceitful; in order to secure the good will of others, and a favorable hearing for his exhortations to altruism, he would have to pretend that he was himself prepared to accept altruistic principles. But again, that would be all right; from the egoist's point of view, this would merely be a matter of adopting the necessary means to the achievement of his goal—and while we might not approve of this, there is nothing inconsistent about it. Again, it might be said: "He advocates one thing, but does another. Surely *that's* inconsistent." But it is not; for what he advocates and what he does are both calculated as means to an end (the *same* end, we might note); and as such, he is doing what is rationally required in each case. Therefore, contrary to the previous argument, there is nothing inconsistent in the ethical egoist's view. He cannot be refuted by the claim that he contradicts himself.

Is there, then, no way to refute the ethical egoist? If by "refute" we mean show that he has made some *logical* error, the answer is that there is not. However, there is something more that can be said. The egoist challenge to our ordinary moral convictions amounts to a demand for an explanation of why we should adopt certain policies of action, namely policies in which the good of others is given importance. We can give an answer to this demand, albeit an indirect one. The reason one ought not to do actions that would hurt other people is: other people would be hurt. The reason one ought to do actions that would benefit other people is: other people would be benefited. This may at first seem like a piece of philosophical sleight-of-hand, but it is not. The point is that the welfare of human beings is something that most of us value *for its own sake,* and not merely for the sake of something else. Therefore, when *further* reasons are demanded for valuing the welfare of human beings, we cannot point to anything further to satisfy this demand. It is not that we have no reason for pursuing these policies, but that our reason is that these policies are for the good of human beings.

So: if we are asked "Why shouldn't I set fire to this department store?" one answer would be "Because if you do, people may be burned to death." This is a complete, sufficient reason which does not require qualification or supplementation of any sort. If someone seriously wants to know why this action shouldn't be done, that's the reason. If we are pressed further and asked the sceptical question "But why shouldn't I do actions that will harm others?" we may not know what to say—but this is because the questioner has included in his question the very answer we would like to give: "Why shouldn't you do actions that will harm others? Because, doing those actions would harm others."

The egoist, no doubt, will not be happy with this. He will protest that *we* may accept this as a reason, but *he* does not. And here the argument stops: there are limits to what can be accomplished by argument, and if the egoist really doesn't care about other people—if he honestly doesn't care whether they are helped or hurt by his actions—then we have reached those limits. If we want to persuade him to act decently toward his fellow humans, we will have to make our appeal to such other attitudes as he does possess, by threats, bribes, or other cajolery. That is all that we can do.

Though some may find this situation distressing (we would like to be able to show that the egoist is just *wrong*), it holds no embarrassment for common morality. What we have come up against is simply a fundamental requirement of rational action, namely, that the existence of reasons for action always depends on the prior existence of certain attitudes in the agent. For example, the fact that a certain course of action would make the agent a lot of money is a reason for doing it only if the agent wants to make money; the fact that practicing at chess makes one a better player is a reason for practicing only if one wants to be a better player; and so on. Similarly, the fact that a certain action would help the agent is a reason for doing the action only if the agent cares about his own welfare, and the fact that an action would help others is a reason for doing it only if the agent cares about others. In this respect ethical egoism and what we might call ethical altruism are in exactly the same fix: both require that the agent *care* about himself, or about other people, before they can get started.

So a nonegoist will accept "It would harm another person" as a reason not to do an action simply because he cares about what happens to that other person. When the egoist says that he does *not* accept that as a reason, he is saying something quite extraordinary. He is saying that he has no affection for friends or family, that he never feels pity or compassion, that he is the sort of person who can look on scenes of human misery with complete indifference, so long as he is not the one suffering. Genuine egoists, people who really don't care at all about anyone other than themselves, are rare. It is important to keep this in mind when thinking about ethical egoism; it is easy to forget just how fundamental to human psychological makeup the feeling of sympathy is. Indeed, a man without any sympathy at all would scarcely be recognizable as a man; and that is what makes ethical egoism such a disturbing doctrine in the first place.

IV

There are, of course, many different ways in which the sceptic might challenge the assumptions underlying our moral practice. In this essay I have discussed only two of them, the two put forward by Glaucon in the passage that I cited from Plato's *Republic*. It is important that the assumptions underlying our moral practice should not be confused with particular judgments made within that practice. To defend one is not to defend the other. We may assume—quite properly, if my analysis has been correct—that the virtue of beneficence does, and indeed should, occupy an important place in "the moral institution of life"; and yet we may make constant and miserable errors when it comes to judging when and in what ways this virtue is to be exercised. Even worse, we may often be able to make accurate moral judgments, and know what we ought to do, but not do it. For these ills, philosophy alone is not the cure.

Notes

1. *The Republic of Plato,* translated by F. M. Cornford (Oxford, 1941), p. 45.
2. Or, as it is sometimes said, "It gives him a clear conscience," or "He couldn't sleep at night if he had done otherwise," or "He would have been ashamed of himself for not doing it," and so on.
3. Frank C. Sharp, *Ethics* (New York, 1928), pp. 74–75. Quoted from the Springfield (Ill.) *Monitor* in the *Outlook,* vol. 56, p. 1059.
4. *The Works of Joseph Butler,* edited by W. E. Gladstone (Oxford, 1896), vol. II, p. 26. It should be noted that most of the points I am making against psychological egoism were first made by Butler. Butler made all the important points; all that is left for us is to remember them.
5. The capacity for altruistic behavior is not unique to human beings. Some interesting experiments with rhesus monkeys have shown that these animals will refrain from operating a device for securing food if this causes other animals to suffer pain. See Masserman, Wechkin, and Terris, "'Altruistic' Behavior in Rhesus Monkeys," *The American Journal of Psychiatry,* vol. 121 (1964), 584–585.
6. I take this to be the view of Ayn Rand, in so far as I understand her confusing doctrine.
7. Cf. Thomas Hobbes, *Leviathan* (London, 1651), Ch. 17.
8. See, for example, Brian Medlin, "Ultimate Principles and Ethical Egoism," *Australasian Journal of Philosophy,* vol. 35 (1957), 111–118; and D. H. Monro, *Empiricism and Ethics* (Cambridge, 1967), Ch. 16.

EGOISM, ALTRUISM, AND SOCIOBIOLOGY
Peter Singer

Peter Singer is Professor of Philosophy and Director of the Centre for Human Bioethics at Monash University, Australia. In addition to being editor of A Companion to Ethics *(1991), he is author of many books, including* Animal Liberation *(1975),* Rethinking Life and Death *(1994), and* How Are We to Live? *(1995). Singer appeals to recent work in sociobiology to argue that there are good reasons for supposing that evolution favors genuinely altruistic behavior, and he illustrates this point by reference to a puzzle called the "Prisoner's Dilemma."*

Every human society has some code of behavior for its members. This is true of nomads and city-dwellers, of hunter-gatherers and of industrial civilizations, of Eskimos in Greenland and Bushmen in Africa, of a tribe of twenty Australian aborigines and of the billion people that make up China. Ethics is part of the natural human condition.

That ethics is natural to human beings has been denied. More than three hundred years ago Thomas Hobbes wrote in his *Leviathan:*

During the time men live without a common Power to keep them all in awe they are in that condition called War; and such a war, as is of every man against every other man. . . . To this war of every man against every man, this also is consequent; that nothing can be Unjust. The notions of Right and Wrong, Justice and Injustice have there no place.

Hobbes's guess about human life in the state of nature was no better than Rousseau's idea that we were naturally solitary. It is not the force of the state that persuades us to act ethically. The state, or some other form of social power, may reinforce our tendency to observe an ethical code, but that tendency exists before the social power is established. The primary role Hobbes gave to the state was always suspect on philosophical grounds, for it invites the question why, having agreed to set up a power to enforce the law, human beings would trust each other long enough to make the agreement work. Now we also have biological grounds for rejecting Hobbes's theory.

Occasionally there are claims that a group of human beings totally lacking any ethical code has been discovered. The Ik, a northern Uganda tribe described by Colin Turnbull in *The Mountain People,* is the most recent example. The biologist Garrett Hardin has even claimed that the Ik are an incarnation of Hobbes's natural man, living in a state of war of every Ik against every other Ik. The Ik certainly were, at the time of Turnbull's visit, a most unfortunate people. Originally nomadic hunters and gatherers, their hunting ground was turned into a national park. They were forced to become farmers in an arid mountain area in which they had difficulty supporting themselves; a prolonged drought and consequent famine was the final blow. As a result, according to Turnbull, Ik society collapsed. Parents turned their three-year-old children out to fend for themselves, the strong took food from the mouths of the weak, the sufferings of the old and sick were a source of laughter, and anyone who helped another was considered a fool. The Ik, Turnbull says, abandoned family, cooperation, social life, love, religion, and everything else except the pursuit of self-interest. They teach us that our much vaunted human values are, in Turnbull's words, "luxuries that can be dispensed with."

The idea of a people without human values holds a certain repugnant fascination. *The Mountain People* achieved a rare degree of fame for a work of anthropology. It was reviewed in *Life*, talked about over cocktails, and turned into a stage play by the noted director Peter Brook. It was also severely criticized by some anthropologists. They pointed out the subjective nature of many of Turnbull's observations, the vagueness of his data, contradictions between *The Mountain People* and an earlier report Turnbull had published (in which he described the Ik as fun-loving, helpful and "great family people"), and contradictions within *The Mountain People* itself. In reply Turnbull admitted that "the data in the book are inadequate for anything approaching proof" and recognized the existence of evidence pointing toward a different picture of Ik life.

Even if we take the picture of Ik life in *The Mountain People* at face value, there is still ample evidence that Ik society has an ethical code. Turnbull refers to disputes over the theft of berries which reveal that, although stealing takes place, the Ik retain notions of private property and the wrongness of theft. Turnbull mentions the Ik's attachment to the mountains and the reverence with which they speak of Mount Morungole, which seems to be a sacred place for them. He observes that the Ik like to sit together in groups and insist on living together in villages. He describes a code that has to be followed by an Ik husband who intends to beat his wife, a code that gives the wife a chance to leave first. He reports that the obligations of a pact of mutual assistance known as *nyot* are invariably carried out. He tells us that there is a strict prohibition on Ik killing each other or even drawing blood. The Ik may let each other starve, but they apparently do not think of other Ik as they think of any non-human animals they find—that is, as potential food. A normal well-fed reader will take the prohibition of cannibalism for granted, but under the circumstances in which the Ik were living human flesh would have been a great boost to the diets of stronger Ik; that they refrain from this source of food is an example of the continuing strength of their ethical code despite the crumbling of almost everything that had made their lives worth living.

Under extreme conditions like those of the Ik during famine, the individual's need to survive becomes so dominant that it may seen as if all other values have ceased to matter, when in fact they continue to exercise an influence. If any conditions can be worse than those the Ik endured they were the conditions of the inmates of Soviet labor camps and, more horrible still, the Nazi death camps. Here too, it has been said that "the doomed devoured each other," that "all trace of human solidarity vanished," that all values were erased and every man fought for himself. Nor should it be surprising if this were so, for the camps deliberately and systematically dehumanized their inmates, stripping them naked, shaving their hair, assigning them numbers, forcing them to soil their clothing with excrement, letting them know in a hundred ways that their lives were of no account, beating them, torturing them, and starving them. The astonishing thing is that despite all this, life in the camps was *not* every man for himself. Again and again, survivors' reports show that prisoners helped each other. In Auschwitz prisoners risked their lives to pick up strangers who had fallen in the snow at roll call; they built a radio and disseminated news to keep up morale; though they were starving, they shared food with those still more needy. There were also ethical rules in the camps. Though theft occurred, stealing from one's fellow prisoners was strongly condemned and those caught stealing were punished by the prisoners themselves. As Terrence Des Pres observes in *The Survivor,* a book based on reports by those who survived the camps: "The assumption that there was no moral or social order in the camps is wrong. . . . Through innumerable small acts of humanness, most of them covert but everywhere in evidence, survivors were able to maintain societal structures workable enough to keep themselves alive and morally sane." . . .

Early in the previous chapter, we accepted a definition of altruism in terms of behavior—"altruistic behavior is behavior which benefits others at some cost to oneself"—without inquiring into motivation. Now we must note that when people talk of altruism they are normally thinking not simply of behavior but also of motivation. To be faithful to the generally accepted meaning of the term, we should redefine altruistic behavior as behavior which benefits others at some initial cost to oneself, and is motivated by the desire to benefit others. To what extent human beings are altruistically motivated is a question I shall consider in a later chapter. Meanwhile we should note that according to the common meaning of the term, which I shall use from now on, an act may in fact benefit me in the long run, and yet—perhaps because I didn't foresee that the act would redound to my advantage—still be altruistic because my intention was to benefit someone else.

Robert Trivers has offered a sociobiological explanation for our moral preference for altruistic motivation. People who are altruistically motivated will make more reliable partners than those motivated by self-interest. After all, one day the calculations of self-interest may turn out differently. Looking at the shabby clothes I have left on the beach, a self-interested potential rescuer may decide that the prospects of a sizable reward are dim. In an exchange in which cheating is difficult to detect, a self-interested partner is more likely to cheat than a partner with real concern for my welfare. Evolution would therefore favor people who could distinguish self-interested from altruistic motivation in others, and then select only the altruistic as beneficiaries of their gifts or services.

Psychologists have experimented with the circumstances that lead people to behave altruistically, and their results show that we are more ready to act altruistically toward those we regard as genuinely altruistic than to those we think have ulterior motives for their apparently altruistic acts. As one review of the literature concludes: "When the legitimacy of the apparent altruism is questioned, reciprocity is less likely to prevail." Another experiment proved something most of us know from our own attitudes: we find genuine altruism a more attractive character trait than a pretense of altruism covering self-interested motives.

Here an intriguing and important point emerges; if there are advantages in being a partner in a reciprocal exchange, and if one is more likely to be selected as a partner if one has genuine concern for others, there is an evolutionary advantage in having genuine concern for others. (This assumes, of course, that potential partners can see through a pretense of altruism by those who are really self-interested—something that is not always easy, but which we spend a lot of time trying to do, and often can do. Evolutionary theory would predict that we would get better at detecting pretense, but at the same time the performance of the pretenders would improve, so the task would never become a simple one.)

This conclusion is highly significant for understanding ethics, because it cuts across the tendency of sociobiological reasoning to explain behavior in terms of self-interest or the interests of one's kin. Properly understood, sociobiology does not imply that behavior is actually motivated by the desire to further one's own interests or those of one's kin. Sociobiology says nothing about motivation, for it remains on the level of the objective consequences of types of behavior. That a piece of behavior in fact benefits oneself does not mean that the behavior is motivated by self-interest, for one might be quite unaware of the benefits to oneself the behavior will bring. Nevertheless, it is a common assumption that sociobiology implies that we are motivated by self-interest, not by genuine altruism. This assumption gains credibility from some of the things sociobiologists write. We can now see that sociobiology itself can explain the existence of genuinely altruistic motivation. The implications of this I shall take up in a later chapter, but it may be useful to make the underlying mechanism more explicit. This can be done by reference to a puzzle known as the Prisoner's Dilemma.

In the cells of the Ruritanian secret police are two political prisoners. The police are trying to persuade them to confess to membership in an illegal opposition party. The prisoners know that if neither of them confesses, the police will not be able to make the charge stick, but they will be interrogated in the cells for another three months before the police give up and let them go. If one of them confesses, implicating the other, the one who confesses will be released immediately but the other will be sentenced to eight years in jail. If both of them confess, their helpfulness will be taken into account and they will get five years in jail. Since the prisoners are interrogated separately, neither can know if the other has confessed or not.

The dilemma is, of course, whether to confess. The point of the story is that circumstances have been so arranged that if either prisoner reasons from the point of view of self-interest, she will find it to her advantage to confess; whereas taking the interests of the two prisoners together, it is obviously in their interests if neither confesses. Thus the first prisoner's self-interested calculations go like this: "If the other prisoner confesses, it will be better for me if I have also confessed, for then I will get five years instead of eight; and if the other prisoner does not confess, it will still be better for me if I confess, for then I will be released immediately, instead of being interrogated for another three months. Since we are interrogated separately, whether the other prisoner confesses has nothing to do with whether I confess—our choices are entirely independent of each other. So whatever happens, it will be better for me if I confess." The second prisoner's self-interested reasoning will, of course, follow exactly the same route as the first prisoner's, and will come to the same conclusion. As a result, both prisoners, if self-interested, will confess, and both will spend the next five years in prison. There was a way for them both to be out in three months, but because they were locked into purely self-interested calculations, they could not take that route.

What would have to be changed in our assumptions about the prisoners to make it rational for them both to refuse to confess? One way of achieving this would be for the prisoners to make an agreement that would bind them both to silence. But how could each prisoner be confident that the other would keep the agreement? If one prisoner breaks the agreement, the other will be in prison for a long time, unable to punish the cheater in any way. So each prisoner will reason: "If the other one breaks the agreement, it will be better for me if I break it too; and if the other one keeps the agreement, I will still be better off if I break it. So I will break the agreement."

Without sanctions to back it up, an agreement is unable to bring two self-interested individuals to the outcome that is best for both of them, taking their interests together. What has to be changed to reach this result is the assumption that the prisoners are motivated by self-interest alone. If, for instance, they are altruistic to the extent of caring as much for the interests of their fellow prisoner as they care for their own interests, they will reason thus: "If the other prisoner does not confess it will be better for us both if I do not confess, for then between us we will be in prison for a total of six months, whereas if I do confess the total will be eight years; and if the other prisoner does confess it will still be better if I do not confess, for then the total served will be eight years, instead of ten. So whatever happens, taking our interests together, it will be better if I don't confess." A pair of altruistic prisoners will therefore come out of this situation better than a pair of self-interested prisoners, *even from the point of view of self-interest.*

Altruistic motivation is not the only way to achieve a happier solution. Another possibility is that the prisoners are conscientious, regarding it as morally wrong to inform on a fellow prisoner; or if they are able to make an agreement, they might believe they have a duty to keep their promises. In either case, each will be able to rely on the other not confessing and they will be free in three months.

The Prisoner's Dilemma shows that, paradoxical as it may seem, we will sometimes be better off if we are not self-interested. Two or more people motivated by self-interest alone may not be able to promote their interests as well as they could if they were more altruistic or more conscientious.

The Prisoner's Dilemma explains why there could be an evolutionary advantage in being genuinely altruistic instead of making reciprocal exchanges on the basis of calculated self-interest. Prisons and confessions may not have played a substantial role in early human evolution, but other forms of cooperations surely did. Suppose two early humans are attacked by a sabertooth cat. If both flee, one will be picked off by the cat; if both stand their ground, there is a very good chance that they can fight the cat off; if one flees and the other stands and fights, the fugitive will escape and the fighter will be killed. Here the odds are sufficiently like those in the Prisoner's Dilemma to produce a similar result. From a self-interested point of view, if your partner flees your chances of survival are better if you flee too (you have a 50 percent chance rather than none at all) and if your partner stands and fights you still do better to run (you are sure of escape if you flee, whereas it is only probable, not certain, that together you and your partner can overcome the cat). So two purely self-interested early humans would flee, and one of them would die. Two early humans who cared for each other, however, would stand and fight, and most likely neither would die. Let us say, just to be able to put a figure on it, that two humans cooperating can defeat a sabertooth cat on nine out of every ten occasions and on the tenth occasion the cat kills one of them. Let us also say that when a sabertooth cat pursues two fleeing humans it always catches one of them, and which one it catches is entirely random, since differences in human running speed are negligible in comparison to the speed of the cat. Then one of a pair of purely self-interested humans would not, on average, last more than a single encounter with a sabertooth cat; but one of a pair of altruistic humans would on average survive ten such encounters.

If situations analogous to this imaginary sabertooth cat attack were common, early humans would do better hunting with altruistic comrades than

with self-interested partners. Of course, an egoist who could find an altruist to go hunting with him would do better still; but altruists who could not
detect—and refuse to assist—purely self-interested partners would be
selected against. Evolution would therefore favor those who are genuinely
altruistic to other genuine altruists, but are not altruistic to those who seek
to take advantage of their altruism. We can add, again, that the same goal
could be achieved if, instead of being altruistic, early humans were moved
by something like a sense that it is wrong to desert a partner in the face
of danger.

CHAPTER 3

Ethics by Authority

THE DIVINE COMMAND THEORY
AND RELATIVISM

MORALITY IS BASED ON GOD'S COMMANDS
Robert C. Mortimer

Robert C. Mortimer, Anglican Bishop of Exeter, is author of the influential Christian Ethics (1950). In the following selection taken from that book, Mortimer defends what is known as the divine command theory of ethics, according to which the rightness or wrongness of an action depends on God's commands. According to Mortimer, then, God's commands set forth a universally valid set of basic moral principles that are revealed to human beings in the Bible.

T he Christian religion is essentially a revelation of the nature of God. It tells men that God has done certain things. And from the nature of these actions we can infer what God is like. In the second place the Christian religion tells men what is the will of God for them, how they must live if they would please God. This second message is clearly dependent on the first. The kind of conduct which will please God depends on the kind of person God is. This is what is meant by saying that belief influences conduct. The once popular view that it does not matter what a man believes so long as he acts decently is nonsense. Because what he considers decent depends on what he believes. If you are a Nazi you will behave as a Nazi, if you are a Communist you will behave as a Communist, and if you are a Christian you will behave as a Christian. At least, in general; for a man does not always do what he

From *Christian Ethics* by Robert C. Mortimer, Hutchinson's University Library, 1950.

knows he ought to do, and he does not always recognize clearly the implications for conduct of his belief. But in general, our conduct, or at least our notions of what constitutes right conduct, are shaped by our beliefs. The man who knows about God—has a right faith—knows or may learn what conduct is pleasing to God and therefore right.

The Christian religion has a clear revelation of the nature of God, and by means of it instructs and enlightens the consciences of men. The first foundation is the doctrine of God the Creator. God made us and all the world. Because of that He has an absolute claim on our obedience. We do not exist in our own right, but only as His creatures, who ought therefore to do and be what He desires. We do not possess anything in the world, absolutely, not even our own bodies; we hold things in trust for God, who created them, and are bound, therefore, to use them only as He intends that they should be used. This is the doctrine contained in the first chapters of Genesis. God created man and placed him in the Garden of Eden with all the animals and the fruits of the earth at his disposal, subject to God's own law. "Of the fruit of the tree of the knowledge of good and evil thou shall not eat." Man's ownership and use of the material world is not absolute, but subject to the law of God.

From the doctrine of God as the Creator and source of all that is, it follows that a thing is not right simply because we think it is, still less because it seems to be expedient. It is right because God commands it. This means that there is a real distinction between right and wrong which is independent of what we happen to think. It is rooted in the nature and will of God. When a man's conscience tells him that a thing is right, which is in fact what God wills, his conscience is true and its judgment correct; when a man's conscience tells him a thing is right which is, in fact, contrary to God's will, his conscience is false and telling him a lie. It is a lamentably common experience for a man's conscience to play him false, so that in all good faith he does what is wrong, thinking it to be right. "Yea the time cometh that whoever killeth you will think that he doeth God service." But this does not mean that whatever you think is right is right. It means that even conscience can be wrong: that the light which is in you can be darkness. . . .

The pattern of conduct which God has laid down for man is the same for all men. It is universally valid. When we speak of Christian ethics we do not mean that there is one law for Christians and another for non-Christians. We mean the Christian understanding and statement of the one common law for all men. Unbelievers also know or can be persuaded of that law or of part of it: Christians have a fuller and better knowledge. The reason for this is that Christians have by revelation a fuller and truer knowledge both of the nature of God Himself and of the nature of man.

The Revelation in the Bible plays a three-fold part. In the first place it recalls and restates in simple and even violent language fundamental moral judgments which men are always in danger of forgetting or explaining away. It thus provides a norm and standard of human behavior in the broadest and simplest outline. Man's duty to worship God and love the truth, to respect lawful authority, to refrain from violence and robbery, to live in chastity, to be fair and even merciful in his dealings with his neighbor—and all this as the declared will of God, the way man *must* live if he would achieve his end—this is the constant theme of the Bible. The effect of it is not to reveal something new which men could not have found out for themselves, but to recall them to what they have forgotten or with culpable blindness have failed to perceive. . . .

And this leads to the second work of Revelation. The conduct which God demands of men, He demands out of His own Holiness and Righteousness. "Be ye perfect, as your Father in Heaven is perfect." Not the service of the lips but of the heart, not obedience in the letter but in the Spirit is commanded. The standard is too high: the Judge too all-seeing and just. The grandeur and majesty of the moral law proclaims the weakness and impotence of man. It shatters human pride and self-sufficiency: it overthrows that complacency with which the righteous regard the tattered robes of their partial virtues, and that satisfaction with which rogues rejoice to discover other men more evil than themselves. The revelation of the holiness of God and His Law, once struck home, drives men to confess their need of grace and brings them to Christ their Savior.

Lastly, revelation, by the light which it throws on the nature of God and man, suggests new emphases and new precepts, a new scale of values which could not at all, or could not easily, have been perceived. . . . Thus it comes about that Christian ethics is at once old and new. It covers the same ground of human conduct as the law of the Old Testament and the "law of the Gentiles written in their hearts." Many of its precepts are the same precepts. Yet all is seen in a different light and in a new perspective—the perspective of God's love manifested in Christ. It will be worth while to give one or two illustrations of this.

Revelation throws into sharp relief the supreme value of each individual human being. Every man is an immortal soul created by God and designed for an eternal inheritance. The love of God effected by the Incarnation the restoration and renewal of fallen human nature in order that all men alike might benefit thereby. The Son of God showed particular care and concern for the fallen, the outcast, the weak and the despised. He came, not to call the righteous, but sinners to repentance. Like a good shepherd, He sought especially for the sheep which was lost. Moreover, the divine drama of Calvary which was the cost of man's redemption, the price necessary to give him again a clear picture of what human nature was designed to be and to provide him with the inspiration to strive towards it and the assurance that he is not irrevocably tied and bound to his sinful, selfish past, makes it equally clear that in the eyes of the Creator His creature man is of infinite worth and value.

The lesson is plain and clear: all men equally are the children of God, all men equally are the object of His love. In consequence of this, Christian ethics has always asserted that every man is a person possessed of certain inalienable rights, that he is an end in himself, never to be used merely as a means to something else. And he is this in virtue of his being a man, no matter what his race or color, no matter how well or poorly endowed with talents, no matter how primitive or developed. And further, since man is an end in himself, and that end transcends this world of time and space, being fully attained only in heaven, it follows that the individual takes precedence over society, in the sense that society exists for the good of its individual members, not those members for society. However much the good of the whole is greater than the good of any one of its parts, and whatever the duties each man owes to society, individual persons constitute the supreme value, and society itself exists only to promote the good of those persons.

This principle of the infinite worth of the individual is explicit in Scripture, and in the light of it all totalitarian doctrines of the State stand condemned. However, the implications of this principle for human living and for the organization of society are not explicit, but need to be perceived and worked out by the human conscience. How obtuse that conscience can be, even when illumined by revelation, is startlingly illustrated by the long centuries in which Christianity tolerated the institution of slavery. In view of the constant tendency of man to exploit his fellow men and use them as the instruments of his greed and selfishness, two things are certain. First, that the Scriptural revelation of the innate inalienable dignity and value of the individual is an indispensable bulwark of human freedom and growth. And second, that our knowledge of the implication of this revelation is far indeed from being perfect; there is constant need for further refinement of our moral perceptions, a refinement which can only emerge as the fruit of a deeper penetration of the Gospel of God's love into human life and thought.

Another illustration of the effect of Scripture upon ethics is given by the surrender of the principle of exact retribution in favor of the principle of mercy. Natural justice would seem to require exact retributive punishment, an eye for an eye, a tooth for a tooth. The codes of primitive peoples, and the long history of blood feuds show how the human conscience has approved of this concept. The revelation of the divine love and the explicit teaching of the Son of God have demonstrated the superiority of mercy, and have pointed the proper role of punishment as correction and not vengeance. Because of the revelation that in God justice is never unaccompanied by mercy, in Christian ethics there has always been an emphasis on the patient endurance of wrongs in imitation of Calvary, and on the suppression of all emotions of vindictive anger. As a means to soften human relations, as a restraint of human anger and cruelty, so easily disguised under the cloak of justice, the history of the world has nothing to show comparable to this Christian emphasis on patience and mercy, this insistence that even the just satisfaction of our wrongs yields to the divine example of forebearance. We are to be content with the reform or at least the restraint of the evil-doer, never to seek or demand vengeance.

MORALITY WITHOUT GOD
John Arthur

John Arthur is professor of philosophy and director of the Program in Law and Society at State University of New York, Binghampton. Arthur considers the commonly held belief that morality somehow depends on religion. Against this he first argues that religion is unnecessary in order either to act morally or to attain moral understanding. After rejecting the idea that God is necessary in order to make sense of morality's being objective, Arthur considers the divine command theory, according to which morality depends on God's will. As Arthur points out, this theory implies that morality is arbitrary (it just so happens that God forbids cruelty; He has no reason for doing so). Furthermore, if we accept the divine command theory, we cannot make sense of the idea that God is good. But if morality is independent of God's will, so that God discovers rather than creates morality, then God's powers are limited. So either way—whether morality is dependent on or independent of God—there are difficulties. (We find expression of this dilemma in Plato's dialogue Euthyphro.*) Having examined the various claims about the connection between morality and religion, Arthur concludes by suggesting how theists and atheists might agree on which moral rules should be adopted by society.*

T he issue which I address in this paper is the nature of the connection, if any, between morality and religion. I will argue that although there are a

From *Morality and Moral Controversies*, 2nd edition, John Arthur, ed. (Prentice-Hall, Inc., 1986), pp. 10-15. Copyright © John Arthur, 1986. Reprinted by permission of John Arthur.

variety of ways the two could be connected, in fact morality is independent of religion, both logically and psychologically. First, however, it will be necessary to say something about the subjects: just what are we referring to when we speak of morality and of religion?

A useful way to approach the first question—the nature of morality—is to ask what it would mean for a society to exist without a moral code. What would such a society look like? How would people think? And behave? The most obvious thing to say is that its members would never feel any moral responsibilities or any guilt. Words like duty, rights, fairness, and justice would never be used, except in the legal sense. Feelings such as that I ought to remember my parents' anniversary, that he has a moral responsibility to help care for his children after the divorce, that she has a right to equal pay for equal work, and that discrimination on the basis of race is unfair would be absent in such a society. In short, people would have no tendency to evaluate or criticize the behavior of others, nor to feel remorse about their own behavior. Children would not be taught to be ashamed when they steal or hurt others, nor would they be allowed to complain when others treat them badly.

Such a society lacks a moral code. What, then, of religion? Is it possible that a society such as the one I have described would have religious beliefs? It seems clear that it is possible. Suppose every day these same people file into their place of worship to pay homage to God (they may believe in many gods or in one all-powerful creator of heaven and earth). Often they can be heard praying to God for help in dealing with their problems and thanking Him for their good fortune. Whenever a disaster befalls them, the people assume that God is angry with them; when things go well they believe He is pleased. Frequently they give sacrifices to God, usually in the form of money spent to build beautiful temples and churches.

To have a moral code, then, is to tend to evaluate (perhaps without even expressing it) the behavior of others and to feel guilt at certain actions when we perform them. Religion, on the other hand, involves beliefs in supernatural power(s) that created and perhaps also control nature, along with the tendency to worship and pray to those supernatural forces or beings. The two—religion and morality—are thus very different. One involves our attitudes toward various forms of behavior (lying and killing, for example), typically expressed using the notions of rules, rights, and obligations. The other, religion, typically involves a different set of activities (prayer, worship) together with beliefs about the supernatural.

We come, then, to the central question: What is the connection, if any, between a society's moral code and its religious beliefs? Many people have felt that there must be a link of some sort between religious beliefs and morality. But is that so? What sort of connection might there be? In what follows I distinguish various ways in which one might claim that religion is necessary for a moral code to function in society. I argue, however, that such connections are not necessary, and indeed that often religion is detrimental to society's attempt to encourage moral conduct among its members.

One possible role which religion might play in morality relates to motives people have. Can people be expected to behave in any sort of decent way towards one another without religious faith? Religion, it is often said, is necessary so that people will DO right. Why might somebody think that? Often, we know, doing what is right has costs: you don't cheat on the test, so you flunk the course; you return the lost billfold, so you don't get the contents. Religion can provide motivation to do the right thing. God rewards those who follow His commands by providing for them a place in heaven and by insuring that they prosper and are happy on earth. He also punishes with damnation those who disobey. Other people emphasize less selfish ways in which religious motives may encourage people to act rightly. God is the creator of the universe and has ordained that His plan should be followed. How better to live one's life than to participate in this divinely ordained plan? Only by living a moral life, it is said, can people live in harmony with the larger, divinely created order.

But how are we to assess the relative strength of these various motives for acting morally, some of which are religious, others not? How important is the fear of hell or the desire to live as God wishes in motivating people? Think about the last time you were tempted to do something you knew to be wrong. Surely your decision not to do so (if that was your decision) was made for a variety of reasons: "What if I get caught? What if somebody sees me—what will he or she think? How will I feel afterwards? Will I regret it?" Or maybe the thought of cheating just doesn't occur to you. You were raised to be an honest person, and that's what you want to be—period. There are thus many motives for doing the right thing which have nothing whatsoever to do with religion. Most of us in fact do worry about getting caught, about being blamed and looked down on by others. We also may do what is right just for that reason, because it's our duty, or because we don't want to hurt others. So to say that we need religion to act morally is mistaken; indeed it seems to me that most of us, when it really gets down to it, don't give much of a thought to religion when making moral decisions. All those other reasons are the ones which we tend to consider, or else we just don't consider cheating and stealing at all. So far, then, there seems to be no reason to suppose that people can't be moral yet irreligious at the same time.

Another oft-heard argument that religion is necessary for people to do right questions whether people would know how to do the right thing without the guidance of religion. In other words, however much people may *want* to do the right thing, it is only with the help of God that true moral understanding can be achieved. People's own intellect is simply inadequate to this task; we must consult revelation for help.

Again, however, this argument fails. Just consider what we would need to know in order for religion to provide moral guidance. First we must be sure that there is a God. And then there's the question of which of the many religions is true. How can anybody be sure his or her religion is the right one? After all, if you had been born in China or India or Iran your religious views would almost certainly not have been the ones you now hold. And even if we can somehow convince ourselves that the Judeo-Christian God is the real one, we still need to find out just what it is He wants us to do. Revelation comes in at least two forms, according to theists, and not even Christians agree which form is real. Some hold that God tells us what He wants by providing us with His words: the Ten Commandments are an example. Many even believe, as Billy Graham once said, that the entire *Bible* was written by God using 39 secretaries. Others doubt that every word of the *Bible* is literally true, believing instead that it is merely an historical account of the *events* in history whereby God revealed Himself. So on this view revelation is not understood as statements made by God but, instead, as His intervening into historical events, such as leading His people from Egypt, testing Job, and sending His son as an example of the ideal life. But if we are to use revelation as a guide we must know what is to count as revelation—words given us by God, events, or both? Supposing that we could somehow solve all those puzzles, the problems of relying on revelation are still not over. Even if we can agree on who God is and on how and when He reveals Himself, we still must interpret that revelation. Some feel that the *Bible* justifies various forms of killing, including war and capital punishment, on the basis of such statements as "An eye for an eye." Others, emphasizing such sayings as "Judge not lest ye be judged" and "Thou shalt not kill," believe the *Bible* demands absolute pacifism. How are we to know which interpretation is correct?

Far from providing a short-cut to moral understanding, looking to revelation for guidance just creates more questions and problems. It is much simpler to address problems such as abortion, capital punishment, and war directly than to seek answers in revelation. In fact, not only is religion unnecessary to provide moral understanding, it is actually a hindrance. (My own hunch is that often those who are most likely to appeal to Scripture as justification for their moral beliefs are really just rationalizing positions they already believe.)

Far from religion being necessary for people to do the right thing, it often gets in the way. People do not need the motivation of religion; they for the most part are not motivated by religion as much as by other factors; and religion is of no help in discovering what our moral obligations are. But others give a different reason for claiming morality depends on religion. They think religion, and especially God, is necessary for morality because without God there could BE no right or wrong. The idea was expressed by Bishop

R. C. Mortimer: "God made us and all the world. Because of that He has an absolute claim on our obedience. . . . From [this] it follows that a thing is not right simply because we think it is. . . . It is right because God commands it."[1]

What Mortimer has in mind can best be seen by comparing moral rules with legal ones. Legal statutes, we know, are created by legislatures. So if there had been no law passed requiring that people limit the speed they travel then there would be no such legal obligation. Without the commands of the legislature statutes simply would not exist. The view defended by Mortimer, often called the divine command theory, is that God has the same relation to moral law as the legislature does to statutes. Without God's commands there would be no moral rules.

Another tenet of the divine command theory, besides the belief that God is the author of morality, is that only the divine command theory is able to explain the objective difference between right and wrong. This point was forcefully argued by F. C. Copleston in a 1948 British Broadcasting Corporation radio debate with Bertrand Russell.

RUSSELL. But aren't you now saying in effect "I mean by God whatever is good or the sum total of what is good—the system of what is good, and, therefore, when a young man loves anything that is good he is loving God." Is that what you're saying, because if so, it wants a bit of arguing.

COPLESTON. I don't say, of course, that God is the sum total or system of what is good . . . but I do think that all goodness reflects God in some way and proceeds from Him, so that in a sense the man who loves what is truly good, loves God even if he doesn't advert to God. But still I agree that the validity of such an interpretation of man's conduct depends on the recognition of God's existence, obviously. . . . Let's take a look at the Commandant of the [Nazi] concentration camp at Belsen. That appears to you as undesirable and evil and to me too. To Adolph Hitler we suppose it appeared as something good and desirable. I suppose you'd have to admit that for Hitler it was good and for you it is evil.

RUSSELL. No, I shouldn't go so far as that. I mean. I think people can make mistakes in that as they can in other things. If you have jaundice you see things yellow that are not yellow. You're making a mistake.

COPLESTON. Yes, one can make mistakes, but can you make a mistake if it's simply a question of reference to a feeling or emotion? Surely Hitler would be the only possible judge of what appealed to his emotions.

RUSSELL. . . . you can say various things about that; among others, that if that sort of thing makes that sort of appeal to Hitler's emotions, then Hitler makes quite a different appeal to my emotions.

COPLESTON. Granted. But there's no objective criterion outside feeling then for condemning the conduct of the Commandant of Belsen, in your view. . . . The human being's idea of the content of the moral law depends certainly to a large extent on education and environment, and a man has to use his reason in assessing the validity of the actual moral ideas of his social group. But the possibility of criticizing the accepted moral code presupposes that there is an objective standard, that there is an ideal moral order, which imposes itself. . . . It implies the existence of a real foundation of God.[2]

God, according to Copleston, is able to provide the basis for the distinction, which we all know to exist, between right and wrong. Without that objective basis for defining human obligation we would have no real reason for condemning the behavior of anybody, even Nazis. Morality would be little more than an expression of personal feeling.

Before assessing the divine command theory, let's first consider this last point. Is it really true that only the commands of God can provide an objective basis for moral judgments? Certainly many philosophers . . . have felt that morality rests on its own, perfectly sound footing; to prejudge those efforts or others which may be made in the future as unsuccessful seems mistaken. And, second, if it were true that there is no nonreligious basis for claiming moral objectivity, then perhaps that means there simply is no such basis. Why suppose that there *must* be such a foundation?

What of the divine command theory itself? Is it reasonable, even though we need not do so, to equate something's being right with its being commanded by God? Certainly the expressions "is commanded by God" and "is morally required" do not *mean* the same thing; atheists and agnostics use moral words without understanding them to make any reference to God. And while it is of course true that God (or any other moral being for that matter) would tend to want others to do the right thing, this hardly shows that being right and being commanded by God are the same thing. Parents want their children to do the right thing, too, but that doesn't mean they, or anybody else, can make a thing right just by commanding it!

I think that, in fact, theists themselves if they thought about it would reject the divine command theory. One reason is because of what it implies. Suppose we grant (just for the sake of argument) that the divine command theory is correct. Notice what we have now said: Actions are right just because they are commanded by God. And the same, of course, can be said about those deeds which we believe are wrong. If God hadn't commanded us not to do them, they would not be wrong. (Recall the comparison made with the commands of the legislature, which would not be law except for the legislature having passed a statute.)

But now notice this. Since God is all-powerful, and since right is determined solely by His commands, is it not possible that He might change the rules and make what we now think of as wrong into right? It would seem that according to the divine command theory it is possible that tomorrow God will decree that virtues such as kindness and courage have become vices while actions which show cruelty and cowardice are the right actions. Rather than it being right for people to help each other out and prevent innocent people from suffering unnecessarily, it would be right to create as much pain among innocent children as we possibly can! To adopt the divine command theory commits its advocate to the seemingly absurd position that even the greatest atrocities might be not only acceptable but morally required if God were to command them.

Plato made a similar point in the dialogue *Euthyphro*. Socrates is asking Euthyphro what it is that makes the virtue of holiness a virtue, just as we have been asking what makes kindness and courage virtues. Euthyphro has suggested that holiness is just whatever all the gods love.

SOCRATES. Well, then, Euthyphro, what do we say about holiness? Is it not loved by all the gods, according to your definition?

EUTHYPHRO. Yes.

SOCRATES. Because it is holy, or for some other reason?

EUTHYPHRO. No, because it is holy.

SOCRATES. Then it is loved by the gods because it is holy: it is not holy because it is loved by them?

EUTHYPHRO. It seems so.

SOCRATES. . . . Then holiness is not what is pleasing to the gods, and what is pleasing to the gods is not holy as you say, Euthyphro. They are different things.

EUTHYPHRO. And why, Socrates?

SOCRATES. Because we are agreed that the gods love holiness because it is holy: and that it is not holy because they love it.[3]

Having claimed that virtues are what is loved by the gods why does Euthyphro so readily agree that the gods love holiness *because* it's holy? One possibility is that he is assuming whenever the gods love something they do so with good reason, not just arbitrarily. If something is pleasing to gods, there must be a reason. To deny this and say that it is simply the gods' love which makes holiness a virtue would mean that the gods have no basis for their opinions, that they are arbitrary. Or to put it another way, if we say that it is simply God's loving something that makes it right, then what sense does it make to say God wants us to do right? All that could mean is that God wants us to do what He wants us to do. He would have no reason for wanting it. Similarly "God is good" would mean little more than "God does what He pleases." Religious people who find this an unacceptable consequence will reject the divine command theory.

But doesn't this now raise another problem? If God approves kindness because it is a virtue, then it seems that God discovers morality rather than inventing it. And haven't we then suggested a limitation on God's power, since He now, being a good God, must love kindness and command us not to be cruel? What is left of God's omnipotence?

But why should such a limitation on God be unacceptable for a theist? Because there is nothing God cannot do? But is it true to say that God can do absolutely anything? Can He, for example, destroy Himself? Can God make a rock so heavy that He cannot lift it? Or create a universe which was never created by Him? Many have thought that God's inability to do these sorts of things does not constitute a genuine limitation on His power because these are things which cannot logically be done. Thomas Aquinas, for example, wrote that, "whatever implies contradiction does not come within the scope of divine omnipotence, because it cannot have the aspect of possibility. Hence it is more appropriate to say that such things cannot be done than that God cannot do them."[4] Many theists reject the view that there is nothing which God cannot do.

But how, then, ought we to understand God's relationship to morality if we reject the divine command theory? Can religious people consistently maintain their faith in God the Creator and yet deny that what is right is right because He commands it? I think the answer to this is "yes." First, note that there is still a sense in which God could change morality (assuming, of course, there is a God). Whatever moral code we decide is best (most justified), that choice will in part depend on such factors as how we reason, what we desire and need, and the circumstances in which we find ourselves. Presumably, however, God could have constructed us or our environment very differently, so that we didn't care about freedom, weren't curious about nature, and weren't influenced by others' suffering. Or perhaps our natural environment could be altered so that it is less hostile to our needs and desires. If He had created either nature or us that way, then it seems likely that the most justified moral code might be different in important ways from the one it is now rational for us to support. In that sense, then, morality depends on God whether or not one supports the divine command theory.

In fact, it seems to me that it makes little difference for ethical questions whether a person is religious. The atheist will treat human nature simply as a given, a fact of nature, while the theist may regard it as the product of divine intention. But in any case the right thing to do is to follow the best moral code, the one that is most justified. Instead of relying on revelation to discover morality, religious and nonreligious people alike can inquire into which system is best.

In sum, I have argued first that religion is neither necessary nor useful in providing moral motivation or guidance. My objections to the claim that without God there would be no morality are somewhat more complex. First, it is wrong to say that only if God's will is at its base can morality be objective. The idea of the best moral code—the one fully rational persons would support—may prove to provide sound means to evaluate one's own code as well as those of other societies. Furthermore, the divine command theory should not be accepted even by those who are religious. This is because it implies what clearly seems absurd, namely that God might tomorrow change the moral rules and make performing the most extreme acts of cruelty an obligation we all should meet. And, finally, I discussed how the theist and atheist might hope to find common ground about the sorts of moral rules to teach our children and how we should evaluate each other's behavior. Far from helping resolve moral disputes, religion does little more than sow confusion. Morality does not need religion and religion does not need morality.

Notes

1. R. C. Mortimer, *Christian Ethics* (London: Hutchinson's University Library, 1950), pp. 7–8.
2. This debate was broadcast on the Third Program of the British Broadcasting Corporation in 1948.
3. Plato, *Euthyphro,* tr. H. N. Fowler (Cambridge, Mass.: Harvard University Press, 1947).
4. Thomas Aquinas, *Summa Theologica,* Part I, Q. 25, Art. 3.

A DEFENSE OF ETHICAL RELATIVISM
Ruth Benedict

Ruth Benedict (1887–1948) was a pioneering American anthropologist and wrote Patterns of Culture *(1935), an important work in comparative anthropology. Benedict argues that careful study of the cultural practices of different peoples supports the idea that what is and is not behaviorally normal is culturally determined. She argues for a similar point in connection with such moral distinctions as good and bad, and right and wrong. She suggests that phrases like "it is morally good" should be understood as being synonymous with "it is habitual."*

From "Anthropology and the Abnormal," by Ruth Benedict, *The Journal of General Psychology,* 1934, vol. 10, pp. 59-82. Reprinted by permission of Helen Dwight Ried Educational Foundation. Published by Heldref Publications, Washington, D.C.

Modern social anthropology has become more and more a study of the varieties and common elements of cultural environment and the consequences of these in human behavior. For such a study of diverse social orders primitive peoples fortunately provide a laboratory not yet entirely vitiated by the spread of a standardized worldwide civilization. Dyaks and Hopis, Fijians and Yakuts are significant for psychological and sociological study because only among these simpler peoples has there been sufficient isolation to give opportunity for the development of localized social forms. In the higher cultures the standardization of custom and belief over a couple of continents has given a false sense of the inevitability of the particular forms that have gained currency, and we need to turn to a wider survey in order to check the conclusions we hastily base upon this near-universality of familiar customs. Most of the simpler cultures did not gain the wide currency of the one which, out of our experience, we identify with human nature, but this was for various historical reasons, and certainly not for any that gives us as its carriers a monopoly of social good or of social sanity. Modern civilization, from this point of view, becomes not a necessary pinnacle of human achievement but one entry in a long series of possible adjustments.

These adjustments, whether they are in mannerisms like the ways of showing anger, or joy, or grief in any society, or in major human drives like those of sex, prove to be far more variable than experience in any one culture would suggest. In certain fields, such as that of religion or of formal marriage arrangements, these wide limits of variability are well known and can be fairly described. In others it is not yet possible to give a generalized account, but that does not absolve us of the task of indicating the significance of the work that has been done and of the problems that have arisen.

One of these problems relates to the customary modern normal-abnormal categories and our conclusions regarding them. In how far are such categories culturally determined, or in how far can we with assurance regard them as absolute? In how far can we regard inability to function socially as diagnostic of abnormality, or in how far is it necessary to regard this as a function of the culture?

As a matter of fact, one of the most striking facts that emerges from a study of widely varying cultures is the ease with which our abnormals function in other cultures. It does not matter what kind of "abnormality" we choose for illustration, those which indicate extreme instability, or those which are more in the nature of character traits like sadism or delusions of grandeur or of persecution, there are well-described cultures in which these abnormals function at ease and with honor, and apparently without danger or difficulty to the society.

The most notorious of these is trance and catalepsy. Even a very mild mystic is aberrant in our culture. But most peoples have regarded even extreme psychic manifestations not only as normal and desirable, but even as characteristic of highly valued and gifted individuals. This was true even in our own cultural background in that period when Catholicism made the ecstatic experience the mark of sainthood. It is hard for us, born and brought up in a culture that makes no use of the experience, to realize how important a role it may play and how many individuals are capable of it, once it has been given an honorable place in any society. . . .

Cataleptic and trance phenomena are, of course, only one illustration of the fact that those whom we regard as abnormals may function adequately in other cultures. Many of our culturally discarded traits are selected for elaboration in different societies. Homosexuality is an excellent example, for in this case our attention is not constantly diverted, as in the consideration of trance, to the interruption of routine activity which it implies. Homosexuality poses the problem very simply. A tendency toward this trait in our culture exposes an individual to all the conflicts to which all aberrants are always exposed, and we tend to identify the consequences of this conflict with homosexuality. But these consequences are obviously local and cultural. Homosexuals in many societies are not incompetent, but they may be such if the culture asks adjustments of them that would strain any man's vitality. Wherever homosexuality has been given an honorable place in any society, those to whom it is congenial have filled adequately the honorable roles society assigns to them. Plato's *Republic* is, of course, the most convincing statement of such a reading of homosexuality. It is presented as one of the major means to the good life, and it was generally so regarded in Greece at that time.

The cultural attitude toward homosexuals has not always been on such a high ethical plane, but it has been very varied. Among many American Indian tribes there exists the institution of the berdache, as the French called them. These men-women were men who at puberty or thereafter took the dress and the occupations of women. Sometimes they married other men and lived with them. Sometimes they were men with no inversion, persons of weak sexual endowment who chose this role to avoid the jeers of the women. The berdaches were never regarded as of first-rate supernatural power, as similar men-women were in Siberia, but rather as leaders in women's occupations, good healers in certain diseases, or, among certain tribes, as the genial organizers of social affairs. In any case, they were socially placed. They were not left exposed to the conflicts that visit the deviant who is excluded from participation in the recognized pattern of his society.

The most spectacular illustrations of the extent to which normality may be culturally defined are those cultures where an abnormality of our culture is the cornerstone of their social structure. It is not possible to do justice to these possibilities in a short discussion. A recent study of an island of northwest Melanesia by Fortune describes a society built upon traits which we regard as beyond the border of paranoia. In this tribe the exogamic groups look upon each other as prime manipulators of black magic, so that one marries always into an enemy group which remains for life one's deadly and unappeasable foes. They look upon a good garden crop as a confession of theft, for everyone is engaged in making magic to induce into his garden the productiveness of his neighbors'; therefore no secrecy in the island is so rigidly insisted upon as the secrecy of a man's harvesting of his yams. Their polite phrase at the acceptance of a gift is, "And if you now poison me, how shall I repay you this present?" Their preoccupation with poisoning is constant; no woman ever leaves her cooking pot for a moment untended. Even the great affinal economic exchanges that are characteristic of this Melanesian culture area are quite altered in Dobu since they are incompatible with this fear and distrust that pervades the culture. They go farther and people the whole world outside their own quarters with such malignant spirits that allnight feasts and ceremonials simply do not occur here. They have even rigorous religiously enforced customs that forbid the sharing of seed even in one family group. Anyone else's food is deadly poison to you, so that communality of stores is out of the question. For some months before harvest the whole society is on the verge of starvation, but if one falls to the temptation and eats up one's seed yams, one is an outcast and a beachcomber for life. There is no coming back. It involves, as a matter of course, divorce and the breaking of all social ties.

Now in this society where no one may work with another and no one may share with another, Fortune describes the individual who was regarded by all his fellows as crazy. He was not one of those who periodically ran amok and, beside himself and frothing at the mouth, fell with a knife upon anyone he could reach. Such behavior they did not regard as putting anyone outside the pale. They did not even put the individuals who were known to be liable to these attacks under any kind of control. They merely fled when they saw the attack coming on and kept out of the way. "He would be all right tomorrow." But there was one man of sunny, kindly disposition who liked work and liked to be helpful. The compulsion was too strong for him to repress it in favor of the opposite tendencies of his culture. Men and women never spoke of him without laughing; he was silly and simple and definitely crazy. Nevertheless, to the ethnologist used to a culture that has, in Christianity, made his type the model of all virtue, he seemed a pleasant fellow. . . .

. . . Among the Kwakiutl it did not matter whether a relative had died in bed of disease, or by the hand of an enemy, in either case death was an affront to be wiped out by the death of another person. The fact that one had been caused to mourn was proof that one had been put upon. A chief's sister and her daughter had gone up to Victoria, and either because they drank bad whiskey or because their boat capsized they never came back. The chief called together his warriors, "Now I ask you, tribes, who shall wail? Shall I do it or shall another?" The spokesman answered, of course, "Not you, Chief. Let some other of the tribes." Immediately they set up the war pole to announce their intention of wiping out the injury, and gathered a war party. They set out, and found seven men and two children asleep and killed them. "Then they felt good when they arrived at Sebaa in the evening."

The point which is of interest to us is that in our society those who on that occasion would feel good when they arrived at Sebaa that evening would be the definitely abnormal. There would be some, even in our society, but it is not a recognized and approved mood under the circumstances. On the Northwest Coast those are favored and fortunate to whom that mood under those circumstances is congenial, and those to whom it is repugnant are unlucky. This latter minority can register in their own culture only by doing violence to their congenial responses and acquiring others that are difficult for them. The person, for instance, who, like a Plains Indian whose wife has been taken from him, is too proud to fight, can deal with the Northwest Coast civilization only by ignoring its strongest bents. If he cannot achieve it, he is the deviant in that culture, their instance of abnormality.

This head-hunting that takes place on the Northwest Coast after a death is no matter of blood revenge or of organized vengeance. There is no effort to tie up the subsequent killing with any responsibility on the part of the victim for the death of the person who is being mourned. A chief whose son has died goes visiting wherever his fancy dictates, and he says to his host, "My prince has died today, and you go with him." Then he kills him. In this, according to their interpretation, he acts nobly because he has not been downed. He has thrust back in return. The whole procedure is meaningless without the fundamental paranoid reading of bereavement. Death, like all the other untoward accidents of existence, confounds man's pride and can only be handled in the category of insults.

Behavior honored upon the Northwest Coast is one which is recognized as abnormal in our civilization, and yet it is sufficiently close to the attitudes of our own culture to be intelligible to us and to have a definite vocabulary with which we may discuss it. The megalomaniac paranoid trend is a definite danger in our society. It is encouraged by some of our major preoccupations, and it confronts us with a choice of two possible attitudes. One is to brand it as abnormal and reprehensible, and is the attitude we have chosen in our civilization. The other is to make it an essential attribute of ideal man, and this is the solution in the culture of the Northwest Coast.

These illustrations, which it has been possible to indicate only in the briefest manner, force upon us the fact that normality is culturally defined. An adult shaped to the drives and standards of either of these cultures, if he were transported into our civilization, would fall into our categories of abnormality. He would be faced with the psychic dilemmas of the socially unavailable. In his own culture, however, he is the pillar of society, the end result of socially inculcated mores, and the problem of personal instability in his case simply does not arise.

No one civilization can possibly utilize in its mores the whole potential range of human behavior. Just as there are great numbers of possible phonetic articulations, and the possibility of language depends on a selection and standardization of a few of these in order that speech communication may be possible at all, so the possibility of organized behavior of every sort, from the fashions of local dress and houses to the dicta of a people's ethics and religion, depends upon a similar selection among the possible behavior traits. In the field of recognized economic obligations or sex tabus this selection is as nonrational and subconscious a process as it is in the field of phonetics. It is a process which goes on in the group for long periods of time and is historically conditioned by innumerable accidents of isolation or of contact of peoples. In any comprehensive study of psychology, the selection that different cultures have made in the course of history within the great circumference of potential behavior is of great significance.

Every society, beginning with some slight inclination in one direction or another, carries its preference farther and farther, integrating itself more and more completely upon its chosen basis, and discarding those types of behavior that are uncongenial. Most of those organizations of personality that seem to us most incontrovertibly abnormal have been used by different civilizations in the very foundations of their institutional life. Conversely the most valued traits of our normal individuals have been looked on in differently organized cultures as aberrant. Normality, in short, within a very wide range, is culturally defined. It is primarily a term for the socially elaborated segment of human behavior in any culture; and abnormality, a term for the segment that that particular civilization does not use. The very eyes with which we see the problem are conditioned by the long traditional habits of our own society.

It is a point that has been made more often in relation to ethics than in relation to psychiatry. We do not any longer make the mistake of deriving the morality of our locality and decade directly from the inevitable constitution of human nature. We do not elevate it to the dignity of a first principle. We recognize that morality differs in every society, and is a convenient term for socially approved habits. Mankind has always preferred to say, "It is morally good," rather than "It is habitual," and the fact of this preference is matter enough for a critical science of ethics. But historically the two phrases are synonymous.

The concept of the normal is properly a variant of the concept of the good. It is that which society has approved. A normal action is one which falls well within the limits of expected behavior for a particular society. Its variability among different peoples is essentially a function of the variability of the behavior patterns that different societies have created for themselves, and can never be wholly divorced from a consideration of culturally institutionalized types of behavior.

Each culture is a more or less elaborate working-out of the potentialities of the segment it has chosen. In so far as a civilization is well integrated and consistent within itself, it will tend to carry farther and farther, according to its nature, its initial impulse toward a particular type of action, and from the point of view of any other culture those elaborations will include more and more extreme and aberrant traits.

Each of these traits, in proportion as it reinforces the chosen behavior patterns of that culture, is for that culture normal. Those individuals to whom it is congenial either congenitally, or as the result of childhood sets, are accorded prestige in that culture, and are not visited with the social contempt or disapproval which their traits would call down upon them in a society that was differently organized. On the other hand, those individuals whose characteristics are not congenial to the selected type of human behavior in that community are the deviants, no matter how valued their personality traits may be in a contrasted civilization.

The Dobuan who is not easily susceptible to fear of treachery, who enjoys work and likes to be helpful, is their neurotic and regarded as silly. On the Northwest Coast the person who finds it difficult to read life in terms of an insult contest will be the person upon whom fall all the difficulties of the culturally unprovided for. The person who does not find it easy to humiliate a neighbor, nor to see humiliation in his own experience, who is genial and loving, may, of course, find some unstandardized way of achieving satisfactions in his society, but not in the major patterned responses that his culture requires of him. If he is born to play an important role in a family with many hereditary privileges, he can succeed only by dong violence to his whole personality. If he does not succeed, he has betrayed his culture; that is, he is abnormal.

I have spoken of individuals as having sets toward certain types of behavior, and of these sets as running sometimes counter to the types of behavior which are institutionalized in the culture to which they belong. From all that we know of contrasting cultures it seems clear that differences of temperament occur in every society. The matter has never been made the subject of investigation, but from the available material it would appear that these temperament types are very likely of universal recurrence. That is, there is an ascertainable range of human behavior that is found wherever a sufficiently large series of individuals is observed. But the proportion in which behavior types stand to one another in different societies is not universal. The vast majority of individuals in any group are shaped to the fashion of that culture. In other words, most individuals are plastic to the moulding force of the society into which they are born. In a society that values trance, as in India, they will have supernormal experience. In a society that institutionalizes homosexuality, they will be homosexual. In a society that sets the gathering of possessions as the chief human objective, they will amass property. The deviants, whatever the type of behavior the culture has institutionalized, will remain few in number, and there seems no more difficulty in moulding the vast malleable majority to the "normality" of what we consider an aberrant trait, such as delusions of reference, than to the normality of such accepted behavior patterns as acquisitiveness. The small proportion of the number of the deviants in any culture is not a function of the sure instinct with which the society has built itself upon the fundamental sanities, but of the universal fact that, happily, the majority of mankind quite readily take any shape that is presented to them. . . .

THE CHALLENGE OF CULTURAL RELATIVISM
James Rachels

James Rachels is University Professor of Philosophy at the University of Alabama at Birmingham. He is author of The End of Life: Euthanasia and Morality *(1986) and* The Elements of Moral Philosophy, *2d ed. (1993). Rachels critically considers* Cultural Relativism, *according to which what is right or wrong or good or bad is relative to the moral code of one's society. After criticizing the so-called* Cultural Differences Argument *often used to support cultural relativism, Rachels argues that there are good reasons to reject cultural relativism.*

> Morality differs in every society, and is a convenient term for socially approved habits.
> —Ruth Benedict, *Patterns of Culture* (1934)

From James Rachels, *The Elements of Moral Philosophy* (New York: McGraw-Hill, 1986). Reprinted by permission of McGraw-Hill Publishing Company.

How Different Cultures Have Different Moral Codes

Darius, a king of ancient Persia, was intrigued by the variety of cultures he encountered in his travels. He had found, for example, that the Callatians (a tribe of Indians) customarily ate the bodies of their dead fathers. The Greeks, of course, did not do that—the Greeks practiced cremation and regarded the funeral pyre as the natural and fitting way to dispose of the dead. Darius thought that a sophisticated understanding of the world must include an appreciation of such differences between cultures. One day, to teach this lesson, he summoned some Greeks who happened to be present at his court and asked them what they would take to eat the bodies of their dead fathers. They were shocked, as Darius knew they would be, and replied that no amount of money could persuade them to do such a thing. Then Darius called in some Callatians, and while the Greeks listened asked them what they would take to burn their dead fathers' bodies. The Callatians were horrified and told Darius not even to mention such a dreadful thing.

This story, recounted by Herodotus in his *History,* illustrates a recurring theme in the literature of social science: different cultures have different moral codes. What is thought right within one group may be utterly abhorrent to the members of another group, and vice versa. Should we eat the bodies of the dead or burn them? If you were a Greek, one answer would seem obviously correct; but if you were a Callatian, the opposite would seem equally certain.

It is easy to give additional examples of the same kind. Consider the Eskimos. They are a remote and inaccessible people. Numbering only about 25,000, they live in small, isolated settlements scattered mostly along the northern fringes of North America and Greenland. Until the beginning of this century, the outside world knew little about them. Then explorers began to bring back strange tales.

Eskimo customs turned out to be very different from our own. The men often had more than one wife, and they would share their wives with guests, lending them for the night as a sign of hospitality. Moreover, within a community, a dominant male might demand—and get—regular sexual access to other men's wives. The women, however, were free to break these arrangements simply by leaving their husbands and taking up with new partners— free, that is, so long as their former husbands chose not to make trouble. All in all, the Eskimo practice was a volatile scheme that bore little resemblance to what we call marriage.

But it was not only their marriage and sexual practices that were different. The Eskimos also seemed to have less regard for human life. Infanticide, for example, was common. Knud Rasmussen, one of the most famous early explorers, reported that he met one woman who had borne twenty children but had killed ten of them at birth. Female babies, he found, were especially liable to be destroyed, and this was permitted simply at the parents' discretion, with no social stigma attached to it. Old people also, when they became too feeble to contribute to the family, were left out in the snow to die. So there seemed to be, in this society, remarkably little respect for life.

To the general public, these were disturbing revelations. Our own way of living seems so natural and right that for many of us it is hard to conceive of others living so differently. And when we do hear of such things, we tend immediately to categorize those other peoples as "backward" or "primitive." But to anthropologists and sociologists, there was nothing particularly surprising about the Eskimos. Since the time of Herodotus, enlightened observers have been accustomed to the idea that conceptions of right and wrong differ from culture to culture. If we assume that *our* ideas of right and wrong will be shared by all peoples at all times, we are merely naive.

Cultural Relativism

To many thinkers, this observation—"Different cultures have different moral codes"—has seemed to be the key to understanding morality. The idea of universal truth in ethics, they say, is a myth. The customs of different societies are all that exist. These customs cannot be said to be "correct" or "incorrect," for that implies we have an independent standard of right and wrong by which they may be judged. But there is no such independent standard; every standard is culture-bound. The great pioneering sociologist William Graham Sumner, writing in 1906, put the point like this:

The "right" way is the way which the ancestors used and which has been handed down. The tradition is its own warrant. It is not held subject to verification by experience. The notion of right is in the folkways. It is not outside of them, of independent origin, and brought to test them. In the folkways, whatever is, is right. This is because they are traditional, and therefore contain in themselves the authority of the ancestral ghosts. When we come to the folkways we are at the end of our analysis.

This line of thought has probably persuaded more people to be skeptical about ethics than any other single thing. *Cultural Relativism,* as it has been called, challenges our ordinary belief in the objectivity and universality of moral truth. It says, in effect, that there is no such thing as universal truth in ethics; there are only the various cultural codes, and nothing more. Moreover, our own code has no special status; it is merely one among many. . . .

The Cultural Differences Argument

Cultural Relativism is a theory about the nature of morality. At first blush it seems quite plausible. However, like all such theories, it may be evaluated by subjecting it to rational analysis; and when we analyze Cultural Relativism we find that it is not so plausible as it first appears to be.

The first thing we need to notice is that at the heart of Cultural Relativism there is a certain *form of argument*. The strategy used by cultural relativists is to argue from facts about the differences between cultural outlooks to a conclusion about the status of morality. Thus we are invited to accept this reasoning:

1. The Greeks believed it was wrong to eat the dead, whereas the Callatians believed it was right to eat the dead.

2. Therefore, eating the dead is neither objectively right nor objectively wrong. It is merely a matter of opinion, which varies from culture to culture.

Or, alternatively:

1. The Eskimos see nothing wrong with infanticide, whereas Americans believe infanticide is immoral.

2. Therefore, infanticide is neither objectively right nor objectively wrong. It is merely a matter of opinion, which varies from culture to culture.

Clearly, these arguments are variations of one fundamental idea. They are both special cases of a more general argument, which says:

1. Different cultures have different moral codes.

2. Therefore, there is no objective "truth" in morality. Right and wrong are only matters of opinion, and opinions vary from culture to culture.

We may call this the *Cultural Differences Argument*. To many people, it is very persuasive. But from a logical point of view, is it a *sound* argument?

It is not sound. The trouble is that the conclusion does not really follow from the premise—that is, even if the premise is true, the conclusion still might be false. The premise concerns what people *believe*: in some societies, people believe one thing; in other societies, people believe differently. The conclusion, however, concerns *what really is the case*. The trouble is that this sort of conclusion does not follow logically from this sort of premise.

Consider again the example of the Greeks and Callatians. The Greeks believed it was wrong to eat the dead; the Callatians believed it was right. Does it follow, *from the mere fact that they disagreed,* that there is no objective truth in the matter? No, it does not follow; for it *could* be that the practice was objectively right (or wrong) and that one or the other of them was simply mistaken.

To make the point clearer, consider a very different matter. In some societies, people believe the earth is flat. In other societies, such as our own, people believe the earth is (roughly) spherical. Does it follow, *from the mere fact that they disagree,* that there is no "objective truth" in geography? Of course not; we would never draw such a conclusion because we realize that, in their beliefs about the world, the members of some societies might simply be wrong. There is no reason to think that if the world is round everyone must know it. Similarly, there is no reason to think that if there is moral truth everyone must know it. The fundamental mistake in the Cultural Differences Argument is that it attempts to derive a substantive conclusion about a subject (morality) from the mere fact that people disagree about it.

It is important to understand the nature of the point that is being made here. We are *not* saying (not yet, anyway) that the conclusion of the argument is false. Insofar as anything being said here is concerned, it is still an open question whether the conclusion is true. We *are* making a purely logical point and saying that the conclusion does not *follow from* the premise. This is important, because in order to determine whether the conclusion is true, we need arguments in its support. Cultural Relativism proposes this argument, but unfortunately the argument turns out to be fallacious. So it proves nothing.

The Consequences of Taking Cultural Relativism Seriously

Even if the Cultural Differences Argument is invalid, Cultural Relativism might still be true. What would it be like if it were true?

In the passage quoted above, William Graham Sumner summarizes the essence of Cultural Relativism. He says that there is no measure of right and wrong other than the standards of one's society: "The notion of right is in the folkways. It is not outside of them, of independent origin, and brought to test them. In the folkways, whatever is, is right."

Suppose we took this seriously. What would be some of the consequences?

1. *We could no longer say that the customs of other societies are morally inferior to our own.* This, of course, is one of the main points stressed by Cultural Relativism. We would have to stop condemning other societies merely because they are "different." So long as we concentrate on certain

examples, such as the funerary practices of the Greeks and Callatians, this may seem to be a sophisticated, enlightened attitude.

However, we would also be stopped from criticizing other, less benign practices. Suppose a society waged war on its neighbors for the purpose of taking slaves. Or suppose a society was violently anti-Semitic and its leaders set out to destroy the Jews. Cultural Relativism would preclude us from saying that either of these practices was wrong. We would not even be able to say that a society tolerant of Jews is *better* than the anti-Semitic society, for that would imply some sort of transcultural standard of comparison. The failure to condemn *these* practices does not seem "enlightened"; on the contrary, slavery and anti-Semitism seem wrong *wherever* they occur. Nevertheless, if we took Cultural Relativism seriously, we would have to admit that these social practices also are immune from criticism.

2. *We could decide whether actions are right or wrong just by consulting the standards of our society.* Cultural Relativism suggests a simple test for determining what is right and what is wrong: all one has to do is ask whether the action is in accordance with the code of one's society. Suppose a resident of South Africa is wondering whether his country's policy of *apartheid*—rigid racial segregation—is morally correct. All he has to do is ask whether this policy conforms to his society's moral code. If it does, there is nothing to worry about, at least from a moral point of view.

This implication of Cultural Relativism is disturbing because few of us think that our society's code is perfect—we can think of ways it might be improved. Yet Cultural Relativism would not only forbid us from criticizing the codes of *other* societies; it would stop us from criticizing our *own*. After all, if right and wrong are relative to culture, this must be true for our own culture just as much as for others.

3. *The idea of moral progress is called into doubt.* Usually, we think that at least some changes in our society have been for the better. (Some, of course, may have been changes for the worse.) Consider this example: Throughout most of Western history the place of women in society was very narrowly circumscribed. They could not own property; they could not vote or hold political office; with a few exceptions, they were not permitted to have paying jobs; and generally they were under the almost absolute control of their husbands. Recently much of this has changed, and most people think of it as progress.

If Cultural Relativism is correct, can we legitimately think of this as progress? Progress means replacing a way of doing things with a *better* way. But by what standards do we judge the new ways as better? If the old ways were in accordance with the social standards of their time, then Cultural Relativism would say it is a mistake to judge them by the standards of a different time. Eighteenth-century society was, in effect, a different society from the one we have now. To say that we have made progress implies a judgment that present-day society is better, and that is just the sort of transcultural judgment that, according to Cultural Relativism, is impermissible.

Our idea of social *reform* will also have to be reconsidered. A reformer such as Martin Luther King, Jr., seeks to change his society for the better. Within the constraints imposed by Cultural Relativism, there is one way this might be done. If a society is not living up to its own ideals, the reformer may be regarded as acting for the best: the ideals of the society are the standard by which we judge his or her proposals as worthwhile. But the "reformer" may not challenge the ideals themselves, for those ideals are by definition correct. According to Cultural Relativism, then, the idea of social reform makes sense only in this very limited way.

These three consequences of Cultural Relativism have led many thinkers to reject it as implausible on its face. It does make sense, they say, to condemn some practices, such as slavery and anti-Semitism, wherever they occur. It makes sense to think that our own society has made some moral progress, while admitting that it is still imperfect and in need of reform. Because Cultural Relativism says that these judgments make no sense, the argument goes, it cannot be right.

CHAPTER 4

The Natural Law Theory

TREATISE ON LAW
St. Thomas Aquinas

Aquinas (1225–1274) is one of the most important figures in Western intellectual history. In the following passage from his Summa Theologica, *he presents a classical version of the natural law theory of morality. Aquinas defines law as "an ordinance of reason for the common good, promulgated by him who has care of the community." He then distinguishes four sorts of law: external, natural, human, and divine. Natural law is the part of God's eternal law that involves how human beings ought to conduct themselves. The first precept of natural law is that "good is to be done and promoted, evil is to be avoided." Human beings have natural inclinations to seek their own good, including such things as self-preservation, continuance of the species, education, and living in society. Such ends, then, are good for human beings, and the first precept of natural law enjoins us to preserve and maintain them. Thus, for Aquinas, basic moral precepts are derived from facts about human nature.*

QUESTION 90

First Article: Whether law is something pertaining to reason?

. . . It belongs to the law to command and to forbid. But it belongs to reason to command, as was stated above. Therefore law is something pertaining to reason. . . . Law is a rule and measure of acts, whereby man is induced to act or is restrained from acting; for *lex* (law) is derived from

From Anton C. Pegis, ed., *Basic Writings of St. Thomas Aquinas* (New York: Random House, 1945). Reprinted by permission of the A. C. Pegis Estate.

ligare (*to bind*), because it binds one to act. Now the rule and measure of human acts is the reason, which is the first principle of human acts, as is evident from what has been stated above. For it belongs to the reason to direct to the end, which is the first principle in all matters of action. . . .

Second Article: Whether law is always directed to the common good?

. . . Isidore says that *laws are enacted for no private profit, but for the common benefit of the citizens.* . . . As we have stated above, law belongs to that which is a principle of human acts, because it is their rule and measure. Now as reason is a principle of human acts, so in reason itself there is something which is the principle in respect of all the rest. Hence to this principle chiefly and mainly law must needs be referred. Now the first principle in practical matters, which are the object of the practical reason, is the last end: and the last end of human life is happiness or beatitude, as we have stated above. Consequently, law must needs concern itself mainly with the order that is in beatitude. Moreover, since every part is ordained to the whole as the imperfect to the perfect, and since one man is a part of the perfect community, law must needs concern itself properly with the order directed to universal happiness. Therefore the Philosopher, in the above definition of legal matters, mentions both happiness and the body politic, since he says that we call those legal matters *just which are adapted to produce and preserve happiness and its parts for the body politic.* For the state is a perfect community, as he says in *Politics* i. . . . Since law is chiefly ordained to the common good, any other precept in regard to some individual work must needs be devoid of the nature of a law, save in so far as it regards the common good. Therefore every law is ordained to the common good. . . .

Third Article: Whether the reason of any man is competent to make laws?

. . . Isidore says, and the *Decretals* repeat: *A law is an ordinance of the people, whereby something is sanctioned by the Elders together with the Commonalty.* Therefore not everyone can make laws. . . . A law, properly speaking, regards first and foremost the order to the common good. Now to order anything to the common good belongs either to the whole people, or to someone who is the viceregent of the whole people. Hence the making of a law belongs either to the whole people or to a public personage who has care of the whole people; for in all other matters the directing of anything to the end concerns him to whom the end belongs. . . .

As was stated above, a law is in a person not only as in one that rules, but also, by participation, as in one that is ruled. In the latter way, each one is a law to himself, in so far as he shares the direction that he receives from one who rules him. Hence the same text goes on: *Who show the work of the law written in their hearts (Rom.* 2:15).

Fourth Article: Whether promulgation is essential to law?

. . . It is laid down in the *Decretals* that *laws are established when they are promulgated.* . . . As was stated above, a law is imposed on others as a rule and measure. Now a rule or measure is imposed by being applied to those who are to be ruled and measured by it. Therefore, in order that a law obtain the binding force which is proper to a law, it must needs be applied to the men who have to be ruled by it. But such application is made by its being made known to them by promulgation. Therefore promulgation is necessary for law to obtain its force. . . . Law is nothing else than an ordinance of reason for the common good, promulgated by him who has the care of the community. . . .

The natural law is promulgated by the very fact that God has instilled it into man's mind so as to be known by him naturally. . . .

QUESTION 91

First Article: Whether there is an eternal law?

. . . As we have stated above, law is nothing else but a dictate of practical reason emanating from the ruler who governs a perfect community. Now it is evident, granted that the world is ruled by divine providence, as was stated in the First Part, that the whole community of the universe is governed by the divine reason. Therefore the very notion of the government of things in God, the ruler of the universe, has the nature of a law. And since the divine reason's conception of things is not subject to time, but is eternal, according to *Prov.* 8:23, therefore it is that this kind of law must be called eternal. . . .

Promulgation is made by word of mouth or in writing, and in both ways the eternal law is promulgated, because both the divine Word and the writing of the Book of Life are eternal. . . .

Second Article: Whether there is in us a natural law?

. . . The *Gloss* on *Rom.* 2:14 (*When the Gentiles, who have not the law, do by nature those things that are of the law*) comments as follows: *Although they have no written law, yet they have the natural law, whereby each one knows, and is conscious of, what is good and what is evil.* . . . As we have stated above, law, being a rule and measure, can be in a person in two ways: in one way, as in him that rules and measures; in another way, as in that which is ruled and measured, since a thing is ruled and measured in so far as it partakes of the rule or measure. Therefore, since all things subject to divine providence are ruled and measured by the eternal law, as was stated above, it is evident that all things partake in some way in the eternal law, in so far as, namely, from its being imprinted on them, they derive their respective inclinations to their proper acts and ends. Now among all others, the rational creature is subject to divine providence in a more excellent way, in so far as it itself partakes of a share of providence, by being provident both for itself and for others. Therefore it has a share of the eternal reason, whereby it has a natural inclination to its proper act and end; and this participation of the eternal law in the rational creature is called the natural law. Hence the Psalmist, after saying (Ps. 4:6): *Offer up the sacrifice of justice,* as though someone asked what the works of justice are, adds: *Many say, Who showeth us good things?* in answer to which question he says: *The light of Thy countenance, O Lord, is signed upon us.* He thus implies that the light of natural reason, whereby we discern what is good and what is evil, which is the function of the natural law, is nothing else than an imprint on us of the divine light. It is therefore evident that the natural law is nothing else than the rational creature's participation of the eternal law.

Third Article: Whether there is a human law?

. . . Augustine distinguishes two kinds of law, the one eternal, the other temporal, which he calls human. . . . As we have stated above, a law is a dictate of the practical reason. . . . Accordingly, we conclude that, just as in the speculative reason, from naturally known indemonstrable principles we draw the conclusions of the various sciences, the knowledge of which is not imparted to us by nature, but acquired by the efforts of reason, so too it is that from the precepts of the natural law, as from common and indemonstrable principles, the human reason needs to proceed to the more particular determination of certain matters. These particular determinations, devised by human reason, are called human laws, provided that the other essential conditions of law be observed, as was stated above. Therefore Tully says in his *Rhetoric* that *justice has its source in nature; thence certain things came into custom by reason of their utility; afterwards these things which emanated from nature, and were approved by custom, were sanctioned by fear and reverence for the law.* . . . Just as on the part of the speculative reason, by a natural participation of divine wisdom, there is in us the knowledge of certain common principles, but not a proper knowledge of each single truth, such as that contained in the divine wisdom, so, too, on the part of the practical reason, man has a natural participation of the eternal law, according to certain common principles, but not as regards the particular determinations of individual cases, which are, however, contained in the eternal law. Hence the need for human reason to proceed further to sanction them by law.

Fourth Article: Whether there was any need for a divine law?

. . . Besides the natural and the human law it was necessary for the direct-ing of human conduct to have a divine law. And this for four reasons. First, because it is by law that man is directed how to perform his proper acts in view of his last end. Now if man were ordained to no other end than that which is proportionate to his natural ability, there would be no need for man to have any further direction, on the part of his reason, in addition to the natural law and humanly devised law which is derived from it. But since man is ordained to an end of eternal happiness which exceeds man's natural ability, as we have stated above, therefore it was necessary that, in addition to the natural and the human law, man should be directed to his end by a law given by God.

Secondly, because, by reason of the uncertainty of human judgment, espe-cially on contingent and particular matters, different people form different judgments on human acts; whence also different and contrary laws result. In order, therefore, that man may know without any doubt what he ought to do and what he ought to avoid, it was necessary for man to be directed in his proper acts by a law given by God, for it is certain that such a law cannot err.

Thirdly, because man can make laws in those matters of which he is com-petent to judge. But man is not competent to judge of interior movements, that are hidden, but only of exterior acts which are observable; and yet for the perfection of virtue it is necessary for man to conduct himself rightly in both kinds of acts. Consequently, human law could not sufficiently curb and direct interior acts, and it was necessary for this purpose that a divine law should supervene.

Fourthly, because, as Augustine says, human law cannot punish or forbid all evil deeds, since, while aiming at doing away with all evils, it would do away with many good things, and would hinder the advance of the common good, which is necessary for human living. In order, therefore, that no evil might remain unforbidden and unpunished, it was necessary for the divine law to supervene, whereby all sins are forbidden.

Fifth Article: Whether there is but one divine law?

. . . Things may be distinguished in two ways. First, as those things that are altogether specifically different, *e.g.,* a horse and an ox. Secondly, as perfect and imperfect in the same species, *e.g.,* a boy and a man; and in this way the divine law is distinguished into Old and New. Hence the Apostle (*Gal.* 3:24, 25) compares the state of man under the Old Law to that of a child *under a pedagogue;* but that state under the New Law, to that of a full grown man, who is *no longer under a pedagogue.*

Now the perfection and imperfection of these two laws is to be taken in connection with the three conditions pertaining to law, as was stated above. For, in the first place, it belongs to law to be directed to the common good as to its end, as was stated above. This good may be twofold. It may be a sensible and earthly good, and to this man was directly ordained by the Old Law. Hence it is that, at the very outset of the Law, the people were invited to the earthly kingdom of the Chananaceans (*Exod.* 3:8, 17). Again it may be an intelligible and heavenly good, and to this, man is ordained by the New Law. Therefore, at the very beginning of His preaching, Christ invited men to the kingdom of heaven, saying (*Matt.* 4:17): *Do penance, for the kingdom of heaven is at hand.* Hence Augustine says that *promises of temporal goods are contained in the Old Testament, for which reason it is called old; but the promise of eternal life belongs to the New Testament.*

Secondly, it belongs to law to direct human acts according to the order of justice; wherein also the New Law surpasses the Old Law, since it directs our internal acts, according to *Matt.* 5:20: *Unless your justice abound more than that of the Scribes and Pharisees, you shall not enter into the kingdom of heaven.* Hence the saying that *the Old Law restrains the hand, but the New Law controls the soul.*

Thirdly, it belongs to law to induce men to observe its commandments. This the Old Law did by the fear of punishment, but the New Law, by love, which is poured into our hearts by the grace of Christ, bestowed in the New Law, but foreshadowed in the Old. Hence Augustine says that *there is little difference between the Law and the Gospel—fear* [timor] *and love* [amor]. . . .

QUESTION 94

Second Article: Whether the natural law contains several precepts, or only one?

. . . The precepts of the natural law are to the practical reason what the first principles of demonstrations are to the speculative reason, because both are self-evident principles. Now a thing is said to be self-evident in two ways: first, in itself; secondly, in relation to us. Any proposition is said to be self-evident in itself, if its predicate is contained in the notion of the subject; even though it may happen that to one who does not know the definition of the subject, such a proposition is not self-evident. For instance, this proposition, *Man is a rational being,* is, in its very nature, self-evident, since he who says *man,* says *a rational being;* and yet to one who does not know what a man is, this proposition is not self-evident. Hence it is that, as Boethius says, certain axioms or propositions are universally self-evident to all; and such are the propositions whose terms are known to all, as, *Every whole is greater than its part,* and *Things equal to one and the same are equal to one another.* But some propositions are self-evident only to the wise, who understand the meaning of the terms of such propositions. Thus to one who understands that an angel is not a body, it is self-evident that an angel is not circumscriptively in a place. But this is not evident to the unlearned, for they cannot grasp it.

Now a certain order is to be found in those things that are apprehended by men. For that which first falls under apprehension, is *being,* the understanding of which is included in all things whatsoever a man apprehends. Therefore the first indemonstrable principle is that *the same thing cannot be affirmed and denied at the same time,* which is based on the notion of *being and not-being:* and on this principle all others are based, as is stated in *Metaph.* iv. Now as *being* is the first thing that falls under the apprehension absolutely, so *good* is the first thing that falls under the apprehension of the practical reason, which is directed to action (since every agent acts for an end, which has the nature of good). Consequently, the first principle in the practical reason is one founded on the nature of good, viz., that *good is that which all things seek after.* Hence, this is the first precept of law, that *good is to be done and promoted, and evil is to be avoided.* All other precepts of the natural law are based upon this; so that all the things which the practical reason naturally apprehends as man's good belong to the precepts of the natural law under the form of things to be done or avoided.

Since, however, good has the nature of an end, and evil, the nature of the contrary, hence it is that all those things to which man has a natural inclination are naturally apprehended by reason as being good, and consequently as objects of pursuit, and their contraries as evil, and objects of avoidance. Therefore, the order of the precepts of the natural law is according to the order of natural inclinations. For there is in man, first of all, an inclination to good in accordance with the nature which he has in common with all substances, inasmuch, namely, as every substance seeks the preservation of its own being, according to its nature; and by reason of this inclination, whatever is a means of preserving human life, and of warding off its obstacles, belongs to the natural law. Secondly, there is in man an inclination to things that pertain to him more specially, according to that nature which he has in common with other animals; and in virtue of this inclination, those things are said to belong to the natural law *which nature has taught to all animals,* such as sexual intercourse, the education of offspring, and so forth. Thirdly, there is in man an inclination to good according to the nature of his reason, which nature is proper to him. Thus man has a natural inclination to know the truth about God, and to live in society; and in this respect, whatever pertains to this inclination belongs to the natural law: *e.g.,* to shun ignorance, to avoid offending those among whom one has to live, and other such things regarding the above inclination. . . .

All these precepts of the law of nature have the character of one natural law, inasmuch as they flow from one first precept. . . .

All the inclination of any parts whatsoever of human nature, *e.g.,* of the concupiscible and irascible parts, in so far as they are ruled by reason, belong to the natural law; and are reduced to one first precept, as was stated above. And thus the precepts of the natural law are many in themselves, but they are based on one common foundation. . . .

Third Article: Whether all the acts of the virtues are prescribed by the natural law?

. . . We may speak of virtuous acts in two ways: first, in so far as they are virtuous; secondly, as such and such acts considered in their proper species. If, then, we are speaking of the acts of the virtues in so far as they are virtuous, thus all virtuous acts belong to the natural law. For it has been stated that to the natural law belongs everything to which a man is inclined according to his nature. Now each thing is inclined naturally to an operation that is suitable to it according to its form: *e.g.,* fire is inclined to give heat. Therefore, since the rational soul is the proper form of man, there is in every man a natural inclination to act according to reason; and this is to act according to virtue. Consequently, considered thus, all the acts of the virtues are prescribed by the natural law, since each one's reason naturally dictates to him to act virtuously. But if we speak of virtuous acts, considered in themselves, *i.e.,* in their proper species, thus not all virtuous acts are prescribed by the natural law. For many things are done virtuously, to which nature does not primarily incline, but which, through the inquiry of reason, have been found by men to be conducive to well-living. . . .

Temperance is about the natural concupiscences of food, drink and sexual matters, which are indeed ordained to the common good of nature, just as other matters of law are ordained to the moral common good. . . .

By human nature we may mean either that which is proper to man, and in this sense all sins, as being against reason, are also against nature, as Damascene states; or we may mean that nature which is common to man and other animals, and in this sense, certain special sins are said to be against nature: *e.g.,* contrary to sexual intercourse, which is natural to all animals, is unisexual lust, which has received the special name of the unnatural crime. . . .

Fourth Article: Whether the natural law is the same in all men?

. . . As we have stated above, to the natural law belong those things to which a man is inclined naturally; and among these it is proper to man to be inclined to act according to reason. Now it belongs to the reason to proceed from what is common to what is proper, as is stated in *Physics* i. The speculative reason, however, is differently situated, in this matter, from the practical reason. For, since the speculative reason is concerned chiefly with necessary things, which cannot be otherwise than they are, its proper conclusions, like the universal principles, contain the truth without fail. The practical reason, on the other hand, is concerned with contingent matters, which is the domain of human actions; and, consequently, although there is necessity in the common principles, the more we descend towards the particular, the more frequently we encounter defects. Accordingly, then, in speculative matters truth is the same in all men, both as to principles and as to conclusions; although the truth is not known to all as regards the conclusions, but only as regards the principles which are called *common notions*. But in matters of action, truth or practical rectitude is not the same for all as to what is particular, but only as to the common principles; and where there is the same rectitude in relation to particulars, it is not equally known to all.

It is therefore evident that, as regards the common principles whether of speculative or of practical reason, truth or rectitude is the same for all, and is equally known by all. But as to the proper conclusions of the speculative reason, the truth is the same for all, but it is not equally known to all. Thus, it is true for all that the three angles of a triangle are together equal to two right angles, although it is not known to all. But as to the proper conclusions of the practical reason, neither is the truth or rectitude the same for all, nor, where it is the same, is it equally known by all. Thus, it is right and true for all to act according to reason, and from this principle it follows, as a proper conclusion, that goods entrusted to another should be restored to their owner. Now this is true for the majority of cases. But it may happen in a particular case that it would be injurious, and therefore unreasonable, to restore goods held in trust; for instance, if they are claimed for the purpose of fighting against one's country. And this principle will be found to fail the more, according as we descend further towards the particular, *e.g.,* if one were to say that goods held in trust should be restored with such and such a guarantee, or in such and such a way; because the greater the number of conditions added, the greater the number of ways in which the principle may fail, so that it be not right to restore or not to restore.

Consequently, we must say that the natural law, as to the first common principles, is the same for all, both as to rectitude and as to knowledge. But as to certain more particular aspects, which are conclusions, as it were, of those common principles, it is the same for all in the majority of cases, both as to rectitude and as to knowledge; and yet in some few cases it may fail, both as to rectitude, by reason of certain obstacles (just as natures subject to generation and corruption fail in some few cases because of some obstacle), and as to knowledge, since in some the reason is perverted by passion, or evil habit, or an evil disposition of nature. Thus at one time theft, although it is expressly contrary to the natural law, was not considered wrong among the Germans, as Julius Caesar relates.

THE ETHICS OF NATURAL LAW
C. E. Harris

C. E. Harris is associate professor of philosophy at Texas A & M University. In the selection below he presents a version of the natural-law theory, including a discussion of the principle of double effect, which plays an important role in modern natural-law thinking.

What Is Natural Law?   The name *natural law* can be misleading. It implies that ethical laws are like "laws of nature" or scientific laws. An example of a scientific law is Boyle's law in physics, which states that the product of the pressure and the specific volume of a gas at constant temperature is constant. But scientific laws are *descriptive;* they state how phenomena in nature do in fact always behave. Ethical laws, on the other hand, are *prescriptive;* they stipulate how people *should* behave, whether or not they do so. Natural-law theorists assume that human beings have free will and that they can decide whether to act as they ought to act. This discussion implies that the word *law* has more in common with civil laws than with natural laws, because both civil and ethical laws can be disobeyed. Natural phenomena presumably always act according to the laws of nature, whereas people are not necessarily compelled to behave legally or morally.

But the analogy with civil laws can also be misleading, for the point of the term *natural* is to contrast ethical laws with the laws of governments. When the Roman jurists were looking for legal concepts that could apply throughout the Roman empire, they turned to the philosophy of natural law precisely because it proposed that certain ethical laws are "natural" rather than "conventional"; that is, they apply equally to all human beings, regardless of the

From *Applying Moral Theories* by C. E. Harris, Jr. © 1986 by Wadsworth, Inc. Reprinted by permission of the publisher.

conventions, customs, or beliefs of their particular society. These natural laws for all human behavior thus could serve as a basis for judging the actions of people throughout the Roman empire. Therefore we can say that *natural law* refers to ethical guidelines or rules that stipulate what people ought to do rather than what they in fact do and that apply equally to all humanity because they are rooted in human nature itself.

The term *natural law* can be misleading because it inevitably brings to mind some kind of ethical legalism—the belief that hard-and-fast guidelines cover every possible detail of conduct. This characterization, however, is unfair to the natural-law tradition. The greatest exponent of natural law, Thomas Aquinas (1225–1274), believed that the basic outlines of proper human behavior are relatively clear. But he also taught that, the closer we come to particular moral judgments, the more prone we are to error and the more room we make for differences of opinion. Some contemporary natural-law theorists even believe that natural law has a historical dimension, so that what is right in one epoch may not be right in another. Whether or not this view is accepted, the lively discussions of ethical issues in the Roman Catholic Church, where natural-law thinking is especially prominent, show that natural-law theorists by no means believe that all ethical problems have already been solved. The word *law* merely refers to the prescriptive character of the rules that should govern human behavior.

The natural-law theorist does, however, believe in an objective standard for morality: Moral truth exists just as scientific truth exists. The natural-law theorist cannot be a radical ethical relativist or an ethical sceptic. He generally believes we know the basic outlines of this standard, but this belief does not mean we have interpreted the implications of this standard correctly in every case. In ethics, as in science, human beings continually search for truth. The belief in objective truth should be no more stifling of human freedom and creativity in ethics than it is in science.

Human Nature and Natural Inclinations.   What is that standard of truth in ethics? As an approximation we can say that the standard is human nature. People should do whatever promotes the fulfillment of human nature. Here again we can point out the similarity between natural law and egoism. But natural-law theorists have always believed that the individual alone cannot determine what counts as human nature. How then do we determine what human nature is?

Let us consider some analogous situations that illustrate the difficulty in describing human nature. It is often useful to describe something's nature in terms of its function—that is, in terms of the purpose it serves. For example, we can describe the nature of a pencil in terms of its function or purpose of enabling humans to make marks on paper. A "good" pencil is one that performs this function well—without smudging or scratching or breaking, for example. Similarly, if an automobile's function is to provide transportation, a good automobile is one that provides comfortable and reliable transportation. The function of a tomato plant is to produce tomatoes, and a good tomato plant is one that produces an abundance of tomatoes of high quality.

We can also determine the function of human beings if we confine a person to one particular social role. The function of a farmer is to grow food, and a good farmer produces food efficiently and with proper care for the animals and the land for which he has responsibility. By similar reasoning we can say that a good father is one who attends diligently to the welfare of his children. But now let us take human beings out of their social roles and ask simply "What is the function of a human being?" Here we see the problem faced by those who attempt to base ethics on human nature. Generally speaking, the more complex the animal, the more varied its behavior and presumably the less clearly defined is its "nature." The freedom of action possessed by human beings makes it plausible to argue, as some philosophers have, that human beings are characterized precisely by the fact that they have no set nature or function. How can we make sense out of natural law in the face of these problems?

Fortunately we can take another, more promising approach to discovering what human nature is like. One way to determine the characteristics of a thing is to observe its behavior. In chemistry we learn about the nature of iron by observing how it reacts with other elements. Perhaps we can find out what human nature is like by ascertaining those "natural inclinations," as Aquinas put it, that human beings have in common. To put it another way, perhaps we can discover what human nature is by identifying those goals that human beings generally tend to seek. These values would presumably reflect the structure of our human nature, which natural law directs us to follow. Therefore we shall propose the following statement as the moral standard of natural law:

MS: *Those actions are right that promote the values specified by the natural inclinations of human beings.*

How do we find out what these natural inclinations are? We might first consult psychologists, sociologists, or anthropologists. Some contemporary natural-law theorists use studies from the social sciences to defend their conclusions. However, the natural-law tradition developed before the rise of the social sciences, and a more informal method of observation was used to discover the basic human inclinations. Most natural-law theorists would maintain that these observations are still valid. We can divide the values specified by natural human inclination into two basic groups: (1) biological values, which are strongly linked with our bodies and which we share with other animals, and (2) characteristically human values, which are closely connected with our more specifically human aspects. (We will not call this second group uniquely human values because some of the inclinations that point to these values, such as the tendency to live in societies, are not unique to human beings.) We can summarize the values and the natural inclinations that point to them as follows:

1. Biological Values

   a. Life. From the natural inclinations that we and all other animals have to preserve our own existence, we can infer that life is good, that we have an obligation to promote our own health, and that we have the right of self-defense. Negatively, this inclination implies that murder and suicide are wrong.

   b. Procreation. From the natural inclination that we and all animals have to engage in sexual intercourse and to rear offspring, we can infer that procreation is a value and that we have an obligation to produce and rear children. Negatively, this inclination implies that such practices as sterilization, homosexuality, and artificial contraception are wrong.

2. Characteristically Human Values

   a. Knowledge. From the natural tendency we have to know, including the tendency to seek knowledge of God, we can infer that knowledge is a value and that we have an obligation to pursue knowledge of the world and of God. Negatively, this inclination implies that the stifling of intellectual curiosity and the pursuit of knowledge is wrong. It also implies that a lack of religion is wrong.

   b. Sociability. From the natural tendency we have to form bonds of affection and love with other human beings and to associate with others in societies, we can infer that friendship and love are good and that the state is a natural institution and therefore good. We thus have an obligation to pursue close relationships with other human beings and to submit to the legitimate authority of the state. We can also infer that war can be justified under certain conditions if it is necessary to defend the state. Negatively, this inclination implies that activities that interfere with proper human relationships, such as spreading slander and lies, are wrong. Actions that destroy the power of the state are also wrong, so natural law finds a basis for argument against revolution and treason, except when the state is radically unjust.

These natural inclinations are reflections of human nature, and the pursuit of the goods they specify is the way to individual fulfillment. Aquinas himself makes it clear that the list of values, which in most respects follows his account, is incomplete; other natural-law theorists have expanded the list to include such things as play and aesthetic experience. However the list given here has had the greatest historical influence, and we shall assume it is basically complete.

The more important issue raised by this list is the potential for conflict between the various values. What should we do when our need to defend ourselves requires that we kill someone else? What should we do when sterilization is necessary to prevent a life-threatening pregnancy? What should be done when contraception seems necessary in order to limit family size so that families can properly educate the children they already have? In each of these examples, one aspect of natural law seems to conflict with another, and the question arises whether these values have a hierarchy on which a decision can be based. The answer to this question brings into focus one of the most important and controversial aspects of natural law—moral absolutism.

Moral Absolutism and Its Qualifying Principles

Moral Absolutism.   Suppose you were on a military convoy from the United States to England during World War II. Your ship was attacked and sunk. Your life raft was carrying 24 persons, although it was designed to carry only 20. You had good reason to believe that the raft would sink unless four people were eliminated, and four people on board were so seriously injured in the catastrophe that they were probably going to die anyhow. Because no one volunteered to jump overboard, you, as the ranking officer on the boat, decided to have them pushed overboard. Were you morally justified in doing so? Many of us would say that under the circumstances you were, but natural-law theorists would say that you were not justified, even if everyone on the raft would have died otherwise.

Consider another wartime example. Suppose you know that some prisoners have information that will save a large number of lives. The only way to obtain the information is to threaten to kill the prisoners, but you know that they will not reveal what they know unless your threat is absolutely serious. To show them how serious you are, you have another prisoner shot before their eyes. As a result of your action, the information is revealed and many lives are saved. Is this action justified? Many people would say that under these extreme circumstances it is justified, but natural-law theorists would say that it is not.

Finally, . . . the traditional natural-law position is that practicing "artificial" contraception, undergoing sterilization, or practicing homosexuality is wrong. For the natural-law theorist, these prohibitions are valid even if the consequences are that parents produce children they cannot afford to educate or that the life of the mother is endangered or if homosexual relationships are the only sexual relationships a person can have with any satisfaction. These examples point out one of the most significant aspects of natural-law theory—namely, its absolutism.

Moral absolutism can refer either to the belief that some objective standard of moral truth exists independently of us or that certain actions are right or wrong regardless of their consequences. Natural law is an absolutist moral theory in both senses, but the second meaning of absolutism is highlighted by the illustrations provided. Natural-law theorists believe that *none of the values specified by natural inclinations may be directly violated.* Innocent people may not be killed for any reason, even if other innocent people can thus be saved. The procreative function that is a part of our biological nature may not be violated by such practices as contraception and sterilization, even if these practices are necessary to preserve other values, such as a child's education or even the mother's life. Similarly, homosexuality violates the value of procreation and is prohibited, even if it is the only kind of sex a person can enjoy.

Natural-law theorists have two reasons to hold that basic values specified by natural inclinations cannot be violated whatever the consequences. First, *basic values cannot be measured or compared;* that is, basic values cannot be quantified or measured by some common unit, so they cannot be traded off for one another. For example, we cannot divide the good of knowledge into units of value and the good of procreation into units of value so that the two can be compared on a common scale. Nor can the good of a single life be compared with the good of a number of lives; thus we cannot say that a single life may be sacrificed to preserve a number of other lives. This idea is sometimes called the "absolute value" or "infinite value" of a human life, suggesting that a human life cannot be weighed against anything else, including another human life. Natural-law theorists also make this point by saying that basic values are *incommensurable.* Because we cannot measure values, we cannot calculate which consequences of an action are more important. Therefore consequences cannot be used to determine the moral status of actions.

Second, consequences cannot be used to determine moral judgments because *we must make moral judgments by evaluating the motives of the person performing the action.* The *motive* of an action is what a person wants to accomplish by performing the action. For example, a person can give money to charity because he wants a good reputation in the community. The consequences of the action are good, but the motive is not morally praiseworthy. Some moral philosophers distinguish between a moral evaluation of the consequences of an action and a moral evaluation of the motives of the person performing the action; with this distinction we can say the action of giving money to charity was praiseworthy but the person giving the money was not praiseworthy, because the motives were bad. Natural-law theorists always place primary emphasis on motives.

Qualifying Principles.   Because values are incommensurable and may not ever be directly violated, we may find ourselves in a situation in which any action we could perform violates some value and hence is apparently immoral. For example, self-defense may sometimes require that we override the natural inclination of another human being to self-preservation. If we do nothing, we allow ourselves to be killed; if we defend ourselves, we kill someone else. To avoid this paralysis of action and to gain deeper insight into the dynamics of situations of moral choice, natural-law theorists have developed two ideas that are absolutely crucial in making moral judgments: the principle of forfeiture and the principle of double effect.

According to the *principle of forfeiture*, a person who threatens the life of an innocent person forfeits his or her own right to life. (An *innocent* person is one who has not threatened anyone's life.) Suppose you are a pioneer who is tilling his land. Your wife and small child are in a log cabin on the hill. Two men approach you and express an intent to kill you and your family in order to take the land. Is it morally permissible for you to defend yourself, even to the point of killing them? Natural-law theorists answer the question in the affirmative. Even though you might have to violate the lives of your would-be assailants, they have forfeited their innocence by unjustifiably threatening your life. Therefore they have forfeited their claim to have their lives respected. We can make this point by distinguishing between killing and murder. *Killing* is taking the life of a non-innocent person, whereas *murder* is taking the life of an innocent person. When you take the life of a person who is attempting to kill you, you are killing him but you are not committing murder.

The principle of forfeiture can be used to justify not only acts of individual self-defense, but also war and capital punishment. A defensive war may be justified under certain conditions, even though it involves killing other people, because the aggressors have forfeited their right to life. Similarly, murderers may justly be put to death because they have forfeited their right to life by killing others.

According to the *principle of double effect*, it is morally permissible to perform an action that has two effects, one good and the other bad, if (1) the bad effect is unavoidable if the good effect is to be achieved, (2) the bad effect is unintended—that is, not a direct means to the good effect, and (3) a proportionally serious reason exists for performing the action.

The best way to explain this principle is by example. A pregnant woman who has tuberculosis wants to take a drug that will cure her disease, but the drug has the side effect of aborting the pregnancy. Is taking the drug morally permissible? The principle of double effect justifies taking the drug in this case, because all three of its conditions are met.

First, the bad effect is unavoidable in that the good effect cannot be achieved without also producing the bad effect. Presumably no other drug will cure the woman's tuberculosis and the abortion cannot be prevented once the drug is taken.

Second, the bad effect is unintended in that it is not a direct means to achieving the good effect. We must clarify here what natural-law theorists mean. The bad effect is certainly foreseen; the woman knows the drug will produce an abortion. However, the bad effect is not intended as a direct means to the good effect: An abortion is not a necessary step in curing the tuberculosis; rather, it is an unfortunate and unintended side effect. Evidence that the abortion is unintended even though it is foreseen is that the woman would presumably choose a different treatment that did not kill the fetus if it were equally effective and readily available.

Third, a proportionally serious reason exists for performing the abortion. The death of the fetus is at least balanced by the saving of the mother's life. If the bad effect were serious (as in this case), but the good effect were relatively insignificant, the action would not be justifiable by the principle of double effect, even if the other conditions were met. Here, consequences do play a part in natural-law reasoning. But note that consequences can be considered *only* when the other two conditions have been met.

Two other examples will show more clearly how the principle of double effect works. Suppose I want to turn on a light so that I can read a book on ethics, but I know that turning on the light will electrocute a worker on the floor below. If I cannot get the reading done except by electrocuting the worker, we can say that the electrocution is unavoidable. The bad effect is unintended in that electrocuting a worker is not a direct means to reading philosophy, but rather only an unfortunate and unintended side effect. But the third condition of the principle of double effect is not satisfied. The killing of a human being, even if unintended and unavoidable in the circumstances, is not outweighed by the value of reading a book on ethics. Therefore, turning on the light is not justified by the principle of double effect. The existence of a proportionally serious reason is often difficult to determine, as are the questions of the action's ultimate intention and avoidability. But in this case the application of the principle is clear.

Consider another example. A woman's egg is fertilized in the fallopian tube; as the fertilized egg developed it will rupture the tube, killing both the mother and the fetus. Is an abortion justified by the principle of double effect? The bad effect (the abortion) is unavoidable; the mother's life cannot be saved without it. The bad effect is not unintended, though, since removing the fetus from the fallopian tube is the direct means of saving the mother's life. The principle of proportionality is satisfied, because we have a case of life against life. However, since the second condition is not met, the abortion in this case cannot be justified by the principle of double effect.

This case is, of course, tragic for natural-law theorists, and various attempts have been made to justify the abortion on other grounds. For example, some natural-law theorists argue that the principle of forfeiture can be invoked, since the fetus is actually an aggressor on the life of the mother. Even though the fetus is innocent of any conscious motive to harm its mother, the actual effect of its growth is to threaten the life of its mother. Natural-law theorists sometimes say that the fetus, having no malicious motive, is subjectively innocent but not objectively innocent, because it does threaten the mother's life. Whether this argument justifies an abortion is left to the reader to decide. . . .

Applying the Ethics of Natural Law

We can now apply natural law to some cases involving moral decision. . .

CASE 1: A CASE OF EUTHANASIA

A 36-year-old accountant, married and the father of three young children, is diagnosed as having immunoblastic lymphadenopathy, a fatal malignant tumor of the lymph nodes. He has been receiving a variety of treatments, yet his condition has steadily worsened. He knows that all surgical and medical measures have been exhausted. He suffers daily from excruciating nerve-root pain; he must take addicting doses of narcotics but still is not free from pain. The expenses of his treatment are rapidly exhausting his family's financial resources. His wife and family are beginning to withdraw from him emotionally, in anticipation of his inevitable death. Having reconciled himself to his death, he asks the doctor for the means of killing himself in order to end his pain, the suffering of his family, and the depletion of the funds that are so important for his family's future well-being. Is it morally permissible for the physician to acquiesce in this request?[1]

1. Obviously, administering a drug to end the accountant's life is a direct action against one of the four fundamental values of natural law—namely, the value of life.

2. The only question is whether either of the two qualifying principles applies. The accountant is not guilty of any action that would cause him to forfeit his own right to life, so the principle of forfeiture does not apply.

3. The principle of double effect might be used to justify two kinds of actions the physician could perform to alleviate his patient's suffering. First, it could justify the use of a pain killer, even if the pain killer had the

indirect effect of shortening the patient's life. (a) If no other drug could alleviate pain as effectively, the use of that particular drug could be considered unavoidable. (b) The direct intent of administering the pain killer would be to alleviate pain; the tendency of the pain killer to shorten life would be unintended because the shortening of life is not the direct means to eliminating pain. (c) Although some might argue that an action that shortens life is not justified by the desire to alleviate pain, most natural-law theorists would probably accept the use of the principle of proportionality in this case.

The principle of double effect could also justify the physician's decision not to use "heroic measures" to prolong the accountant's life. Natural-law theorists distinguish between "ordinary" and "extraordinary" means for preserving life. Father Gerald Kelly defines these two terms in the following way:

Ordinary means of preserving life are all medicines, treatments, and operations [that] offer a reasonable hope of benefit for the patient and [that] can be obtained and used without excessive expense, pain, or other inconvenience. . . .

Extraordinary means of preserving life [are] all medicines, treatments, and operations [that] cannot be obtained without excessive expense, pain, or other inconvenience, or [that], if used, would not offer a reasonable hope of benefit.[2]

The failure to use heroic or extraordinary means satisfies all three criteria of double effect. (a) The shortening of life is inevitable if extraordinary means are not used. (b) The shortening of life is unintended, because it is not a direct means to the use of ordinary means, and is simply an unfortunate side effect of the use of ordinary means. (c) The principle of proportionality is satisfied, since the use of extraordinary means would only prolong the accountant's dying process, not restore him to health. Therefore the decision not to use extraordinary means can be justified by the principle of double effect.

But the accountant's request goes far beyond the two measures described here. He is asking the physician to cooperate actively in directly ending his life. (a) The good effect of relieving the accountant's pain cannot be achieved without also producing the bad effect—namely, the accountant's death. So the first criterion is met. (b) However, the accountant's death is the direct means of achieving the release from pain, so the accountant's death is intended. The second criterion is not satisfied. (c) No proportionally serious reason exists for administering the lethal drug, since relief from pain cannot justify directly killing an innocent person, an act that is actually murder.

4. Because the physician's action in administering a lethal drug to the accountant is a violation of a fundamental value and because the qualifying principles of forfeiture and double effect do not apply, the action is morally impermissible.

CASE 2: THE MORALITY OF OBLITERATION
BOMBING IN WORLD WAR II

During World War II, both the Germans and the Allied Forces bombed civilian residential areas, a practice called "obliteration bombing." Probably the two most famous examples of this practice, in which conventional explosives were used, were the German bombing of London and the Allied bombing of Dresden, Germany. Let us confine ourselves to the fire bombing of Dresden and ask whether this action was permissible by the principles of natural law.

1. The first question is whether the bombing of Dresden violated the value of life. The answer is that it did, so the action must be morally impermissible unless one of the two qualifying principles applies.

2. The principle of forfeiture would apply if civilians in wartime can be considered non-innocent. If we assume that the criteria of just-war theory were met—that is, the Allied Forces were fighting a just war and the Germans were not fighting a just war—then the Germans in uniform were non-innocent and attacking them was morally justified. But most civilians in large cities were connected with the war effort in a very indirect way. Many had little direct knowledge of the reasons for war and certainly had no part in starting it. Therefore, the principle of forfeiture does not justify the bombing.

3. Some have argued that an appeal to the principle of double effect could justify the bombing. According to this argument, the intended effect of the bombing was to destroy war industries, communications, and military installations, whereas the damage to civilian life was unintentional and not a means to the production of the good effect. But a careful analysis of the conditions of the bombing will not sustain this argument. (a) Although killing of civilians truly is sometimes unavoidable when military targets are attacked, the massive civilian deaths in Dresden could have been avoided. (b) If the Allies were engaged in strategic bombing of war plants, with the direct intent to destroy the plants, and if the destruction of human life was unintended and unavoidable, the second condition of the principle of double effect would be satisfied. But, in this case, the maiming and death of hundreds of civilians was an immediate result of the bombing, and the undermining of civilian morale through terror was, on the testimony of military documents themselves, an object of the bombing. This goal of demoralization is impossible without a direct intent to injure and kill civilians. If one intends to create terror, one cannot escape intending the principal means of obtaining that end. Therefore the second condition of double effect is not met. (c) We can also question the allegation that the principle of proportionality was satisfied by the belief that obliteration bombing would shorten the war. The goal was speculative, futuristic, and problematic, whereas the evil effect was definite, immediate, and widespread. Thus we must conclude that the principle of double effect does not apply.

4. Because the Allied attack on Dresden involved the destruction of innocent human life and because the qualifying principles of forfeiture and double effect do not apply, we must conclude that the action was morally
impermissible by natural-law theory.

CASE 3: THE MORALITY OF HOMOSEXUALITY

James has known since he was five years old that he was somehow different. Even then he enjoyed watching male athletes and seemed to "love" his
older male playmates. In high school he was active in sports and his attraction to members of his own sex became obvious to him and to some of his
friends. He has never been attracted to women sexually, although he likes
some of them as friends, and the thought of sex with a woman has always
repelled him. In college he began to associate with other homosexuals. He
has talked to several counselors, and he now feels ready to admit to himself
and to others, including his family, that he is a homosexual. However he
still wonders about the morality of homosexuality, especially because he is
a Roman Catholic. Is homosexuality wrong by natural law?

1. The determination of whether homosexuality violates natural law is
more difficult than it might at first appear. The traditional natural-law argument against homosexuality was based on the view that homosexual relationships involved a perversion or misuse of the sexual organs. Because the
sex organs are made for procreation, using them for purposes other than this
"natural end" is immoral. This same argument also leads to the conclusion
that masturbation is immoral, because it uses the sex organs for pleasure
rather than procreation. By a similar argument, oral sex and anal sex, even
between married partners, is immoral. Thus, it is also wrong for a woman to
refuse to breast-feed her child. If female breasts have the natural function of
lactation, a mother who decides not to breast-feed her child acts directly
against this natural function and does something wrong. This so-called
perverted-faculty argument leads to so many absurd conclusions that it is
being increasingly rejected. It does not even seem to be in agreement with
Thomas Aquinas' basic understanding of natural law. For homosexuality to
be immoral by our version of natural law, it must involve a direct action
against a fundamental value.

Of course, homosexuals who engage in sexual activity have no intention
of producing children; they know that their sexual activity cannot be procreative. But a married heterosexual couple who engage in sex during a non-
fertile period also know that they cannot produce children, yet their action
is not immoral by natural law. Neither the homosexual nor the married couple has done anything directly to violate the procreative function. The same
statement applies to masturbation, oral sex, and anal sex; they do not seem
directly to violate the value of procreation.

Some, perhaps many, homosexual acts are immoral because they violate the value of sociability. If the acts are demeaning or destructive or if they involved trickery or deception, they are wrong because they violate the value of loving, supportive human relationships. But the same is true of some heterosexual relationships, even if they occur within marriage. So we must look elsewhere for an argument that homosexual acts are wrong simply because they are homosexual.

Although it seems mistaken to say that homosexuals act directly to violate the value of procreation in the same straightforward sense that the use of contraceptives does, either case involves sex that is closed to the possibility of procreation. In fact, an exclusively homosexual lifestyle is closed to the possibility of procreation in a more decisive way than contraceptive sex or other types of nonprocreative sex by a married couple, because a homosexual's nonprocreative sex lasts throughout a lifetime. Therefore we can say that, although homosexual acts do not constitute a direct violation of the value of procreation, the homosexual lifestyle is antiprocreative.

2. Since homosexuality is not a direct threat to life, the principle of forfeiture is inapplicable.

3. James might argue that choosing a homosexual lifestyle is justifiable by the principle of double effect. (a) He might believe that the criterion of unavoidability is met, because it is impossible for him to have a fulfilling sex life without also failing to produce children. (b) He could say that his direct intent is to promote a fulfilling relationship and that any violation of the value of procreation is an unintended side effect. The nonproduction of children is not, after all, a direct means to his end of having a fulfilling sex life; he might even want to have children. (c) He could argue that the principle of proportionality is satisfied because the value of a meaningful relationship outweighs the failure to have children.

The first argument is weak because a fulfilling sex life is not a fundamental value, but the second criterion presents the main problem with this argument. Although it is true that the absence of children is not, as such, a direct means to James's goal of a fulfilling lifestyle, nonprocreative sex is a part of the means to this end. Whether the principle of double effect is applicable depends on the conceptual issue of whether the absence of children or nonprocreative sex is considered the undesirable effect. The absence of children is arguably an unintended side effect, but nonprocreative sex is a means to the desired end.

4. We have found problems with the argument that homosexual acts violate the value of procreation and with the application of the principle of double effect. However, virtually all natural-law theorists have concluded that homosexual acts are morally impermissible. Ask yourself whether you agree with this conclusion.

Notes

1. This case was supplied by Harry S. Lipscomb, M.D. Used with permission.
2. Gerald Kelly, *Medico-Moral Problems* (St. Louis, Mo.: The Catholic Hospital Association, 1958), p. 120. Quoted in Paul Ramsey, *The Patient as Person,* p. 122.

THE DOCTRINE OF DOUBLE EFFECT
Philippa Foot

Philippa Foot is professor emeritus of philosophy at the University of California at Los Angeles and honorary fellow at Somerville College, Oxford. She has written many influential essays in moral philosophy, some of them to be found in Virtues and Vices *(1978). According to the doctrine (or principle) of double effect, it is sometimes permissible to perform an action that will knowingly bring about a bad effect so long as one does not directly intend the bad effect. Foot is critical of this doctrine. After explaining why some philosophers have thought that certain problematic cases calling for moral response require that we accept the doctrine, she goes on to argue that (1) those same cases can be understood in terms of the distinction between the negative duty to avoid injury to others and the positive duty to render aid (and so the cases in question do not require accepting the doctrine), and (2) that since there are cases where the doctrine of double effect yields counterintuitive results about what is morally right, we should reject it.*

I

I shall not, of course, discuss all the principles that may be used in deciding how to act where the interests or rights of human beings conflict. What I want to do is to look at one particular theory, known as the "doctrine of the double effect" which is invoked by Catholics in support of their views on abortion but supposed by them to apply elsewhere. . . .

The doctrine of the double effect is based on a distinction between what a man foresees as a result of his voluntary action and what, in the strict sense, he intends. He intends in the strictest sense both those things that he

Originally published in *Oxford Review,* 5, 1967. Reprinted by permission of the author.

aims at as ends and those that he aims at as means to his ends. The latter may be regretted in themselves but nevertheless desired for the sake of the end, as we may intend to keep dangerous lunatics confined for the sake of our safety. By contrast a man is said not strictly, or directly, to intend the foreseen consequences of his voluntary actions where these are neither the end at which he is aiming nor the means to this end. Whether the word "intention" should be applied in both cases is not of course what matters: Bentham spoke of "oblique intention," contrasting it with the "direct intention" of ends and means, and we may as well follow his terminology. Everyone must recognise that some such distinction can be made, though it may be made in a number of different ways, and it is the distinction that is crucial to the doctrine of the double effect. The words "double effect" refer to the two effects that an action may produce: the one aimed at, and the one foreseen but in no way desired. By "the doctrine of the double effect" I mean the thesis that it is sometimes permissible to bring about by oblique intention what one may not directly intend. Thus the distinction is held to be relevant to moral decision in certain difficult cases. It is said for instance that the operation of hysterectomy involves the death of the foetus as the foreseen but not strictly or directly intended consequence of the surgeon's act, while other operations kill the child and count as the direct intention of taking an innocent life, a distinction that has evoked particularly bitter reactions on the part of non-Catholics. If you are permitted to bring about the death of the child, what does it matter how it is done? The doctrine of the double effect is also used to show why in another case, where a woman in labour will die unless a craniotomy operation is performed, the intervention is not to be condoned. There, it is said, we may not operate but must let the mother die. We foresee her death but do not directly intend it, whereas to crush the skull of the child would count as direct intention of its death.[1] . . .

The first point that should be made clear, in fairness to the theory, is that no one is suggesting that it does not matter what you bring about as long as you merely foresee and do not strictly intend the evil that follows. We might think, for instance, of the (actual) case of wicked merchants selling, for cooking, oil they knew to be poisonous and thereby killing a number of innocent people, comparing and contrasting it with that of some unemployed gravediggers, desperate for custom, who got hold of this same oil and sold it (or perhaps they secretly gave it away) in order to create orders for graves. They strictly (directly) intend the deaths they cause, while the merchants could say that it was not part of their plan that anyone should die. In morality, as in law, the merchants, like the gravediggers, would be considered as murderers; nor are the supporters of the doctrine of the double effect bound to say that there is the least difference between them in respect of moral turpitude. What they are committed to is the thesis that *sometimes* it makes a difference to the permissibility of an action involving harm to others that this harm, although foreseen, is not part of the agent's direct intention. An end such as earning one's living is clearly not such as to justify *either* the direct or oblique intention of the death of innocent people, but in certain cases one is justified in bringing about knowingly what one could not directly intend.

It is now time to say why this doctrine should be taken seriously in spite of the fact that it sounds rather odd, that there are difficulties about the distinction on which it depends, and that it seemed to yield one sophistical conclusion when applied to the problem of abortion. The reason for its appeal is that its opponents have often *seemed* to be committed to quite indefensible views. Thus the controversy has raged around examples such as the following. Suppose that a judge or magistrate is faced with rioters demanding that a culprit be found for a certain crime and threatening otherwise to take their own bloody revenge on a particular section of the community. The real culprit being unknown, the judge sees himself as able to prevent the bloodshed only by framing some innocent person and having him executed. Beside this example is placed another in which a pilot whose aeroplane is about to crash is deciding whether to steer from a more to a less inhabited area. To make the parallel as close as possible it may rather be supposed that he is the driver of a runaway tram which he can only steer from one narrow track on to another; five men are working on one track and one man on the other; anyone on the track he enters is bound to be killed. In the case of the riots the mob have five hostages, so that in both the exchange is supposed to be one man's life for the lives of five. The question is why we should say, without hesitation, that the driver should steer for the less occupied track, while most of us would be appalled at the idea that the innocent man could be framed. It may be suggested that the special feature of the latter case is that it involves the corruption of justice, and this is, of course, very important indeed. But if we remove that special feature, supposing that some private individual is to kill an innocent person and pass him off as the criminal we still find ourselves horrified by the idea. The doctrine of double effect offers us a way out of the difficulty, insisting that it is one thing to steer towards someone foreseeing that you will kill him and another to aim at his death as part of your plan. . . .

Another pair of examples poses a similar problem. We are about to give a patient who needs it to save his life a massive dose of a certain drug in short supply. There arrive, however, five other patients each of whom could be saved by one-fifth of that dose. We say with regret that we cannot spare our whole supply of the drug for a single patient, just as we should say that we could not spare the whole resources of a ward for one dangerously ill individual when ambulances arrive bringing in victims of a multiple crash. We feel bound to let one man die rather than many if that is our only choice.

Why then do we not feel justified in killing people in the interests of cancer research or to obtain, let us say, spare parts for grafting on to those who need them? We can suppose, similarly, that several dangerously ill people can be saved only if we kill a certain individual and make a serum from his dead body. (These examples are not over-fanciful considering present controversies about prolonging the life of mortally ill patients whose eyes or kidneys are to be used for others.) Why cannot we argue from the case of the scarce drug to that of the body needed for medical purposes? Once again the doctrine of the double effect comes up with an explanation. In one kind of case but not the other we aim at the death of an innocent man. . . .

II

At one time I thought that these arguments in favour of the doctrine of the double effect were conclusive, but I now believe that the conflict should be solved in another way. . . .

Let us speak of negative duties when thinking of the obligation to refrain from such things as killing or robbing, and of the positive duty, e.g., to look after children or aged parents. It will be useful, however, to extend the notion of positive duty beyond the range of things that are strictly called duties, bringing acts of charity under this heading. These are owed only in a rather loose sense, and some acts of charity could hardly be said to be *owed* at all, so I am not following ordinary usage at this point.

Let us now see whether the distinction of negative and positive duties explains why we see differently the action of the steering driver and that of the judge, of the doctors who withhold the scarce drug and those who obtain a body for medical purposes, of those who choose to rescue five men rather than one man from torture and those who are ready to torture the one man themselves in order to save five. In each case we have a conflict of duties, but what kind of duties are they? Are we, in each case, weighing positive duties against positive, negative against negative, or one against the other? Is the duty to refrain from injury, or rather to bring aid?

The steering driver faces a conflict of negative duties, since it is his duty to avoid injuring five men and also his duty to avoid injuring one. In the circumstances he is not able to avoid both, and it seems clear that he should do the least injury he can. The judge, however, is weighing the duty of not inflicting injury against the duty of bringing aid. He wants to rescue the innocent people threatened with death but can do so only by inflicting injury himself. Since one does not in general have the same duty to help people as to refrain from injuring them, it is not possible to argue to a conclusion about what he should do from the steering driver case. It is interesting that, even where the strictest duty of positive aid exists, this still does not weigh as if a negative duty were involved. It is not, for instance, permissible to commit a murder to bring one's starving children food. If the choice is between inflicting injury on one or many there seems only one rational course of action; if the choice is between aid to some at the cost of injury to others, and refusing to inflict the injury to bring the aid, the whole matter is open to dispute. So it is not inconsistent of us to think that the driver must steer for the road on which only one man stands while the judge (or his equivalent) may not kill the innocent person in order to stop the riots. Let us now consider the second pair of examples, which concern the scarce drug on the one hand and on the other the body needed to save lives. Once again we find a difference based on the distinction between the duty to avoid injury and the duty to provide aid. Where one man needs a massive dose of the drug and we withhold it from him in order to save five men, we are weighing aid against aid. But if we consider killing a man in order to use his body to save others, we are thinking of doing him an injury to bring others aid. In an interesting variant of the model, we may suppose that instead of killing someone we deliberately let him die. (Perhaps he is a beggar to whom we are thinking of giving food, but then we say "No, they need bodies for medical research.") Here it does seem relevant that in allowing him to die we are aiming at his death, but presumably we are inclined to see this as a violation of negative rather than positive duty. If this is right, we see why we are unable in either case to argue to a conclusion from the case of the scarce drug. . . .

So far the conclusions are the same as those at which we might arrive following the doctrine of the double effect, but in others they will be different, and the advantage seems to be all on the side of the alternative. Suppose, for instance, that there are five patients in a hospital whose lives could be saved by the manufacture of a certain gas, but that this inevitably releases lethal fumes into the room of another patient whom for some reason we are unable to move. His death, being of no use to us, is clearly a side effect, and not directly intended. Why then is the case different from that of the scarce drug, if the point about that is that we foresaw but did not strictly intend the death of the single patient? Yet it surely is different. The relatives of the gassed patient would presumably be successful if they sued the hospital and the whole story came out. We may find it particularly revolting that someone should be *used* as in the case where he is killed or allowed to die in the interest of medical research, and the fact of *using* may even determine what we would decide to do in some cases, but the principle seems unimportant compared with our reluctance to bring such injury for the sake of giving aid.

My conclusion is that the distinction between direct and oblique intention plays only a quite subsidiary role in determining what we say in these cases, while the distinction between avoiding injury and bringing aid is very important indeed. I have not, of course, argued that there are no other principles. For instance it clearly makes a difference whether our positive duty is a strict duty or rather an act of charity: feeding our own children or feeding those in faraway countries. It may also make a difference whether the person about to suffer is one thought of as uninvolved in the threatened disaster, and whether it is his presence that constitutes the threat to the others. In many cases we find it very hard to know what to say, and I have not been arguing for any general conclusion such as that we may never, whatever the balance of good and evil, bring injury to one for the sake of aid to others, even when this injury amounts to death. I have only tried to show that even if we reject the doctrine of the double effect we are not forced to the conclusion that the size of the evil must always be our guide. . . .

NOTE

1. For discussions of the Catholic doctrine on abortion see Glanville Williams, *The Sanctity of Life and the Criminal Law* (New York, 1957); also N. St. John Stevas, *The Right to Life* (London, 1963).

PROBLEMS FOR NATURAL LAW THEORY
Emmett Barcalow

Emmett Barcalow teaches at Western New England College and is author of Moral Philosophy: Theories and Issues *(1994). Perhaps the most distinctive feature of the natural law theory is its attempt to infer basic moral principles from facts about human nature, and Barcalow raises two problems for this feature of natural-law thinking. First, it is doubtful that one can infer moral principles forbidding adultery, rape, homosexuality, and so forth, either from biological facts about human nature or from facts about the inherent nature of* Homo sapiens. *Second, it is questionable that behavior in accordance with human nature is morally right and behavior not in accord with human nature is morally wrong. For instance, if it turns out that human beings (at least the males) are naturally aggressive, should we infer that war and fighting are morally right?*

Human Nature

Natural law theorists argue in the following way.

Behavior/action X is not in accordance with a human being's inherent nature.

It is contrary to reason for a human being to act in a way that is not in accordance with a human being's inherent nature.

Whatever is contrary to reason is immoral.

Therefore, behavior/action X is immoral.

However, many critics of natural law theory doubt that human nature can provide moral guidance and they doubt that whatever is "natural" or in conformity with an organism's inherent nature must be morally right and good.

The concept of the inherent nature of an organism is complicated. On the one hand it can include purely biological features that all members of a species have. For example, it is part of the inherent nature of whales that they have lungs rather than gills, while it is part of the inherent nature of sharks that they have gills rather than lungs. Consequently, whales must breathe in air and cannot breathe in water while sharks must breathe in water and cannot breathe in air. Similarly, it is part of a chicken's inherent nature that it lays eggs, while it is part of a cow's nature that it bears live calves rather than lays eggs. It is part of a termite's inherent nature that its digestive system can gain nourishment from eating wood, while it is part of a crocodile's nature that its digestive system cannot gain nourishment from eating wood. In this sense of an organism's inherent nature, an organism either physically cannot do certain things because of its inherent nature (lay eggs, breathe in water, digest wood) or it cannot survive and flourish if it acts contrary to its inherent nature.

Human nature includes certain biological features. For example, all human beings have lungs rather than gills; therefore, they breathe in air and cannot breathe in water. Similarly, because of the nature of their digestive systems, human beings cannot digest and gain nourishment from wood or stones. Therefore, a human being who attempted to breathe in water or eat wood would not be acting in accordance with his inherent nature as a human being. However, the biological features of the species *Homo sapiens* do not establish the most common moral laws that natural law theorists claim to derive from human nature. For example, adultery, polygamy, homosexuality, theft, physical assault, cruelty, rape, and killing the innocent are not contrary to the biological nature of human beings the way that breathing in water or eating wood are; they obviously do not have the same effects on a person as eating wood or breathing in water. Therefore, they are not "unnatural" in the sense of being contrary to the biological nature of human beings. If natural law theorists wish to maintain that such behavior is contrary to reason and immoral for human beings because it is not in accordance with human nature, they must appeal to some other conception of what it is to act or not act, to live or not live, in accordance with human nature.

An organism's inherent nature as a member of a certain species often establishes characteristic patterns of behavior common to all or almost all members of the species. For example, spiders spin webs; sparrows build nests; bees construct hives; cats hunt mice and birds; hyenas tend to hunt in packs; polar bears hunt alone. It would be unnatural in the sense of unusual or uncharacteristic for a spider not to spin a web, for a sparrow to spin a web, for a hyena to hunt alone, or for a polar bear to hunt in a pack of polar bears. Similarly, it would be contrary to a lamb's nature to attack a lion, just as it would be contrary to a lion's nature to run from a lamb. In a sense, an organism's inherent nature as a member of a certain species establishes laws of behavior for it that are physical laws of nature.

Critics of natural law theory say that it is doubtful, however, that the inherent nature of *Homo sapiens* establishes laws of behavior for human beings in the same way as it may establish laws of behavior for cats, lions, and polar bears. Human nature is surprisingly diverse. For example, are human beings naturally as fearless and aggressive as lions or are they naturally as timid and pacific as rabbits and lambs? Human nature has room for both kinds of personality. Human beings also don't seem to have the relatively simple inherent or "instinctive" behavior patterns of some of the animals lower on the evolutionary tree. Cats "instinctively" chase mice and birds; therefore, such behavior is natural for them. It is not easy to identify "instinctive" behavior patterns in human beings that are akin to such behavior patterns as cats chasing mice and birds. It is especially difficult because so much of human behavior is shaped by the environment, that is, by deliberate and nondeliberate conditioning, training, and education.

In this sense of an organism's inherent nature, critics think that it is quite doubtful that polygamy, adultery, homosexuality, physical assault, cruelty, rape, or killing the innocent are contrary to the inherent nature of human beings. If that is so, then we cannot appeal to this sense of the inherent nature of human beings in order to show that such behavior is wrong. The challenge facing natural law theorists is to provide a plausible account of the inherent nature of human beings so that they can show that the kinds of behavior they condemn (for example, adultery, homosexuality, theft, and killing the innocent) are immoral because they are contrary to the inherent nature of human beings. Without that, it is not clear how appeals to the inherent nature of human beings can provide moral guidance.

What Is Natural Is Right and
What Is Unnatural Is Wrong?

Natural law theorists assume that it is morally right and good for an organism to act in accordance with its inherent nature. Only on the basis of that assumption can the inherent nature of human beings provide moral laws of conduct for them. However, critics present reasons for doubting that all behavior that is in accordance with an organism's inherent nature is morally good and all behavior not in accordance with its inherent nature is morally bad. For example, biologist Stephen Jay Gould writes of a group of wasps named Ichneumonoidea comprising hundreds of thousands of different species. These wasps reproduce by laying their eggs inside the living body of another insect, most commonly a caterpillar. The wasp stings the caterpillar and then injects its eggs into it. As Gould writes, "Usually, the host is not otherwise inconvenienced for the moment, at least until the eggs hatch and the ichneumon larvae begin their grim work of interior excavation."[1] Then, the larvae slowly eat the helpless caterpillar from the inside out. "[T]he ichneumon larva eats fat bodies and digestive organs first, keeping the caterpillar alive by preserving intact that essential heart and central nervous system. Finally, the larva completes its work and kills its victim, leaving behind the caterpillar's empty shell."[2] Such behavior is in accordance with the inherent nature of Ichneumonoidea wasps. However, one may doubt that such natural behavior is morally praiseworthy.

It may be that human beings, or at least male human beings, are naturally aggressive and prone to violence. After all, war and fighting seem to be such universal pastimes of men in all ages that one might conclude that the inherent nature of male human beings includes a strong tendency to behave violently. If that is so, should men act in accordance with their inherent nature or should they try to resist their inherent natural tendencies? Similarly, many people believe that the image of childhood as a time of innocence and purity is sentimental nonsense. In their view, children are inherently cruel and are brought to extinguish or control their inherent cruelty only through education and socialization. Consider the tendency of children to mercilessly taunt or bully those who are weaker than or different from themselves. We might maintain that the purpose of moral education is not to encourage people to give their inherent natures free rein but rather to tame their inherent natures.

Similarly, suppose that human beings are inherently selfish or primarily self-interested and that altruism is not in accordance with the inherent nature of human beings. If this were true, would it follow that altruism is immoral and contrary to reason because it is not in accordance with the inherent nature of human beings? Many people would deny that altruism is wrong even if it is not in accordance with the inherent nature of human beings. They would say, "So much the worse for the inherent nature of human beings." In their view, moral education often needs to go against rather than with the inherent nature of human beings. They deny that actions in accordance with the inherent nature of human beings are always right and good for human beings and that actions not in accordance with the inherent nature of human beings are always wrong and bad for human beings.

Notes

1. Stephen Jay Gould, "Nonmoral Nature," in Stephen Jay Gould, *Hen's Teeth and Horse's Toes* (New York: W. W. Norton, 1983), p. 34.
2. *Ibid.*, p. 35.

CHAPTER 5

Utilitarianism

THE PRINCIPLE OF UTILITY
Jeremy Bentham

Jeremy Bentham (1748–1832) is often called the father of modern utilitarianism. In this selection from his classic, The Principles of Morals and Legislation *(1789), Bentham presents and defends a hedonistic version of utilitarianism. According to the principle of utility, the morality of an individual action depends on how much utility that action would produce, where utility is measured in amounts of pleasure and pain. Because the focus is on the effects of concrete actions, this view is often called "act utilitarianism."*

After defending the claim that the principle of utility is the basic principle of right conduct, Bentham proceeds to set forth his famous "hedonic calculus"— a list of seven considerations to be used in calculating the utility of actions.

The principle of utility is the foundation of the present work: it will be proper therefore at the outset to give an explicit and determinate account of what is meant by it. By the principle of utility is meant that principle which approves or disapproves of every action whatsoever, according to the tendency which it appears to have to augment or diminish the happiness of the party whose interest is in question: or, what is the same thing in other words, to promote or to oppose that happiness. I say of every action whatsoever; and therefore not only of every action of a private individual, but of every measure of government.

By utility is meant that property in any object, whereby it tends to produce benefit, advantage, pleasure, good, or happiness (all this in the present case comes to the same thing), or (what comes again to the same thing) to prevent the happening of mischief, pain, evil, or unhappiness to the party whose interest is considered: if that party be the community in general, then the happiness of the community: if a particular individual, then the happiness of that individual.

The interest of the community is one of the most general expressions that can occur in the phraseology of morals: no wonder that the meaning of it is often lost. When it has a meaning, it is this. The community is a fictitious *body,* composed of the individual persons who are considered as constituting as it were its *members.* The interest of the community then is, what?—the sum of the interests of the several members who compose it.

It is in vain to talk of the interest of the community, without understanding what is the interest of the individual. A thing is said to promote the interest, or to be *for* the interest, of an individual, when it tends to add to the sum total of his pleasures: or, what comes to the same thing, to diminish the sum total of his pains.

An action then may be said to be conformable to the principle of utility, or, for shortness sake, to utility (meaning with respect to the community at large), when the tendency it has to augment the happiness of the community is greater than any it has to diminish it.

A measure of government (which is but a particular kind of action, performed by a particular person or persons) may be said to be conformable to or dictated by the principle of utility, when in like manner the tendency which it has to augment the happiness of the community is greater than any which it has to diminish it.

When an action, or in particular a measure of government, is supposed by a man to be conformable to the principle of utility, it may be convenient, for the purposes of discourse, to imagine a kind of law or dictate, called a law or dictate of utility: and to speak of the action in question, as being conformable to such law or dictate.

A man may be said to be a partisan of the principle of utility, when the approbation or disapprobation he annexes to any action, or to any measure, is determined by and proportioned to the tendency which he conceives it to have to augment or to diminish the happiness of the community: or in other words, to its conformity or unconformity to the laws or dictates of utility.

Of an action that is conformable to the principle of utility one may always say either that it is one that ought to be done, or at least that it is not one that ought not to be done. One may say also, that it is right it should be done; at least that it is not wrong it should be done: that it is a right action; at least that it is not a wrong action. When thus interpreted, the words *ought,* and *right* and *wrong,* and others of that stamp, have a meaning: when otherwise, they have none.

Has the rectitude of this principle been ever formally contested? It should seem that it had, by those who have not known what they have been meaning. Is it susceptible of any direct proof? it should seem not: for that which is used to prove every thing else, cannot itself be proved: a chain of proofs must have their commencement somewhere. To give such proof is as impossible as it is needless.

Not that there is or ever has been that human creature breathing, however stupid or perverse, who has not on many, perhaps on most occasions of his life, deferred to it. By the natural constitution of the human frame, on most occasions of their lives men in general embrace this principle, without thinking of it: if not for the ordering of their own actions, yet for the trying of their own actions, as well as of those of other men. There have been, at the same time, not many, perhaps, even of the most intelligent, who have been disposed to embrace it purely and without reserve. There are even few who have not taken some occasion or other to quarrel with it, either on account of their not understanding always how to apply it, or on account of some prejudice or other which they were afraid to examine into, or could not bear to part with. For such is the stuff that man is made of: in principle and in practice, in a right track and in a wrong one, the rarest of all human qualities is consistency.

When a man attempts to combat the principle of utility, it is with reasons drawn, without his being aware of it, from that very principle itself. His arguments, if they prove any thing, prove not that the principle is *wrong*, but that, according to the applications he supposes to be made of it, it is *misapplied*. Is it possible for a man to move the earth? Yes; but he must first find out another earth to stand upon.

To disprove the propriety of it by arguments is impossible; but, from the causes that have been mentioned, or from some confused or partial view of it, a man may happen to be disposed not to relish it. Where this is the case, if he thinks the setting of his opinions on such a subject worth the trouble, let him take the following steps, and at length, perhaps, he may come to reconcile himself to it.

Let him settle with himself, whether he would wish to discard this principle altogether; if so, let him consider what it is that all his reasonings (in matters of politics especially) can amount to?

If he would, let him settle with himself, whether he would judge and act without any principle, or whether there is any other he would judge and act by?

If there be, let him examine and satisfy himself whether the principle he thinks he has found is really any separate intelligible principle; or whether it be not a mere principle in words, a kind of phrase, which at bottom expresses neither more nor less than the mere averment of his own unfounded senti-ments; that is, what in another person he might be apt to call caprice?

If he is inclined to think that his own approbation or disapprobation, annexed to the idea of an act, without any regard to its consequences, is a sufficient foundation for him to judge and act upon, let him ask himself whether his sentiment is to be a standard of right and wrong, with respect to every other man, or whether every man's sentiment has the same privi-lege of being a standard to itself?

In the first case, let him ask himself whether his principle is not despot-ical, and hostile to all the rest of human race?

In the second case, whether it is not anarchial, and whether at this rate there are not as many different standards of right and wrong as there are men? and whether even to the same man, the same thing, which is right today, may not (without the least change in its nature) be wrong tomorrow? and whether the same thing is not right and wrong in the same place at the same time? and in either case, whether all argument is not at an end? and whether, when two men have said, "I like this," and "I don't like it," they can (upon such a principle) have any thing more to say?

If he should have said to himself, No: for that the sentiment which he proposes as a standard must be grounded on reflection, let him say on what particulars the reflection is to turn? if on particulars having relation to the utility of the act, then let him say whether this is not deserting his own prin-ciple, and borrowing assistance from the very one in opposition to which he sets it up: or if not on those particulars, on what other particulars?

If he should be for compounding the matter, and adopting his own prin-ciple in part, and the principle of utility in part, let him say how far he will adopt it?

When he has settled with himself where he will stop, then let him ask himself how he justifies to himself the adopting it so far? and why he will not adopt it any farther?

Admitting any other principle than the principle of utility to be a right principle, a principle that it is right for a man to pursue; admitting (what is not true) that the word *right* can have a meaning without reference to utility, let him say whether there is any such thing as a *motive* that a man can have to pursue the dictates of it: if there is, let him say what that motive is, and how it is to be distinguished from those which enforce the dictates of utility: if not, then lastly let him say what it is this other principle can be good for? . . .

Pleasures then, and the avoidance of pains, are the *ends* which the legisla-tor has in view: it behooves him therefore to understand their *value*. Pleasures and pains are the *instruments* he has to work with: it behooves him therefore to understand their force, which is again, in other words, their value.

To a person considered *by himself*, the value of a pleasure or pain considered *by itself*, will be greater or less, according to the four following circumstances:

1. Its *intensity*.

2. Its *duration*.

3. Its *certainty* or *uncertainty*.

4. Its *propinquity* or *remoteness*.

These are the circumstances which are to be considered in estimating a pleasure or a pain considered each of them by itself. But when the value of any pleasure or pain is considered for the purpose of estimating the tendency of any *act* by which it is produced, there are two other circumstances to be taken into the account; these are,

5. Its *fecundity*, or the chance it has of being followed by sensations of the *same* kind: that is, pleasures, if it be a pleasure: pains, if it be a pain.

6. Its *purity*, or the chance it has of *not* being followed by sensations of the *opposite* kind: that is, pains, if it be a pleasure: pleasures, if it be a pain.

These two last, however, are in strictness scarcely to be deemed properties of the pleasure or the pain itself, they are not, therefore, in strictness to be taken into the account of the value of that pleasure or that pain. They are in strictness to be deemed properties only of the act, or other event, by which such pleasure or pain has been produced; and accordingly are only to be taken into the account of the tendency of such act or such event.

To a *number* of persons, with reference to each of whom the value of a pleasure or a pain is considered, it will be greater or less, according to seven circumstances: to wit, the six preceding ones; *viz.*

1. Its *intensity*.

2. Its *duration*.

3. Its *certainty* or *uncertainty*.

4. Its *propinquity* or *remoteness*.

5. Its *fecundity*.

6. Its *purity*.

And one other; to wit:

7. Its *extent;* that is, the number of persons to whom it *extends;* or (in other words) who are affected by it.

To take an exact account then of the general tendency of any act, by which the interests of a community are affected, proceed as follows. Begin with any one person of those whose interests seem most immediately to be affected by it: and take an account,

1. Of the value of each distinguishable *pleasure* which appears to be produced by it in the *first* instance.

2. Of the value of each *pain* which appears to be produced by it in the *first* instance.

3. Of the value of each pleasure which appears to be produced by it *after* the first. This constitutes the *fecundity* of the first *pleasure* and the *impurity* of the first *pain.*

4. Of the value of each *pain* which appears to be produced by it after the first. This constitutes the *fecundity* of the first *pain,* and the *impurity* of the first pleasure.

5. Sum up all the values of all the *pleasures* on the one side, and those of all the pains on the other. The balance, if it be on the side of pleasure, will give the *good* tendency of the act upon the whole, with respect to the interests of that *individual* person; if on the side of pain, the *bad* tendency of it upon the whole.

6. Take an account of the *number* of persons whose interests appear to be concerned; and repeat the above process with respect to each. *Sum up* the numbers expressive of the degrees of *good* tendency, which the act has, with respect to each individual, in regard to whom the tendency of it is *good* upon the whole: do this again with respect to each individual, in regard to whom the tendency of it is *good* upon the whole: do this again with respect to each individual, in regard to whom the tendency of it is *bad* upon the whole. Take the *balance;* which, if on the side of *pleasure,* will give the general *good tendency* of the act, with respect to the total number or community of individuals concerned; if on the side of pain, the general *evil tendency,* with respect to the same community.

It is not to be expected that this process should be strictly pursued previously to every moral judgment, or to every legislative or judicial operation.

It may, however, be always kept in view: and as near as the process actually pursued on these occasions approaches to it, so near will such process approach to the character of an exact one.

The same process is alike applicable to pleasure and pain, in whatever shape they appear: and by whatever denomination they are distinguished: to pleasure, whether it be called *good* (which is properly the cause or instrument of pleasure) or *profit* (which is distant pleasure, or the cause or instrument of distant pleasure), or *convenience,* or *advantage, benefit, emolument, happiness,* and so forth: to pain, whether it be called *evil* (which corresponds to *good*), or *mischief,* or *inconvenience,* or *disadvantage,* or *loss,* or *unhappiness,* and so forth.

Nor is this a novel and unwarranted, any more than it is a useless theory. In all this there is nothing but what the practice of mankind, wheresoever they have a clear view of their own interest, is perfectly conformable to. An article of property, an estate in land, for instance, is valuable, on what account? On account of the pleasures of all kinds which it enables a man to produce, and what comes to the same thing the pains of all kinds which it enables him to avert. But the value of such an article of property is universally understood to rise or fall according to the length or shortness of the time which a man has in it: the certainty or uncertainty of its coming into possession: and the nearness or remoteness of the time at which, if at all, it is to come into possession. As to the *intensity* of the pleasures which a man may derive from it, this is never thought of, because it depends upon the use which each particular person may come to make of it; which cannot be estimated till the particular pleasures he may come to derive from it, or the particular pains he may come to exclude by means of it, are brought to view. For the same reason, neither does he think of the *fecundity* or *purity* of those pleasures. . . .

IN DEFENSE OF UTILITARIANISM
J. S. Mill

John Stuart Mill (1806–1873), a British philosopher, was a leading intellectual of the nineteenth century. In the following excerpt from his book, Utilitarianism *(1863), Mill considers three objections to the utilitarian theory. First, some opponents charge that the emphasis on the pursuit of pleasure makes utilitarianism*

Reprinted from *Utilitarianism* (1863).

"a doctrine worthy of swine." Mill responds by distinguishing higher from lower pleasures. Because utilitarianism considers pursuit of higher, distinctively human pleasures (such as enjoying great literature) as especially important, it is, Mill asserts, a doctrine worthy of human beings. Second, some argue that utilitarian moral theory sets standards that are "too high for humanity." Third, still others object that in ordinary circumstances that call for a moral decision, we lack the time needed for calculating the utility of actions. Mill argues that these latter two objections are based on misunderstandings of the utilitarian theory. After answering these objections, Mill offers what he calls an "indirect proof" of the principle of utility.

The creed which accepts as the foundation of morals, Utility, or the Greatest Happiness Principle, holds that actions are right in proportion as they tend to promote happiness, wrong as they tend to produce the reverse of happiness. By happiness is intended pleasure, and the absence of pain; by unhappiness, pain, and the privation of pleasure. To give a clear view of the moral standard set up by the theory, much more requires to be said; in particular, what things it includes in the ideas of pain and pleasure; and to what extent this is left an open question. But these supplementary explanations do not affect the theory of life on which this theory of morality is grounded—namely, that pleasure, and freedom from pain, are the only things desirable as ends; and that all desirable things (which are as numerous in the utilitarian as in any other scheme) are desirable either for the pleasure inherent in themselves, or as means to the promotion of pleasure and the prevention of pain.

Now, such a theory of life excites in many minds, and among them in some of the most estimable in feeling and purpose, inveterate dislike. To suppose that life has (as they express it) no higher end than pleasure—no better and nobler object of desire and pursuit—they designate as utterly mean and grovelling; as a doctrine worthy only of swine, to whom the followers of Epicurus were, at a very early period, contemptuously likened; and modern holders of the doctrine are occasionally made the subject of equally polite comparisons by its German, French, and English assailants.

When thus attacked, the Epicureans have always answered, that it is not they, but their accusers, who represent human nature in a degrading light; since the accusation supposes human beings to be capable of no pleasures except those of which swine are capable. If this supposition were true, the charge could not be gainsaid, but would then be no longer an imputation; for if the sources of pleasure were precisely the same to human beings and to swine, the rule of life which is good enough for the one would be good enough for the other. The comparison of the Epicurean life to that of beasts is felt as degrading, precisely because a beast's pleasures do not satisfy a human being's conceptions of happiness. Human beings have faculties more elevated than the animal appetites, and when once made conscious of them, do not regard anything as happiness which does not include their gratification. I do not, indeed, consider the Epicureans to have been by any means faultless in drawing out their scheme of consequences from the utilitarian principle. To do this in any sufficient manner, many Stoic, as well as Christian, elements require to be included. But there is no known Epicurean theory of life which does not assign to the pleasures of the intellect, of the feelings and imagination, and of the moral sentiments, a much higher value as pleasures than to those of mere sensation. It must be admitted, however, that utilitarian writers in general have placed the superiority of mental over bodily pleasures chiefly in the greater permanency, safety, uncostliness, etc., of the former—that is, in their circumstantial advantages rather than in their intrinsic nature. And on all these points utilitarians have fully proved their case; but they might have taken the other, and, as it may be called, higher ground, with entire consistency. It is quite compatible with the principle of utility to recognize the fact, that some *kinds* of pleasure are more desirable and more valuable than others. It would be absurd that while, in estimating all other things, quality is considered as well as quantity, the estimation of pleasures should be supposed to depend on quantity alone.

If I am asked, what I mean by difference of quality in pleasures, or what makes one pleasure more valuable than another, merely as a pleasure, except its being greater in amount, there is but one possible answer. Of two pleasures, if there be one to which all or almost all who have experience of both give a decided preference, irrespective of any feeling of moral obligation to prefer it, that is the more desirable pleasure. If one of the two is, by those who are competently acquainted with both, placed so far above the other that they prefer it, even though knowing it to be attended with a greater amount of discontent, and would not resign it for any quantity of the other pleasure which their nature is capable of, we are justified in ascribing to the preferred enjoyment a superiority in quality, so far outweighing quantity as to render it, in comparison, of small account.

Now it is an unquestionable fact that those who are equally acquainted with, and equally capable of appreciating and enjoying, both, do give a most marked preference to the manner of existence which employs their higher faculties. Few human creatures would consent to be changed into any of the lower animals, for a promise of the fullest allowance of a beast's pleasures; no intelligent human being would consent to be a fool, no instructed person would be an ignoramus, no person of feeling and conscience would be selfish and base, even though they should be persuaded that the fool, the dunce, or the rascal is better satisfied with his lot than they are with theirs. They would not resign what they possess more than he for the most complete satisfaction of all the desires which they have in common with him. If they ever fancy they would, it is only in cases of unhappiness so extreme, that to escape from it they would exchange their lot for almost any other, however undesirable in their own eyes. A being of higher faculties requires more to make him happy, is capable probably of more acute suffering, and is certainly accessible to it at more points than one of an inferior type; but in spite of these liabilities, he can never really wish to sink into what he feels to be a lower grade of existence. We may give what explanation we please of this unwillingness; we may attribute it to pride, a name which is given indiscriminately to some of the most and to some of the least estimable feelings of which mankind are capable; we may refer it to the love of liberty and personal independence, an appeal to which was with the Stoics one of the most effective means for the inculcation of it; to the love of power, or to the love of excitement, both of which do really enter into and contribute to it: but its most appropriate appellation is a sense of dignity, which all human beings possess in one form or other, and in some, though by no means in exact, proportion to their higher faculties, and which is so essential a part of the happiness of those in whom it is strong, that nothing which conflicts with it could be, otherwise than momentarily, an object of desire to them. Whoever supposes that this preference takes place at a sacrifice of happiness—that the superior being, in anything like the equal circumstances, is not happier than the inferior—confounds the two very different ideas, of happiness, and content. It is indisputable that the being whose capacities of enjoyment are low, has the greatest chance of having them fully satisfied; and a highly-endowed being will always feel that any happiness which he can look for, as in the world is constituted, is imperfect. But he can learn to bear its imperfections, if they are at all bearable; and they will not make him envy the being who is indeed unconscious of the imperfections, but only because he feels not at all the good which those imperfections qualify. It is better to be a human being dissatisfied than a pig satisfied; better to be Socrates dissatisfied than a fool satisfied. And if the fool, or the pig, is of a different opinion, it is because they only know their own side of the question. The other party to the comparison knows both sides. . . .

. . . The objectors to utilitarianism cannot always be charged with representing it in a discreditable light. On the contrary, those among them who entertain anything like a just idea of its disinterested character, sometimes find fault with its standard as being too high for humanity. They say it is exacting too much to require that people shall always act from the inducement of promoting the general interests of society. But this is to mistake the very meaning of a standard of morals, and to confound the rule of action with the motive of it. It is the business of ethics to tell us what are our duties, or by what test we may know them; but no system of ethics requires that the sole motive of all we do shall be a feeling of duty; on the contrary, ninety-nine hundredths of all our actions are done from other motives, and rightly so done, if the rule of duty does not condemn them. It is the more unjust to utilitarianism that this particular misapprehension should be made a ground of objection to it, inasmuch as utilitarian moralists have gone beyond almost all others in affirming that the motive has nothing to do with the morality of the action, though much with the worth of the agent. He who saves a fellow creature from drowning does what is morally right, whether his motive be duty, or the hope of being paid for his trouble: he who betrays the friend that trusts him, is guilty of a crime, even if his object be to serve another friend to whom he is under greater obligations. But to speak only of actions done from the motive of duty, and in direct obedience to principle: it is a misapprehension of the utilitarian mode of thought, to conceive it as implying that people should fix their minds upon so wide a generality as the world, or society at large. The great majority of good actions are intended, not for the benefit of the world, but for that of individuals, of which the good of the world is made up; and the thoughts of the most virtuous man need not on these occasions travel beyond the particular persons concerned, except so far as is necessary to assure himself that in benefiting them he is not violating the rights—that is, the legitimate and authorized expectations—of any one else. The multiplication of happiness is, according to the utilitarian ethics, the object of virtue: the occasions on which any person (except one in a thousand) has it in his power to do this on an extended scale, in other words, to be a public benefactor, are but exceptional; and on these occasions alone is he called on to consider public utility; in every other case, private utility, the interest or happiness of some few persons, is all he has to attend to. Those alone the influence of whose actions extends to society in general, need concern themselves habitually about so large an object. In the case of abstinences indeed—of things which people forbear to do, from moral considerations, though the consequences in the particular case might be beneficial—it would be unworthy of an intelligent agent not to be consciously aware that the action is of a class which, if practiced generally, would be generally injurious, and that this is the ground of the obligation to abstain from it. The amount of regard for the public interest implied in this recognition, is no greater than is demanded by every system of morals; for they all enjoin to abstain from whatever is manifestly pernicious to society. . . .

. . . Again, defenders of utility often find themselves called upon to reply to such objections as this—that there is not time, previous to action, for calculating and weighing the effects of any line of conduct on the general happiness. This is exactly as if any one were to say that it is impossible to guide our conduct by Christianity, because there is not time, on every occasion on which anything has to be done, to read through the Old and New Testaments. The answer to the objection is, that there has been ample time, namely, the whole past duration of the human species. During all that time mankind have been learning by experience the tendencies of actions; on which experience all the prudence, as well as all the morality of life, is dependent. People talk as if the commencement of this course of experience had hitherto been put off, and as if, at the moment when some man feels tempted to meddle with the property or life of another, he had to begin considering for the first time whether murder and theft are injurious to human happiness. Even then I do not think that he would find the question very puzzling; but, at all events, the matter is now done to his hand. It is truly a whimsical supposition that if mankind were agreed in considering utility to be the test of morality, they would remain without any agreement as to what *is* useful, and would take no measures for having their notions on the subject taught to the young, and enforced by law and opinion. There is no difficulty in proving any ethical standard whatever to work ill, if we suppose universal idiocy to be conjoined with it, but on any hypothesis short of that, mankind must by this time have acquired positive beliefs as to the effects of some actions on their happiness; and the beliefs which have thus come down are the rules of morality for the multitude, and for the philosopher until he has succeeded in finding better. That philosophers might easily do this, even now, on many subjects; that the received code of ethics is by no means of divine right; and that mankind have still much to learn as to the effects of actions on the general happiness, I admit, or rather, earnestly maintain. The corollaries from the principle of utility, like the precepts of every practical art, admit of indefinite improvement, and, in a progressive state of the human mind, their improvement is perpetually going on. But to consider the rules of morality as improvable, is one thing; to pass over the intermediate generalizations entirely, and endeavor to test each individual action directly by the first principle, is another. It is a strange notion that the acknowledgment of a first principle is inconsistent with the admission of secondary ones. To inform a traveller respecting the place of his ultimate destination, is not to forbid the use of landmarks and direction-posts on the way. The proposition that happiness is the end and aim of morality, does not mean that no road ought to be laid down to that goal, or that persons going thither should not be advised to take one direction rather than another. Men really ought to leave off talking a kind of nonsense on this subject, which they would neither talk nor listen to in other matters of practical concernment. Nobody argues that the art of navigation is not founded on astronomy, because sailors cannot wait to calculate the Nautical Almanack. Being rational creatures, they go to sea with it ready calculated; and all rational creatures go out upon the sea of life with their minds made up on the common questions of right and wrong, as well as on many of the far more difficult questions of wise and foolish. And this, as long as foresight is a human quality, is to be presumed they will continue to do. Whatever we adopt as the fundamental principle of morality, we require subordinate principles to apply it by: the impossibility of doing without them, being common to all systems, can afford no argument against any one in particular: but gravely to argue as if no such secondary principles could be had, and as if mankind had remained till now, and always must remain, without drawing any general conclusions from the experience of human life, is as high a pitch, I think, as absurdity has ever reached in philosophical controversy. . . .

Of What Sort of Proof
the Principle of Utility Is Susceptible

It has already been remarked, that questions of ultimate ends do not admit of proof, in the ordinary acceptation of the term. To be incapable of proof by reasoning is common to all first principles; to the first premises of our knowledge, as well as to those of our conduct. But the former, being matters of fact, may be the subject of a direct appeal to the faculties which judge of fact—namely, our senses, and our internal consciousness. Can an appeal be made to the same faculties on questions of practical ends? Or by what other faculty is cognizance taken of them?

Questions about ends are, in other words, questions what things are desirable. The utilitarian doctrine is, that happiness is desirable, and the only thing desirable, as an end; all other things being only desirable as means to that end. What ought to be required of this doctrine—what conditions is it requisite that the doctrine should fulfill—to make good its claim to be believed?

The only proof capable of being given that an object is visible, is that people actually see it. The only proof that a sound is audible, is that people hear it: and so of the other sources of our experience. In like manner, I apprehend, the sole evidence it is possible to produce that anything is desirable, is that people do actually desire it. If the end which the utilitarian doctrine proposes to itself were not, in theory and in practice, acknowledged to be an end, nothing could ever convince any person that it was so. No reason can be given why the general happiness is desirable, except that each person, so far as he believes it to be attainable, desires his own happiness. This, however, being a fact, we have not only all the proof which the case admits of, but all which it is possible to require, that happiness is a good: that each person's happiness is a good to that person, and the general happiness, therefore, a good to the aggregate of all persons. Happiness has made out its title as *one* of the ends of conduct, and consequently one of the criteria of morality.

But it has not, by this alone, proved itself to be the sole criterion. To do that, it would seem, by the same rule, necessary to show, not only that people desire happiness, but that they never desire anything else. Now it is palpable that they do desire things which, in common language, are decidedly distinguished from happiness. They desire, for example, virtue, and the absence of vice, no less really than pleasure and the absence of pain. The desire of virtue is not as universal, but it is as authentic a fact, as the desire of happiness. And hence the opponents of the utilitarian standard deem that they have a right to infer that there are other ends of human action besides happiness, and that happiness is not the standard of approbation and disapprobation.

But does the utilitarian doctrine deny that people desire virtue, or maintain that virtue is not a thing to be desired? The very reverse. It maintains not only that virtue is to be desired, but that it is to be desired disinterestedly, for itself. Whatever may be the opinion of utilitarian moralists as to the original conditions by which virtue is made virtue; however they may believe (as they do) that actions and dispositions are only virtuous because they promote another end than virtue; yet this being granted, and it having been decided, from considerations of this description, what *is* virtuous, they not only place virtue at the very head of the things which are good as means to the ultimate end, but they also recognize as a psychological fact the possibility of its being, to the individual, a good in itself, without looking to any end beyond it; and hold, that the mind is not in a right state, not in a state conformable to Utility, not in the state most conducive to the general happiness, unless it does love virtue in this manner—as a thing desirable in itself, even although, in the individual instance, it should not produce those other desirable consequences which it tends to produce, and on account of which it is held to be virtue. This opinion is not, in the smallest degree, a departure from the Happiness principle. The ingredients of happiness are very various, and each of them is desirable in itself, and not merely when considered as swelling an aggregate. The principle of utility does not mean that any given pleasure, as music, for instance, or any given exemption from pain, as for example health, are to be looked upon as a means to a collective something termed happiness, and to be desired on that account. They are desired and desirable in and for themselves; besides being means, they are a part of the end. Virtue, according to the utilitarian doctrine, is not naturally and originally part of the end, but it is capable of becoming so; and in those who love it disinterestedly it has become so, and is desired and cherished, not as a means to happiness, but as a part of their happiness. . . .

AGAINST MORAL CONSERVATISM
Kai Nielsen

Kai Nielsen is professor of philosophy at Calgary University. He is author of numerous articles on ethics and philosophy of religion, and his books include the influential Ethics Without God *(1973). Nielsen defends utilitarianism against various examples that purport to show that utilitarianism does not cohere with certain deeply held moral convictions. (See the discussion in the Introduction to this book of the coherence criterion.) According to the critics, reflection on certain life-and-death situations supports a deontological moral theory (what Nielsen calls "moral conservatism"). Nielsen responds by considering the examples of the critics and explaining how a utilitarian can account for them.*

I

It is sometimes claimed that any consequentialist view of ethics has monstrous implications which make such a conception of morality untenable. What we must do—so the claim goes—is reject all forms of consequentialism and accept what has been labeled "conservativism" or "moral absolutism." By "conservativism" is meant, here, a normative ethical theory which maintains that there is a privileged moral principle or cluster of moral principles, prescribing determinate actions, with which it would always be wrong not to act in accordance no matter what the consequences. A key example of such a principle is the claim that it is always wrong to kill an innocent human, whatever the consequences of not doing so.

I will argue that such moral conservativism is itself unjustified and, indeed, has morally unacceptable consequences, while consequentialism does not have implications which are morally monstrous and does not contain evident moral mistakes.

A consequentialist maintains that actions, rules, policies, practices, and moral principles are ultimately to be judged by certain consequences: to wit (for a very influential kind of consequentialism), by whether doing them more than, or at least as much as doing anything else, or acting in accordance with them more than or at least as much as acting in accordance with alternative policies, practices, rules or principles, tends, on the whole, and for *everyone* involved, to maximize satisfaction and minimize dissatisfaction. The states of affairs to be sought are those which maximize these things to

From *Ethics*, 82 (1972): 113-124. Reprinted with permission of The University of Chicago Press and the author.

the greatest extent possible for all mankind. But while this all sounds very humane and humanitarian, when its implications are thought through, it has been forcefully argued, it will be seen actually to have inhumane and morally intolerable implications. Circumstances could arise in which one holding such a view would have to assert that one was justified in punishing, killing, torturing, or deliberately harming the innocent, and such a consequence is, morally speaking, unacceptable.[1] As Anscombe has put it, anyone who "really thinks, *in advance,* that it is open to question whether such an action as procuring the judicial execution of the innocent should be quite excluded from consideration—I do not want to argue with him; he shows a corrupt mind."[2]

At the risk of being thought to exhibit a corrupt mind and a shallow consequentialist morality, I should like to argue that things are not as simple and straightforward as Anscombe seems to believe.

Surely, every moral man must be appalled at the judicial execution of the innocent or at the punishment, torture, and killing of the innocent. Indeed, being appalled by such behavior partially defines what it is to be a moral agent. And a consequentialist has very good utilitarian grounds for being so appalled, namely, that it is always wrong to inflict pain for its own sake. But this does not get to the core considerations which divide a conservative position such as Anscombe's from a consequentialist view. There are a series of tough cases that need to be taken to heart and their implications thought through by any reflective person, be he a conservative or a consequentialist. By doing this, we can get to the heart of the issue between conservativism and consequentialism arising over the problem of a "just war."

If we deliberately bomb civilian targets, we do not pretend that civilians are combatants in any simple fashion, but argue that this bombing will terminate hostilities more quickly, and will minimize all around suffering. It is hard to see how any brand of utilitarian will escape Miss Anscombe's objections. We are certainly killing the innocent . . . we are not killing them for the sake of killing them, but to save the lives of other innocent persons. Utilitarians, I think, grit their teeth and put up with this as part of the logic of total war; Miss Anscombe and anyone who thinks like her surely has to either redescribe the situation to ascribe guilt to the civilians or else she has to refuse to accept this sort of military tactics as simply wrong.[3]

It is indeed true that we cannot but feel the force of Anscombe's objections here. But is it the case that anyone shows a corrupt mind if he defends such bombing when, horrible as it is, it will quite definitely lessen appreciably the total amount of suffering and death in the long run, and if he is sufficiently nonevasive not to rationalize such a bombing of civilians into a situation in which all the putatively innocent people—children and all—are somehow in some measure judged guilty? Must such a man exhibit a corrupt moral sense if he refuses to hold that such military tactics are never morally justified? Must this be the monstrous view of a fanatical man devoid of any proper moral awareness? It is difficult for me to believe that this must be so.

Consider the quite parallel actions of guerrilla fighters and terrorists in wars of national liberation. In certain almost unavoidable circumstances, they must deliberately kill the innocent. We need to see some cases in detail here to get the necessary contextual background, and for this reason the motion picture *The Battle of Algiers* can be taken as a convenient point of reference. There we saw Algerian women—gentle, kindly women with children of their own and plainly people of moral sensitivity—with evident heaviness of heart, plant bombs which they had every good reason to believe would kill innocent people, including children; and we also saw a French general, also a human being of moral fiber and integrity, order the torture of Arab terrorists and threaten the bombing of houses in which terrorists were concealed but which also contained innocent people, including children. There are indeed many people involved in such activities who are cruel, sadistic beasts, or simply morally indifferent or, in important ways, morally uncomprehending. But the characters I have referred to from *The Battle of Algiers* were not of that stamp. They were plainly moral agents of a high degree of sensitivity, and yet they deliberately killed or were prepared to kill the innocent. And, with inessential variations, this is a recurrent phenomenon of human living in extreme situations. Such cases are by no means desert-island or esoteric cases.

It is indeed arguable whether such actions are always morally wrong—whether anyone should ever act as the Arab women or French general acted. But what could not be reasonably maintained, *pace* Anscombe, by any stretch of the imagination, is that the characters I described from *The Battle of Algiers* exhibited corrupt minds. Possibly morally mistaken, yes; guilty of moral corruption, no.

Dropping the charge of moral corruption but sticking with the moral issue about what actions are right, is it not the case that my consequentialist position logically forces me to conclude that under some circumstances—where the good to be achieved is great enough—I must not only countenance but actually advocate such violence toward the innocent? But is it not always, no matter what the circumstances or consequences, wrong to countenance, advocate, or engage in such violence? To answer such a question affirmatively is to commit oneself to the kind of moral absolutism or conservativism which Anscombe advocates. But, given the alternatives, should not one be such a conservative or at least hold that certain deontological principles must never be overridden?

I will take, so to speak, the papal bull by the horns and answer that there are circumstances when such violence must be reluctantly assented to or even taken to be something that one, morally speaking, must do. But, *pace* Anscombe, this very much needs arguing, and I shall argue it; but first I would like to set out some further but simpler cases which have a similar bearing. They are, by contrast, artificial cases. I use them because, in their greater simplicity, by contrast with my above examples, there are fewer variables to control and I can more conveniently make the essential conceptual and moral points. But, if my argument is correct for these simpler cases, the line of reasoning employed is intended to be applicable to those more complex cases as well.

II

Consider the following cases embedded in their exemplary tales:

THE CASE OF THE INNOCENT FAT MAN

Consider the story (well known to philosophers) of the fat man stuck in the mouth of a cave on a coast. He was leading a group of people out of the cave when he got stuck in the mouth of the cave and in a very short time high tide will be upon them, and unless he is promptly unstuck, they all will be drowned except the fat man, whose head is out of the cave. But, fortunately or unfortunately, someone has with him a stick of dynamite. The short of the matter is, either they use the dynamite and blast the poor innocent fat man out of the mouth of the cave or everyone else drowns. Either one life or many lives. Our conservative presumably would take the attitude that it is all in God's hands and say that he ought never to blast the fat man out, for it is always wrong to kill the innocent. Must or should a moral man come to that conclusion? I shall argue that he should not.

My first exemplary tale was designed to show that our normal, immediate, rather absolutistic, moral reactions need to be questioned along with such principles as "The direct intention of the death of an innocent person is never justifiable." I have hinted (and later shall argue) that we should *beware* of our moral outrage here—our naturally conservative and unreflective moral reactions—for here the consequentialist has a strong case for what I shall call "moral radicalism." But, before turning to a defense of that, I want to tell another story taken from Philippa Foot but used for my own purposes.[4] This tale, I shall argue, has a different import than our previous tale. Here our unrehearsed, commonsense moral reactions will stand up under moral scrutiny. But, I shall also argue when I consider them in Section III, that our commonsense moral reactions here, initial expectations to the contrary notwithstanding, can be shown to be justified on consequentialist grounds. The thrust of my argument for this case is that we are not justified in opting for a theistic and/or deontological absolutism or in rejecting consequentialism.

THE MAGISTRATE AND THE THREATENING MOB

A magistrate or judge is faced with a very real threat from a large and uncontrollable mob of rioters demanding a culprit for a crime. Unless the criminal is produced, promptly tried, and executed, they will take their own bloody revenge on a much smaller and quite vulnerable section of the community (a kind of frenzied pogrom). The judge knows that the real culprit is unknown and that the authorities do not even have a good clue as to who he may be. But he also knows that there is within easy reach a disreputable, thoroughly disliked, and useless man, who, though innocent could easily be framed so that the mob would be quite convinced that he was guilty and would be pacified if he were promptly executed. Recognizing that he can prevent the occurrence of extensive carnage only by framing some innocent person, the magistrate has him framed, goes through the mockery of a trial, and has him executed. Most of us regard such a framing and execution of such a man in such circumstances as totally unacceptable.[5] There are some who would say that it is categorically wrong—morally inexcusable—*whatever the circumstances*. Indeed, such a case remains a problem for the consequentialist, but here again, I shall argue, one can consistently remain a consequentialist and continue to accept commonsense moral convictions about such matters.

My storytelling is at an end. The job is to see what the stories imply. We must try to determine whether thinking through their implications should lead a clearheaded and morally sensitive man to abandon consequentialism and to adopt some form of theistic absolutism and/or deontological absolutism. I shall argue that it does not.

III

I shall consider the last case first because there are good reasons why the consequentialist should stick with commonsense moral convictions for such cases. I shall start by giving my rationale for that claim. If the magistrate were a tough-minded but morally conscientious consequentialist, he could still, on straightforward consequentialist grounds, refuse to frame and execute the innocent man, even knowing that this would unleash the mob and cause much suffering and many deaths. The rationale for this particular moral stand would be that, by so framing and then executing such an innocent man, he would, in the long run, cause still more suffering through the resultant corrupting effect on the institution of justice. That is, in a case involving such extensive general interest in the issue—without that, there would be no problem about preventing the carnage or call for such extreme measures—knowledge that the man was framed, that the law had prostituted itself, would, surely, eventually leak out. This would encourage mob action in other circumstances, would lead to an increased skepticism about the in-corruptibility or even the reliability of the judicial process, and would set a dangerous precedent for less clearheaded or less scrupulously humane mag-istrates. Given such a potential for the corruption of justice, a utilitarian or consequentialist judge or magistrate could, on good utilitarian or conse-quentialist grounds, argue that it was morally wrong to frame an innocent man. If the mob must rampage if such a sacrificial lamb is not provided, then the mob must rampage.

Must a utilitarian or consequentialist come to such a conclusion? The answer is no. It is the conclusion which is, as things stand, the most rea-sonable conclusion, but that he *must* come to it is far too strong a claim. A consequentialist could *consistently*—I did not say successfully—argue that, in taking the above tough-minded utilitarian position, we have overesti-mated the corrupting effects of such judicial railroading. His circumstance was an extreme one: a situation not often to be repeated even if, instead of acting as he did, he had set a precedent by such an act of judicial murder. A utilitarian rather more skeptical than most utilitarians about the claims of commonsense morality might reason that the lesser evil here is the judicial murder of an innocent man, vile as it is. He would persist in his moral icon-oclasm by standing on the consequentialist rock that the lesser evil is always to be preferred to the greater evil.

The short of it is that utilitarians could disagree, as other consequential-ists could disagree, about what is morally required of us in that case. The dis-agreement here between utilitarians or consequentialists of the same type is not one concerning fundamental moral principles but a disagreement about the empirical facts, about what course of action would in the long run pro-duce the least suffering and the most happiness for *everyone* involved.[6]

However, considering the effect advocating the deliberate judicial killing of an innocent man would have on the reliance people put on common-sense moral beliefs of such a ubiquitous sort as the belief that the innocent must not be harmed, a utilitarian who defended the centrality of common-sense moral beliefs would indeed have a strong utilitarian case here. But the most crucial thing to recognize is that, to regard such judicial bowing to such a threatening mob as unqualifiedly wrong, as morally intolerable, one need not reject utilitarianism and accept some form of theistic or deonto-logical absolutism.

It has been argued, however, that, in taking such a stance, I still have not squarely faced the moral conservative's central objection to the judicial rail-roading of the innocent. I allow, as a consequentialist, that there could be circumstances, at least as far as logical possibilities are concerned, in which such a railroading would be justified but that, as things actually go, it is not and probably never in fact will be justified. But the conservative's point is that in *no circumstances, either actual or conceivable, would it be justified.* No matter what the consequences, it is unqualifiedly unjustified. To say, as I do, that the situations in which it might be justified are desert-island, esoteric cases which do not occur in life, is not to the point, for, as Alan Donagan argues, "Moral theory is *a priori,* as clear-headed utilitarians like Henry Sidgwick recognized. It is, as Leibniz would say, 'true of all possible worlds.'"[7] Thus, to argue as I have and as others have that the counterexamples directed against the consequentialist's appeal to conditions which are never in fact fulfilled or are unlikely to be fulfilled is beside the point.[8] Whether "a moral theory is true or false depends on whether its implications for all possible worlds are true. Hence, whether utilitarianism (or consequentialism) is true or false cannot depend on how the actual world is."[9] It is possible to specify logically conceivable situations in which consequentialism would have implications which are monstrous—for example, certain beneficial judicial murders of the innocent (whether they are even remotely likely to obtain is irrelevant)—hence consequentialism must be false.

We should not take such a short way with consequentialists, for what is true in Donagan's claim about moral theory's being *a priori* will not refute or even render implausible consequentialism, and what would undermine it in such a claim about the *a priori* nature of moral theory and presumably moral claims is not true.

To say that moral theory is *a priori* is probably correct if that means that categorical moral claims—fundamental moral statements—cannot be deduced from empirical statements or nonmoral theological statements, such that it is a contradiction to assert the empirical and/or nonmoral theological statements and deny the categorical moral claims or vice versa.[10] In that fundamental sense, it is reasonable and, I believe, justifiable to maintain that moral theory is autonomous and *a priori.* It is also *a priori* in the sense that moral statements are not themselves a kind of empirical statement. That is, if I assert "One ought never to torture any sentient creature" or "One ought never to kill an innocent man," I am not trying to predict or describe what people do or are likely to do but am asserting what they are *to do.* It is also true that, if a moral statement is true, it holds for all possible worlds *in which situations of exactly the sort characterized in the statement obtain.* If it is true for one, it is true for all. You cannot consistently say that A ought to do B in situation Y and deny that someone exactly like A in a situation exactly like Y ought to do B.

In these ways, moral claims and indeed moral theory are *a priori.* But it is also evident that none of these ways will touch the consequentialist or utilitarian arguments. After all, the consequentialist need not be, and typically has not been, an ethical naturalist—he need not think moral claims are derivable from factual claims or that moral claims are a subspecies of empirical statement and he could accept—indeed, he must accept—what is an important truism anyway, that you cannot consistently say that A ought to do B in situation Y and deny that someone exactly like A in a situation exactly like Y ought to do B. But he could and should deny that moral claims are *a priori* in the sense that rational men must or even will make them without regard for the context, the situation, in which they are made. We say people ought not to drive way over the speed limit, or speed on icy roads, or throw knives at each other. But, if human beings had a kind of metallic exoskeleton and would not be hurt, disfigured, or seriously inconvenienced by knives sticking in them or by automobile crashes, we would not—so evidently at least—have good grounds for saying such speeding or knife throwing is wrong. It would not be so obvious that it was unreasonable and immoral to do these things if these conditions obtained.

In the very way we choose to describe the situation when we make ethical remarks, it is important in making this choice that we know what the world is like and what human beings are like. Our understanding of the situation, our understanding of human nature and motivation cannot but affect our structuring of the moral case. The consequentialist is saying that, as the world goes, there are good grounds for holding that judicial killings are morally intolerable, though he would have to admit that if the world (including human beings) were very different, such killings could be something that ought to be done.

IV

So far, I have tried to show with reference to the case of the magistrate and the threatening mob how consequentialists can reasonably square their normative ethical theories with an important range of commonsense moral convictions. Now, I wish by reference to the case of the innocent fat man to establish that there is at least a serious question concerning whether such fundamental commonsense moral convictions should always function as "moral facts" or a kind of moral ground to test the adequacy of normative ethical theories or positions. I want to establish that careful attention to such cases shows that we are not justified in taking the principles embodied in our commonsense moral reasoning about such cases as normative for all moral decisions. That a normative ethical theory is incompatible with some of our "moral intuitions" (moral feelings or convictions) does not refute the normative ethical theory. What I will try to do here is to establish that this case, no more than the case examined in Section III, gives us adequate grounds for abandoning consequentialism and for adopting moral conservatism.

Forget the levity of the example and consider the case of the innocent fat man. If there really is no other way of unsticking our fat man and if plainly, without blasting him out, everyone in the cave will drown, then, innocent or not, he should be blasted out. This indeed overrides the principle that the innocent should never be deliberately killed, but it does not reveal a callousness toward life, for the people involved are caught in a desperate situation in which, if such extreme action is not taken, many lives will be lost and far greater misery will obtain. Moreover, the people who do such a horrible thing or acquiesce in the doing of it are not likely to be rendered more callous about human life and human suffering as a result. Its occurrence will haunt them for the rest of their lives and is as likely as not to make them more rather than less morally sensitive. It is not even correct to say that such a desperate act shows a lack of respect for persons. We are not treating the fat man merely as a means. The fat man's person—his interest and rights—are not ignored. Killing him is something which is undertaken with the greatest reluctance. It is only when it is quite certain that there is no other way to save the lives of the others that such a violent course of action is justifiably undertaken.

Alan Donagan, arguing rather as Anscombe argues, maintains that "to use any innocent man ill for the sake of some public good is directly to degrade him to being a mere means" and to do this is of course to violate a principle essential to morality, that is, that human beings should never merely be treated as means but should be treated as ends in themselves (as persons worthy of respect).[11] But, as my above remarks show, it need not be the case, and in the above situation it is not the case, that in killing such an innocent man we are treating him *merely* as a means. The action is universalizable, all alternative actions which would save his life are duly considered, the blasting out is done only as a last and desperate resort with the minimum of harshness and indifference to his suffering and the like. It indeed sounds ironical to talk this way, given what is done to him. But if such a terrible situation were to arise, there would always be more or less humane ways of going about one's grim task. And in acting in the more humane ways toward the fat man, as we do what we must do and would have done to ourselves were the roles reversed, we show a respect for his person.[12]

In so treating the fat man—not just to further the public good but to prevent the certain death of a whole group of people (that is to prevent an even greater evil than his being killed in this way)—the claims of justice are not overridden either, for each individual involved, if he is reasoning correctly, should realize that if he were so stuck rather than the fat man, he should in such situations be blasted out. Thus, there is no question of being unfair. Surely we must choose between evils here, but is there anything more reasonable, more morally appropriate, than choosing the lesser evil when doing

or allowing some evil cannot be avoided? That is, where there is no avoiding both and where our actions can determine whether a greater or lesser
evil obtains, should we not plainly always opt for the lesser evil? And is it
not obviously a greater evil that all those other innocent people should suffer and die than that the fat man should suffer and die? Blowing up the fat
man is indeed monstrous. But letting him remain stuck while the whole
group drowns is still more monstrous.

The consequentialist is on strong moral ground here, and, if his reflective
moral convictions do not square either with certain unrehearsed or with certain reflective particular moral convictions of human beings, so much the
worse for such commonsense moral convictions. One could even usefully
and relevantly adapt here—though for a quite different purpose—an argument of Donagan's. Consequentialism of the kind I have been arguing for
provides so persuasive "a theoretical basis for common morality that when
it contradicts some moral intuition, it is natural to suspect that intuition, not
theory, is corrupt."[13] Given the comprehensiveness, plausibility, and overall
rationality of consequentialism, it is not unreasonable to override even a
deeply felt moral conviction if it does not square with such a theory, though,
if it made no sense or overrode the bulk of or even a great many of our considered moral convictions, that would be another matter indeed.

Notes

1. Alan Donagan, "Is There a Credible Form of Utilitarianism?" and H. J.
   McCloskey, "A Non-Utilitarian Approach to Punishment," both in Michael D.
   Bayles, ed., *Contemporary Utilitarianism* (Garden City, N.Y.: Doubleday, 1968).
2. Elizabeth Anscombe, "Modern Moral Philosophy," *Philosophy* 23 (January
   1957): 16–17.
3. Alan Ryan, "Review of Jan Narveson's *Morality and Utility*," *Philosophical Books*
   9, no. 3 (October 1968): 14.
4. Philippa Foot, "The Problem of Abortion and the Doctrine of the Double
   Effect," *Oxford Review*, no. 5 (1967): 5–15.
5. Later, I shall show that there are desert-island circumstances—i.e., highly
   improbable situations—in which such judicial railroading might be a moral
   necessity. But I also show what little force desert-island cases have in the articulation and defense of a normative ethical theory.
6. "Everyone" here is used distributively; i.e., I am talking about the interests of
   each and every one. In that sense, everyone's interests need to be considered.
7. Donagan, "Utilitarianism," p. 189.
8. T. L. S. Sprigge argues in such a manner in his "A Utilitarian Reply to
   Dr. McCloskey," in Michael D. Bayles, ed., *Contemporary Utilitarianism* (Garden City, N.Y.: Doubleday, 1968).
9. Donagan, "Utilitarianism," p. 194.

10. There is considerable recent literature about whether it is possible to derive moral claims from nonmoral claims. See W. D. Hudson, ed., *The Is-Ought Question: A Collection of Papers on the Central Problem in Moral Philosophy* (New York: St. Martin's Press, 1969).
11. Donagan, "Utilitarianism," pp. 199–200.
12. Again, I am not asserting that we would have enough fortitude to assent to it were the roles actually reversed. I am making a conceptual remark about what as moral beings we must try to do and not a psychological observation about what we can do.
13. Donagan, "Utilitarianism," p. 198.

TWO CONCEPTS OF RULES
John Rawls

John Rawls is professor of philosophy at Harvard University and author of A Theory of Justice *(1971) and* Political Liberalism *(1993). In the following article, Rawls proposes a version of what is often called* rule utilitarianism. *The* act utilitarian *claims that the morality of an action is determined by the value of the consequences of individual actions, whereas the* rule utilitarian *maintains that considerations of utility properly pertain to social practices comprised of rules and that the morality of concrete actions is determined by appeal to the utility of the practices under which they fall rather than by appeal to the utility of those actions. The contrast between act and rule utilitarianism is sharpened by considering the practices of punishment and promising. The rule utilitarian claims that we judge the morality of such practices by appealing to considerations of utility, while the morality of specific acts of punishment and promising are to be judged by appealing to those rules that constitute justified practices. Thus, for the rule utilitarian, punishing an innocent person on some rare occasion might have a higher utility than any other manner of treatment, but it does not follow from that fact that the innocent person should be punished. This result is supposed to help save the utilitarian moral theory from the charge that the view fails to cohere with certain of our widely shared and deeply held moral convictions.*

From *The Philosophical Review,* 64 (1955): 3-32. Reprinted by permission of the publisher.

In this paper I want to show the importance of the distinction between justifying a practice and justifying a particular action falling under it, and I want to explain the logical basis of this distinction and how it is possible to miss its significance. While the distinction has frequently been made, and is now becoming commonplace, there remains the task of explaining the tendency either to overlook it altogether, or to fail to appreciate its importance.

To show the importance of the distinction I am going to defend utilitarianism against those objections which have traditionally been made against it in connection with punishment and the obligation to keep promises. I hope to show that if one uses the distinction in question then one can state utilitarianism in a way which makes it a much better explication of our considered moral judgments that these traditional objections would seem to admit. Thus the importance of the distinction is shown by the way it strengthens the utilitarian view regardless of whether that view is completely defensible or not.

To explain how the significance of the distinction may be overlooked, I am going to discuss two conceptions of rules. One of these conceptions conceals the importance of distinguishing between the justification of a rule or practice and the justification of a particular action falling under it. The other conception makes it clear why this distinction must be made and what is its logical basis. . . .

I

The subject of punishment, in the sense of attaching legal penalties to the violation of legal rules, has always been a troubling moral question. The trouble about it has not been that people disagree as to whether or not punishment is justifiable. Most people have held that, freed from certain abuses, it is an acceptable institution. Only a few have rejected punishment entirely, which is rather surprising when one considers all that can be said against it. The difficulty is with the justification of punishment: various arguments for it have been given by moral philosophers, but so far none of them has won any sort of general acceptance; no justification is without those who detest it. I hope to show that the use of the aforementioned distinction enables one to state the utilitarian view in a way which allows for the sound points of its critics.

For our purposes we may say that there are two justifications of punishment. What we may call the retributive view is that punishment is justified on the grounds that wrongdoing merits punishment. It is morally fitting that a person who does wrong should suffer in proportion to his wrongdoing.

That a criminal should be punished follows from his guilt, and the severity of the appropriate punishment depends on the depravity of his act. The state of affairs where a wrongdoer suffers punishment is morally better than the state of affairs where he does not; and it is better irrespective of any of the consequences of punishing him.

What we may call the utilitarian view holds that on the principle that bygones are bygones and that only future consequences are material to present decisions, punishment is justifiable only by reference to the probable consequences of maintaining it as one of the devices of the social order. Wrongs committed in the past are, as such, not relevant considerations for deciding what to do. If punishment can be shown to promote effectively the interest of society it is justifiable, otherwise it is not.

I have stated these two competing views very roughly to make one feel the conflict between them: one feels the force of *both* arguments and one wonders how they can be reconciled. From my introductory remarks it is obvious that the resolution which I am going to propose is that in this case one must distinguish between justifying a practice as a system of rules to be applied and enforced, and justifying a particular action which falls under these rules; utilitarian arguments are appropriate with regard to questions about practices, while retributive arguments fit the application of particular rules to particular cases. . . . But can it really be this simple?

What retributionists have rightly insisted upon is that no man can be punished unless he is guilty, that is, unless he has broken the law. Their fundamental criticism of the utilitarian account is that, as they interpret it, it sanctions an innocent person's being punished (if one may call it that) for the benefit of society. . . . The real question, however, is whether the utilitarian, in justifying punishment, hasn't used arguments which commit him to accepting the infliction of suffering on innocent persons if it is for the good of society (whether or not one calls this punishment). More generally, isn't the utilitarian committed in principle to accepting many practices which he, as a morally sensitive person, wouldn't want to accept? Retributionists are inclined to hold that there is no way to stop the utilitarian principle from justifying too much except by adding to it a principle which distributes certain rights to individuals. Then the amended criterion is not the greatest benefit of society *simpliciter,* but the greatest benefit of society subject to the constraint that no one's rights may be violated. Now while I think that the classical utilitarians proposed a criterion of this more complicated sort, I do not want to argue that point here. What I want to show is that there is *another* way of preventing the utilitarian principle from justifying too much, or at least of making it much less likely to do so: namely, by stating utilitarianism in a way which accounts for the distinction between the justification of an institution and the justification of a particular action falling under it.

I begin by defining the institution of punishment as follows: a person is said to suffer punishment whenever he is legally deprived of some of the normal rights of a citizen on the ground that he has violated a rule of law, the violation having been established by trial according to the due process of law, provided that the deprivation is carried out by the recognized legal authorities of the state, that the rule of law clearly specifies both the offense and the attached penalty, that the courts construe statutes strictly, and that the statute was on the books prior to the time of the offense. This definition specifies what I shall understand by punishment. The question is whether utilitarian arguments may be found to justify institutions widely different from this and such as one would find cruel and arbitrary. . . .

Try to imagine, then, an institution (which we may call "telishment") which is such that the officials set up by it have authority to arrange a trial for the condemnation of an innocent man whenever they are of the opinion that doing so would be in the best interests of society. The discretion of officials is limited, however, by the rule that they may not condemn an innocent man to undergo such an ordeal unless there is, at the time, a wave of offenses similar to that with which they charge him and telish him for. We may imagine that the officials having the discretionary authority are the judges of the higher courts in consultation with the chief of police, the minister of justice, and a committee of the legislature.

Once one realizes that one is involved in setting up an *institution,* one sees that the hazards are very great. For example, what check is there on the officials? How is one to tell whether or not their actions are authorized? How is one to limit the risks involved in allowing such systematic deception? How is one to avoid giving anything short of complete discretion to the authorities to telish anyone they like? In addition to these considerations, it is obvious that people will come to have a very different attitude towards their penal system when telishment is adjoined to it. They will be uncertain as to whether a convicted man has been punished or telished. They will wonder whether or not they should feel sorry for him. They will wonder whether the same fate won't at any time fall on them. If one pictures how such an institution would actually work, and the enormous risks involved in it, it seems clear that it would serve no useful purpose. A utilitarian justification for this institution is most unlikely.

It happens in general that as one drops off the defining features of punishment one ends up with an institution whose utilitarian justification is highly doubtful. One reason for this is that punishment works like a kind of price system: by altering the prices one has to pay for the performance of actions it supplies a motive for avoiding some actions and doing others. The defining features are essential if punishment is to work in this way; so that an institution which lacks these features, e.g., an institution which is set up to "punish" the innocent, is likely to have about as much point as a price system (if one may call it that) where the prices of things change at random from day to day and one learns the price of something after one has agreed to buy it.

II

I shall now consider the question of promises. The objection to utilitarianism in connection with promises seems to be this: it is believed that on the utilitarian view when a person makes a promise the only ground upon which he should keep it, if he should keep it, is that by keeping it he will realize the most good on the whole. So that if one asks the question "Why should I keep *my* promise?" the utilitarian answer is understood to be that doing so in *this* case will have the best consequences. And this answer is said, quite rightly, to conflict with the way in which the obligation to keep promises is regarded.

Now of course critics of utilitarianism are not unaware that one defense sometimes attributed to utilitarians is the consideration involving the practice of promise-keeping.[1] In this connection they are supposed to argue something like this: it must be admitted that we feel strictly about keeping promises, more strictly than it might seem our view can account for. But when we consider the matter carefully it is always necessary to take into account the effect which our action will have on the practice of making promises. The promisor must weigh, not only the effects of breaking his promise on the particular case, but also the effect which his breaking his promise will have on the practice itself. Since the practice is of great utilitarian value, and since breaking one's promise always seriously damages it, one will seldom be justified in breaking one's promise. If we view our individual promises in the wider context of the practice of promising itself we can account for the strictness of the obligation to keep promises. There is always one very strong utilitarian consideration in favor of keeping them, and this will insure that when the question arises as to whether or not to keep a promise it will usually turn out that one should, even where the facts of the particular case taken by itself would seem to justify one's breaking it. In this way the strictness with which we view the obligation to keep promises is accounted for.

Ross has criticized this defense as follows: however great the value of the practice of promising, on utilitarian grounds, there must be some value which is greater, and one can imagine it to be obtainable by breaking a promise. Therefore there might be a case where the promisor could argue that breaking his promise was justified as leading to a better state of affairs on the whole. And the promisor could argue in this way no matter how slight the advantage won by breaking the promise. If one were to challenge the promisor his defense would be that what he did was best on the whole in view of all the utilitarian considerations, which in this case *include* the importance of the practice. Ross feels that such a defense would be unacceptable. I think he is right insofar as he is protesting against the appeal to consequences in general and without further explanation. Yet it is extremely difficult to weigh the force of Ross's argument. The kind of case imagined seems unrealistic and one feels that it needs to be described. One is inclined to think that it would either turn out that such a case came under an exception defined by the practice itself, in which case there would not be an appeal to consequences in general on the particular case, or it would happen that the circumstances were so peculiar that the conditions which the practice presupposes no longer obtained. But certainly Ross is right in thinking that it strikes us as wrong for a person to defend breaking a promise by a general appeal to consequences. For a general utilitarian defense is not open to the promisor: it is not one of the defenses allowed by the practice of making promises.

Ross gives two further counterarguments: First, he holds that it overestimates the damage done to the practice of promising by a failure to keep a promise. One who breaks a promise harms his own name certainly, but it isn't clear that a broken promise always damages the practice itself sufficiently to account for the strictness of the obligation. Second, and more important, I think, he raises the question of what one is to say of a promise which isn't known to have been made except to the promisor and the promisee, as in the case of a promise a son makes to his dying father concerning the handling of the estate. In this sort of case the consideration relating to the practice doesn't weigh on the promisor at all, and yet one feels that this sort of promise is as binding as other promises. The question of the effect which breaking it has on the practice seems irrelevant. The only consequence seems to be that one can break the promise without running any risk of being censured; but the obligation itself seems not the least weakened. Hence it is doubtful whether the effect on the practice ever weighs in the particular case; certainly it cannot account for the strictness of the obligation where it fails to obtain. It seems to follow that a utilitarian account of the obligation to keep promises cannot be successfully carried out. . . .

These arguments and counterarguments . . . fail to make the distinction between the justification of a practice and the justification of a particular action falling under it, and therefore they fall into the mistake of taking it for granted that the promisor . . . is entitled without restriction to bring utilitarian considerations to bear in deciding whether to keep *his* promise. But if one considers what the practice of promising is one will see, I think, that it is such as not to allow this sort of general discretion to the promisor. Indeed, the point of the practice is to abdicate one's title to act in accordance with utilitarian and prudential considerations in order that the future may be tied down and plans coordinated in advance. There are obvious utilitarian advantages in having a practice which denies to the promisor, as a defense, any general appeal to the utilitarian principle in accordance with which the practice itself may be justified. There is nothing contradictory, or surprising, in this: utilitarian (or aesthetic) reasons might properly be given in arguing that the game of chess, or baseball, is satisfactory just as it is, or in arguing that it should be changed in various respects, but a player in a game cannot properly appeal to such considerations as reasons for his making one move rather than another. It is a mistake to think that if the practice is justified on utilitarian grounds then the promisor must have complete liberty to use utilitarian arguments to decide whether or not to keep his promise. The practice forbids this general defense; and it is a purpose of the practice to do this. Therefore what the above arguments presuppose—the idea that if the utilitarian view is accepted then the promisor is bound if, and only if, the application of the utilitarian principle to his own case shows that keeping it is best on the whole—is false. The promisor is bound because he promised: weighing the case on its merits is not open to him.

Is this to say that in particular cases one cannot deliberate whether or not to keep one's promise? Of course not. But to do so is to deliberate whether the various excuses, exceptions and defenses, which are understood by, and which constitute an important part of, the practice, apply to one's own case. Various defenses for not keeping one's promise are allowed, but among them there isn't the one that, on general utilitarian grounds, the promisor (truly) thought his action best on the whole, even though there may be the defense that the consequences of keeping one's promise would have been *extremely* severe. While there are too many complexities here to consider all the necessary details, one can see that the general defense isn't allowed if one asks the following question: what would one say of someone who, when asked why he broke his promise, replied simply that breaking it was best on the whole? Assuming that his reply is sincere, and that his belief was reasonable (i.e., one need not consider the possibility that he was mistaken), I think that one would question whether or not he knows what it means to say "I promise" (in the appropriate circumstances). It would be said of someone who used this excuse without further explanation that he didn't understand what defenses the practice, which defines a promise, allows to him. If a child were to use this excuse one would correct him; for it is part of the way one is taught the concept of a promise to be corrected if one uses this excuse. The point of having the practice would be lost if the practice did allow this excuse.

It is no doubt part of the utilitarian view that every practice should admit the defense that the consequences of abiding by it would have been extremely severe; and utilitarians would be inclined to hold that some reliance on people's good sense and some concession to hard cases is necessary. They would hold that a practice is justified by serving the interests of those who take part in it; and as with any set of rules there is understood a background of circumstances under which it is expected to be applied and which need not—indeed which cannot—be fully stated. Should these circumstances change, then even if there is no rule which provides for the case, it may still be in accordance with the practice that one be released from one's obligation. But this sort of defense allowed by a practice must not be confused with the general option to weigh each particular case on utilitarian grounds which critics of utilitarianism have thought it necessarily to involve. . . .

III

So far I have tried to show the importance of the distinction between the justification of a practice and the justification of a particular action falling under it by indicating how this distinction might be used to defend utilitarianism against two long-standing objections. One might be tempted to close the discussion at this point by saying that utilitarian considerations should be understood as applying to practices in the first instance and not to particular actions falling under them except insofar as the practices admit of it. One might say that in this modified form it is a better account of our considered moral opinions and let it go at that. But to stop here would be to neglect the interesting question as to how one can fail to appreciate the significance of this rather obvious distinction and can take it for granted that utilitarianism has the consequence that particular cases may always be decided on general utilitarian grounds. I want to argue that this mistake may be connected with misconceiving the logical status of the rules of practices; and to show this I am going to examine two conceptions of rules, two ways of placing them within the utilitarian theory.

The conception which conceals from us the significance of the distinction I am going to call the summary view. It regards rules in the following way: one supposes that each person decides what he shall do in particular cases by applying the utilitarian principle; one supposes further that different people will decide the same particular case in the same way and that there will be recurrences of cases similar to those previously decided. Thus it will happen that in cases of certain kinds the same decision will be made either by the same person at different times or by different persons at the same time. If a case occurs frequently enough one supposes that a rule is formulated to cover that sort of case. I have called this conception the summary view because rules are pictured as summaries of past decisions arrived at by the *direct* application of the utilitarian principle to particular cases. Rules are regarded as reports that cases of a certain sort have been found on *other* grounds to be properly decided in a certain way (although, of course, they do not *say* this).

There are several things to notice about this way of placing rules within the utilitarian theory.

1. The point of having rules derives from the fact that similar cases tend to recur and that one can decide cases more quickly if one records past decisions in the form of rules. If similar cases didn't recur, one would be required to apply the utilitarian principle directly, case by case, and rules reporting past decisions would be of no use. . . .

2. Each person is in principle always entitled to reconsider the correctness of a rule and to question whether or not it is proper to follow it in a particular case. As rules are guides and aids, one may ask whether in past decisions there might not have been a mistake in applying the utilitarian principle to get the rule in question, and wonder whether or not it is best in this case. The reason for rules is that people are not able to apply the utilitarian principle effortlessly and flawlessly; there is need to save time and to post a guide. On this view a society of rational utilitarians would be a society without rules in which each person applied the utilitarian principle directly and smoothly, and without error, case by case. On the other hand, ours is a society in which rules are formulated to serve as aids in reaching these ideally rational decisions on particular cases, guides which have been built up and tested by the experience of generations. If one applies this view to rules, one is interpreting them as maxims, as "rules of thumb"; and it is doubtful that anything to which the summary conception did apply would be called a *rule*. Arguing as if one regarded rules in this way is a mistake one makes while doing philosophy.

3. The concept of a *general* rule takes the following form. One is pictured as estimating on what percentage of the cases likely to arise a given rule may be relied upon to express the correct decision, that is, the decision that would be arrived at if one were to correctly apply the utilitarian principle case by case. If one estimates that by and large the rule will give the correct decision, or if one estimates that the likelihood of making a mistake by applying the utilitarian principle directly on one's own is greater than the likelihood of making a mistake by following the rule, and if these considerations held of persons generally, then one would be justified in urging its adoption as a general rule. In this way *general* rules might be accounted for on the summary view. It will still make sense, however, to speak of applying the utilitarian principle case by case, for it was by trying to foresee the results of doing this

that one got the initial estimates upon which acceptance of the rule depends. That one is taking a rule in accordance with the summary conception will show itself in the naturalness with which one speaks of the rule as a guide, or as a maxim, or as a generalization from experience, and as something to be laid aside in extraordinary cases where there is no assurance that the generalization will hold and the case must therefore be treated on its merits. Thus there goes with this conception the notion of a particular exception which renders a rule suspect on a particular occasion.

The other conception of rules I will call the practice conception. On this view rules are pictured as defining a practice. Practices are set up for various reasons, but one of them is that in many areas of conduct each person's deciding what to do on utilitarian grounds case by case leads to confusion, and that the attempt to coordinate behavior by trying to foresee how others will act is bound to fail. As an alternative one realizes that what is required is the establishment of a practice, the specification of a new form of activity; and from this one sees that a practice necessarily involves the abdication of full liberty to act on utilitarian and prudential grounds. It is the mark of a practice that being taught how to engage in it involves being instructed in the rules which define it, and that appeal is made to those rules to correct the behavior of those engaged in it. Those engaged in a practice recognize the rules as defining it. The rules cannot be taken as simply describing how those engaged in the practice in fact behave; it is not simply that they act as if they were obeying the rules. Thus it is essential to the notion of a practice that the rules are publicly known and understood as definitive; and it is essential also that the rules of a practice can be taught and can be acted upon to yield a coherent practice. On this conception, then, rules are not generalizations from the decisions of individuals applying the utilitarian principle directly and independently to recurrent particular cases. On the contrary, rules define a practice and are themselves the subject of the utilitarian principle. . . .

If one compares the two conceptions of rules I have discussed, one can see how the summary conception misses the significance of the distinction between justifying a practice and justifying actions falling under it. On this view rules are regarded as guides whose purpose it is to indicate the ideally rational decision on the given particular case which the flawless application of the utilitarian principle would yield. One has, in principle, full option to use the guides or to discard them as the situation warrants without one's moral office being altered in any way: whether one discards the rules or not, one always holds the office of a rational person seeking case by case to realize the best on the whole. But on the practice conception, if one holds an office defined by a practice then questions regarding one's actions in this office are settled by reference to the rules which define the practice. If one seeks to question these rules, then one's office undergoes a fundamental change: one then assumes the office of one empowered to change and criticize the rules, or the office of a reformer, and so on. The summary conception does away with the distinction of offices and the various forms of argument appropriate to each. On that conception there is one office and so no offices at all. It therefore obscures the fact that the utilitarian principle must, in the case of actions and offices defined by a practice, apply to the practice, so that general utilitarian arguments are not available to those who act in offices so defined. . . .

I have tried to show that when we fit the utilitarian view together with the practice conception of rules, where this conception is appropriate, we can formulate it in a way which saves it from several traditional objections. I have further tried to show how the logical force of the distinction between justifying a practice and justifying an action falling under it is connected with the practice conception of rules and cannot be understood as long as one regards the rules of practices in accordance with the summary view. . . .

Note

1. Ross, *The Right and the Good*, pp. 37–39, and *Foundations of Ethics* (Oxford, 1939), pp. 92–94. I know of no utilitarian who has used this argument except W. A. Pickard-Cambridge in "Two Problems about Duty," *Mind*, n.s., XLI (April, 1932), 153–157, although the argument goes with G. E. Moore's version of utilitarianism in *Principia Ethica* (Cambridge, 1903). To my knowledge it does not appear in the classical utilitarians; and if one interprets their view correctly this is no accident.

THE ETHICS OF FANTASY
J. L. Mackie

J. L. Mackie (1917–1982) was a fellow in philosophy at University College, Oxford. Against act utilitarianism, Mackie raises two objections. First, he argues that, despite the seeming simplicity and unity of the theory, it suffers from indeterminacy. That is, it leaves such questions unanswered as how we are to measure utility and

*whether the utilities of lower animals and future generations should be factored
into our moral calculations. Second, Mackie objects that utilitarianism is not livable or "practicable." That is, the theory requires too much of us and so could not
function as a livable moral code. (Mackie's second argument here should be compared with the second objection Mill considers in his defense of utilitarianism.)
Finally, Mackie argues that the sorts of indeterminacies and difficulties that are
problems for act utilitarianism are also problems for rule utilitarianism.*

A morality in the broad sense would be a general, all-inclusive theory of
conduct: the morality to which someone subscribed would be whatever
body of principles he allowed ultimately to guide or determine his choices
of action. In the narrow sense, a morality is a system of a particular sort of
constraints on conduct—ones whose central task is to protect the interests
of persons other than the agent and which present themselves to an agent
as checks on his natural inclinations or spontaneous tendencies to act. In
this narrow sense, moral considerations would be considerations from some
limited range, and would not necessarily include everything that a man
allowed to determine what he did. In this second sense, someone could say
quite deliberately, "I admit that morality requires that I should do such-and-
such, but I don't intend to: for me other considerations here overrule the
moral ones." And he need not be putting "morality" here into either visible
or invisible inverted commas. It may well be his morality of which he is
speaking, the moral constraints that he himself in general accepts and endorses as such. But because in this narrow sense moral considerations are
only some considerations among others which he also endorses, not an in-
clusive system which incorporates and, where necessary, weighs against one
another all the reasons that this man accepts as reasons for or against doing
anything, it is possible that in some particular situation moral considerations should be overruled. But no-one could, in his choices of action, deliberately overrule what was his morality in the broad sense, though he might
diverge from it through "weakness of will."

There is no point in discussing whether the broad or the narrow sense of
"morality" is the more correct. Both are used, and both have important roots
and connections in our thought. But it is essential not to confuse them, not
to think that what we recognize as (in the narrow sense) peculiarly moral
considerations are (jumping to the broad sense) necessarily finally authori-
tative with regard to our actions. We should not suppose that any general
system of principles of choice which we can on reflection accept must be
constructed wholly of materials that we would call moral in the narrow
sense. . . .

"Morality in the narrow sense" was roughly distinguished as a particular sort of constraints on conduct, and the remainder of that chapter discussed why such constraints were needed for the flourishing of human life. The view sketched there of morality in the narrow sense was therefore utilitarian in the very broad sense that it took general human well-being as in some way the foundation of morality. However, it is not very illuminating to use the term "utilitarianism" as broadly as this; it is better to restrict it, or qualified variants of it, to more specific views about the way in which moral conclusions are to be derived from or founded upon human happiness, to specific methods of determining the content of the first order moral system.

One such view is extreme or act utilitarianism. This holds that where an agent has a choice between courses of action (or inaction) the right act is that which will produce the most happiness, not just for the agent himself but for all who are in any way affected. The greatest possible total happiness or "utility"—or, as it is sometimes rather misleadingly put, "The greatest happiness of the greatest number"—is proposed as the criterion of right action, and happiness is usually interpreted hedonistically as a balance of pleasure over pain. The suggestion is that for each alternative course of action it is possible in principle to measure all the amounts of pleasure it produces for different persons and to add these up, similarly to measure and add up all the amounts of pain or distress it produces, and subtract the sum of pain from the sum of pleasure; then the right action is that for which there is the greatest positive or the least negative balance of pleasure over pain; presumably if for two or more actions the balances are equal, but better than the balances for all others, each of them is *a* right action.

This proposal has several obvious merits. It seems reasonable that morality, if it is to guide conduct, should have something to do with happiness. It seems natural to seek pleasure and to avoid pain and distress, but it also seems sensible to balance these against each other, to put up with a certain amount of pain in order to achieve a quantity of pleasure that outweighs it. In taking the *general* happiness as the standard of right action this proposal seems to satisfy at once the presumptions that moral actions should be unselfish and that moral principles should be fair. It seems to provide a coherent system of conduct; all decisions about what is right or wrong would flow directly from a single source, whereas in other proposed first order moral systems we find a multiplicity of independent rules and principles, perhaps arbitrarily thrown together, possibly conflicting with one another in certain circumstances. Also it has been argued, particularly by Sidgwick, that if we confront utilitarianism with common-sense or intuitionist morality, utilitarianism can swallow up its rival. We can explain many of the common-sense or intuitive rules as being in general justified by their tendency to promote the general happiness, but where two common-sense rules come into conflict we need to appeal directly to utility to decide what to do. Common-sense morality can be seen as a practically convenient approximation to utilitarianism, but not, therefore, something whose requirements can resist those of utility in the rare cases where there is an open conflict between them.

Closer examination, however, reveals cracks in this apparently unitary structure. There are difficulties for and indeterminacies in utilitarianism. What are we to include in "all who are in any way affected"? Does this mean "all human beings" or "all sentient beings"? Are nonhuman animals included? A theory that equates good with pleasure and evil with pain would appear to have no nonarbitrary reason for excluding from consideration any creatures that are capable of feeling either pleasure or pain. Does it include only those who are now alive, or also future generations; and if so, only those who will exist or also those who might exist? We may have to compare alternative courses of action one of which would lead to there being a large population each of whose members was only moderately happy, and another of which would lead to there being a smaller population each of whose members was very happy; in the former there will be more total utility or happiness, in the latter a higher average utility or happiness. For a fixed population, the maxima of total utility and of average utility must coincide, but if the size of the population is itself variable they can fall apart. Which of the two, then, is it whose maximization is to be the criterion of right action? Again, is it really possible to measure quantities of pleasure and pain even for the same person at different times and in different sorts of experience? Is pleasure even sufficiently of the same category as pain to be measurable on the same scale and so to allow a quantity of one to balance a quantity of the other? Interpersonal measurement presents even greater difficulties, and the problem becomes still more acute if the pleasures and pains of nonhuman animals are to be taken into account. It can be argued that utilitarianism only appears to avoid the arbitrariness of some rival methods of ethics. It only pretends to provide a unitary decision procedure, and arbitrariness breaks out within any serious attempt to implement it, in whatever decisions are made in answer to some of these questions and in estimates of the comparative amounts of pleasure and pain that various courses of action will produce.

Again it can be asked whether the proposed criterion is simply the greatest total happiness (or perhaps average happiness), or whether it matters how happiness is distributed. Is a state of affairs in which one person is supremely happy and nine are miserable better than one in which all ten are equally happy, provided only that the total balance of happiness is greater? Are we to interpret utilitarianism as being founded on an aggregative principle alone, or as including a distributive principle as well—and if so, what distributive principle: should happiness be distributed equally or in proportion to some kind of merit? Bentham's remark that "everybody [is] to count for one, nobody for more than one" has been taken as a distributive thesis; but it offers no clear principle of distribution, and is more naturally taken simply as an instruction that there is to be no unequal weighting, that the happiness of an aristocrat is not more important than that of a peasant, which would, however, leave us with only the aggregative requirement that total utility so calculated should be maximized.

There is even a problem about the distribution of happiness within the life of one person. A period of misery followed by one of happiness seems preferable to a period of happiness followed by one of misery, even if the quantities of misery and happiness are respectively equal. However, it could be argued that order as such is indifferent; what makes the difference here is that when one is unhappy the anticipation of future happiness is itself pleasant, whereas the recollection of past happiness is not (but is even, according to Tennyson and Dante, "sorrow's crown of sorrow") while the reverse holds for the anticipation and recollection of misery when one is happy. One can enjoy troubles when they are over. When we take into account these joys and sorrows of anticipation and recollection, the aggregate of happiness is greater when the order is right, even if the quantities of misery and happiness were *otherwise* equal.

The utilitarian might try to deal analogously with problems of interpersonal distribution. Thus the familiar rule that happiness should be proportionate to merit is merely an incentive device for increasing the aggregate of happiness, merit being measured by a person's contribution to the happiness of others. Material goods have a diminishing marginal utility, so a more equal distribution of whatever goods there are is (apart from the just-mentioned incentive requirement) likely to produce a greater aggregate utility. Less plausibly, the utilitarian might say that it is not possible for a less equal distribution (even of happiness as opposed to material goods) to yield a higher aggregate (still apart from incentive effects) on the ground that (starting from a position of equality) one person's happiness cannot be pushed up much by any procedure that essentially involves reducing the happiness of others. A case, though not, I think, in the end a very convincing case, could thus be made out for a utilitarianism based on an aggregative principle only, without any independent principle of distribution.

All these difficulties and interminacies tell, in the first place, only against the claim that utilitarianism offers a peculiarly unitary and systematic basis for morality. A utilitarian can simply decide which of the various options to take up, and he can plausibly argue that rival views are subject to similar indeterminacies. In particular, many thinkers would give some weight to utility, even though they differ from utilitarians in that they recognize other moral requirements as well; such thinkers will obviously have the same problems about how to calculate the utility of which they propose to take account.

The Ethics of Fantasy

However, even if all the difficulties and indeterminacies mentioned in the last section were resolved, by argument or by decision, there would still be a fatal objection to the resulting act utilitarian system. It would be wholly impracticable. The system can, indeed, be looked at in several different ways, but this charge can be sustained against each interpretation in turn. Suppose, first, that it is considered as a morality in the broad sense, as an all-inclusive theory of conduct. Then, when utility or the general happiness is proposed as the immediate criterion of right action, is it intended that each agent should take the happiness of all as his goal? This, surely, is too much to expect. Mill himself conceded this, and replied to this objection by saying that it confuses the rule of action with the motive of it. "The great majority of good actions," he said, "are intended not for the benefit of the world, but for that of individuals . . . and the thoughts of the most virtuous man need not . . . travel beyond the particular persons concerned, except as far as is necessary to assure himself that in benefiting them he is not violating the rights, that is, the legitimate and authorized expectations, of any one else." But even if we accept this clarification, and take utilitarianism to be supplying not the motive but only a test of right actions, the charge of impracticality still stands. We cannot require that the actions of people generally should even pass the test of being such as to maximize the happiness of all, whether or not this is their motive. Even within a small village or commune it is too much to expect that the efforts of all members should be wholly directed towards the promoting of the well-being of all. And such total cooperation is out of the question on the scale of a nation state, let alone where the "all" are to be the whole human race, including its future or possible future members, and perhaps all other sentient beings as well. The question, which moral philosophers sometimes discuss, "What would happen if there were a society of pure act utilitarians?" is purely academic. We can indeed work out an answer, though only with difficulty, because this hypothesis is so far removed from anything within our experience that it is difficult to envisage it consistently and thoroughly. But the answer would have no direct bearing on any policies of practical importance. All real societies, and all those which it is of direct practical use to consider, are ones whose members have to a great extent divergent and conflicting purposes. And we must expect that their actions will consist largely of the pursuit of these divergent and conflicting purposes, and consequently will not only not be motivated by a desire for the general happiness but also will commonly fail the proposed test of being such as to maximize the general happiness.

Act utilitarianism is by no means the only moral theory that displays this extreme of impracticality. The biblical commandment "Thou shalt love thy neighbor as thyself," though it has its roots in a mistranslation of a much more realistic rule, is often taken as prescribing a universal and equal concern for all men. So interpreted, it is, as Mill says, effectively equivalent to the utilitarian principle. And it is similarly impracticable. People simply are not going to put the interests of all their "neighbors" on an equal footing with their own interests and specific purposes and with the interests of those who are literally near to them. Such universal concern will not be the actual motive of their choices, nor will they act as if it were. . . .

But why have moralists and preachers thought it worthwhile to propound rules that obviously have so little chance of being followed? They must surely have thought that by setting up such admittedly unattainable ideals they might induce at least some movement towards them, that if men were told to let universal beneficence guide all their conduct, they would not indeed do this, but would allow some small admixture of universal beneficence to help to direct their actions.

This would amount to proposing utilitarianism (or the doctrine of neighborly love) no longer as a morality in the broad sense but indirectly and in effect as one in the narrow sense: not as an overriding guide to conduct in general, but as a check or corrective on conduct which was very largely otherwise motivated and otherwise directed. I shall discuss utilitarianism, explicitly so presented, in the next section. Here I would remark only that if this is what is intended, it would be much better if it were explicitly so presented. To put forward as a morality in the broad sense something which, even if it were admirable, would be an utterly impossible ideal is likely to do, and surely has in fact done, more harm than good. It encourages the treatment of moral principles not as guides to action but as a fantasy which accompanies actions with which it is quite incompatible. It is a commonplace that religious morality often has little effect on the lives of believers. It is equally true, though not so frequently pointed out, that utilitarian morality is often treated as a topic of purely academic discussion, and is not taken any more seriously as a practical guide. In both cases the mistake is the same. To identify morality with something that certainly will not be followed is a sure way of bringing it into contempt—practical contempt, which combines all too readily with theoretical respect.

But why, it may be asked, are such moralities of universal concern impracticable? Primarily because a large element of selfishness—or, in an older terminology, self-love—is a quite ineradicable part of human nature. Equally, if we distinguish as Butler did the particular passions and affections from self-love, we must admit that they are inevitably the major part of human motivation, and the actions which express and realize them cannot be expected in general to tend towards the *general* happiness. Even what we recognize as unselfishness or benevolence is equally incompatible with *universal* concern.

It takes the form of what Broad called self-referential altruism—concern for others, but for others who have some special connection with oneself; children, parents, friends, workmates, neighbors in the literal, not the metaphorically extended, sense. Wider affections than these usually center upon devotion to some special cause—religious, political, revolutionary, nationalist—not upon the welfare of human beings, let alone sentient beings, in general. It is much easier, and commoner, to display a self-sacrificing love for some of one's fellow men if one can combine this with hostility to others. It is quite implausible for Mill to argue that such an array of limited motives can express themselves in actions which will conform to the utilitarian standard, provided only that the agent assures himself that he is not violating the rights of anyone else. As a proposed general pattern of conduct, there is indeed much to be said for the pursuit of some such array of special and limited goals within bounds set by respect for some "rights" of others. But it is misleading to present such a pattern as a consequence of the act utilitarian standard of right action, and to suggest that each choice that is a component in such a pattern could be validated as that which, out of the options available to that agent at that time, would contribute more than any other to the happiness of all men or of all sentient things.

But could not human nature be changed? I do not know. Of course, given the techniques of mass persuasion adolescents can be turned into Red Guards or Hitler Youth or pop fans, but in each of these we have only fairly superficial redirection of what are basically the same motives. It is far more doubtful whether any agency could effect the far more fundamental changes that would be needed to make practicable a morality of universal concern. Certainly no ordinary processes of education can bring them about.

Besides, if such changes could be effected, they might well prove self-defeating. Thus Bernard Williams has argued that in becoming capable of acting out of universal concern, people would have to be stripped of the motives on which most of what is of value in human life is based—close affections, private pursuits, and many kinds of competition and struggle. Even if our ultimate goal were the utilitarian one of maximizing the general happiness, the cultivation of such changes in human nature as would make an act utilitarian morality practicable might not be the most sensible way of pursuing it. But in any case this is at most a remote possibility, and has little relevance to our present choice of a first order moral system. For the present our terms of reference can be summed up in words close to those of Rousseau: we are to take men as they are and moral laws as they might be.

It may be objected that if we trim down moral demands to fit present human capacity, we bring morality into contempt in another way. But I do not mean that moral demands are to be so minimal that they are likely to be fulfilled by most people pretty well at once. We may well advocate moral principles that are in conflict with established habits of thought and behavior, that prescribe a degree of respect for the claims of others—and of distant others—which can flourish only by overcoming ingrained selfishness and limitations of generosity that are authorized by the existing law and the real conventional morality (as contrasted with the fantasy moralities of utilitarianism and neighborly love). All I am insisting upon is that we should advocate practicable reforms, that we should look for rules or principles of conduct that can fit in with the relatively permanent tendencies of human motives and thought.

Morality in the Narrow Sense

Act utilitarianism, then, is not viable as a morality in the broad sense—an all-inclusive theory of conduct—nor is it wise to propound it as such in the hope that it will then operate as a morality in the narrow sense, as a counterpoise to selfishness or excessively narrow sympathies. But this leaves open the possibility of supporting it explicitly as a morality in the narrow sense. Could it not be one factor among others which we allow to influence choices, but the factor which has the special function of countering the bad effects of limited sympathies? Warnock states, before going on to criticize, this suggestion:

The essential evil to be remedied . . . is the propensity of people to be concerned in practice, if not exclusively with their own, yet with some restricted range of, interests and ends; and surely the *direct* way to counter, or to limit, the evils liable to result from this propensity to counter it *itself*—to inculcate . . . a directly remedial propensity to be concerned with, and in practice to take into account, the welfare, needs, wants, interests of *all*.

Plausible though this suggestion is, I would agree with Warnock in rejecting it, though for reasons other than the ones on which he chiefly relies. My main reason is that such a propensity is too indeterminate to do the trick. It is now being proposed that an agent should either take the general happiness as his overriding aim or act as if he were doing so, but only that he should give it some weight against the more special interests to which he is primarily attached. But how much weight? When should the one consideration override the other? The utilitarian principle now gives no answer. The function we are now assigning it is to set a boundary to the pursuit of selfish or special or narrowly altruistic aims. Now a boundary may be blurred, uncertain, disputed, wavering, and yet still fulfill to some extent its function as a boundary; but it must be at least roughly indicated, at least dimly visible. The utilitarian principle sets up no visible boundary at all. . . .

Rule Utilitarianism

These objections to act utilitarianism as a determination of the content of a first order morality, whether in the broad or in the narrow sense, leave open and indeed naturally lead on to the consideration of rule utilitarianism. This differs from act utilitarianism in that it makes the general happiness not directly but only indirectly, by way of a two-stage procedure, the criterion of right action. It is summed up in Austin's dictum: "Our rules would be fashioned on utility; our conduct, on our rules." To find out whether an individual act is right or not, we must, Austin says, discover its "tendency," that is, we must consider the probable effect upon the general happiness if acts of the class to which this one belongs were generally done rather than generally omitted.

We must not suppose, however, that if a utilitarian gives any place at all to rules he is therefore a rule utilitarian. Act utilitarians regularly admit the use of rules of thumb: the great majority of ordinary decisions will be guided by rules which sum up what has been found or is reasonably believed usually to conduce fairly well to the general happiness, since it would often be either impossible or absurdly laborious to calculate in any detail the likely effect on utility of each available alternative in an individual case. What is distinctive of rule utilitarianism is the suggestion that the two-stage procedure, and the rules which in it intervene between utility and the individual choice, have some substantial merit over and above the economy of quick decision. It has often been suggested that rule utilitarianism can escape some of the more violent conflicts that break out between act utilitarianism and common moral beliefs or "intuitions." It is easy to construct imaginary examples, and not impossible to find real concrete ones, where an act utilitarian would have to say that it is right to kill innocent people, to invade their rights, to torture political opponents, to break solemn agreements, to cheat, or to betray a trust. But the rule utilitarian can say that each such individual act is wrong because the general performance of acts of each of these classes would plainly have a very bad effect on the general happiness. And in the last section we have followed Mill in recognizing the importance of respect for rules which are justified ultimately by their utility.

But before rule utilitarianism can be considered seriously, it has to defend itself against the criticism that it can make no practical difference, that it is extensionally equivalent to act utilitarianism in that the outcome of its two-stage procedure, consistently carried out, will always coincide with that of a direct test of an individual act by reference to its own utility. The essence of the argument for this equivalence can be given as follows, in *reductio ad absurdum* form.

Suppose that the two methods are not extensionally equivalent, and consider some case where there is a discrepancy between them. That is, some individual act *A* would in itself have a higher utility than any alternative, but it is forbidden by a utility-based rule *R*, because it is of a sort *S*—the sort which *R* forbids—the general performance of which would diminish the general happiness. Since the general performance of acts of sort *S* is harmful, whereas the performance of *A* would be beneficial, there must be something distinctive about *A* or its circumstances which explains this contrast. Let this causally relevant difference be *D*; then all acts that are not only of sort *S* but also have this difference *D*—*SD* acts—will be beneficial although the other acts of sort *S*—*S* non-*D* acts—are generally harmful. There is then a possible rule *R'* which will forbid *S* non-*D* acts but enjoin *SD* ones, and *R'* will serve utility better than *R*, since it will still forbid everything harmful that *R* forbids, while enjoining the beneficial acts that *R* forbids. Hence a consistently worked out rule utilitarianism, basing its rules on utility, will incorporate *R'* instead of *R*, and so will agree with act utilitarianism in prescribing *A*. Any apparent discrepancy between the two methods can be similarly resolved. . . .

This proof of equivalence is decisive, however, only if the rules in rule utilitarianism are treated as purely abstract entities, which can be formulated at will in order to fill in a stage in a theoretical two-stage procedure by which actions are tested in terms of utility. The argument may fail if the rules are to be social realities, rules more or less consciously accepted, followed, appealed to in criticism of violations, backed by public opinion, explicitly taught or unobtrusively passed on from one generation to another—that is, if they are to form what Hume called "a general scheme or system of action" that has "the concurrence of mankind." To flourish in this way a rule does not need to be absolutely simple and inflexible; it may not even be neatly formulable in words; but still there are limits to the complexities and qualifications it can incorporate. It may well be that *R* meets these requirements (indeed it may already exist as a social reality) but that the *R'* required to instantiate the proof of equivalence does not.

Rule utilitarianism, thus understood, can therefore resist the threatened collapse into act utilitarianism. Nevertheless I would not defend it, and would not attempt to justify on rule utilitarian grounds the first order moral system that I support. Utilitarian theory is still plagued by the difficulties and indeterminacies mentioned above. We cannot in any strict sense fashion our rules on utility. There is no such common measure of all interests and purposes as happiness or utility is supposed to be. Utilitarians commonly speak as if there were some entity, happiness, which is in some respect homogeneous and in principle measurable, that the different parts or constituents of happiness can somehow be reduced to a single scale and weighed objectively and decisively against one another. They may, indeed, also admit that this can be done only in principle, that in practice we can achieve only very rough estimates and comparisons of utility. But I doubt whether it can be done even in principle. The utilitarian calculus is a myth, and not, I think, a helpful one. There are and no doubt always will be considerable differences between people about what they value or think worthwhile in human life, about what could be called their concepts of happiness or *eudaimonia;* and if we say, with Aristotle, that everyone aims at *eudaimonia* we run the risk of deceiving ourselves by a mere verbal trick into thinking that human purposes are more unitary than they are or ever will be. We can hope to get much more genuine agreement about certain specifiable evils, about the respects in which, as Warnock says, things are liable to go very badly, and it is more realistic to consider morality in the narrow sense as a device for countering such specific evils than to regard morality, in either the broad or the narrow sense, as a system of rules whose function is to maximize a fictitious agreed or objectively determinable positive value, happiness or utility.

CHAPTER 6

Kantian Ethical Theory

THE MORAL LAW AND AUTONOMY
OF THE WILL
Immanuel Kant

Kant (1724–1804) is one of the most important philosophers of the Western world. He wrote three major ethical works: Groundwork of the Metaphysic of Morals *(1785),* Critique of Practical Reason *(1788), and* Metaphysic of Morals *(1797). In the selection below, taken from the first of these works, Kant presents and defends the "categorical imperative" as the fundamental principle of right conduct. He begins by claiming that only a good will—that is, the disposition to act out of a sense of duty—has unqualified moral worth. He then asks what principle of action guides a good will. He claims that a good will is guided by the idea that one's actions should be acceptable to everyone. Thus, people with a good will act in such a way that the principles of their actions (what Kant calls "maxims") should be universal laws for everyone. The idea of acting on maxims that should become universal laws for everyone's behavior is the fundamental principle of right conduct, Kant's categorical imperative.*

Kant proceeds to illustrate the categorical imperative by showing how it applies to cases of suicide, making a lying promise, letting one's talents rust, and failing to help others in need. He next argues that, since human beings have absolute worth—that is, since they exist as ends in themselves—we can alternatively formulate the categorical imperative as the requirement that we "act as to treat humanity, . . . in every case as an end withal, never as a means only."

Reprinted from *The Foundations of the Metaphysic of Morals,* translated by T. K. Abbott (this translation first published in 1873).

154

The Good Will

Nothing can possibly be conceived in the world, or even out of it, which can be called good, without qualification, except a Good Will. Intelligence, wit, judgment, and the other *talents* of the mind, however they may be named, or courage, resolution, perseverance, as qualities of temperament, are undoubtedly good and desirable in many respects; but these gifts of nature may also become extremely bad and mischievous if the will which is to make use of them, and which, therefore, constitutes what is called *character*, is not good. It is the same with the *gifts of fortune*. Power, riches, honor, even health, and the general well-being and contentment with one's condition which is called *happiness*, inspire pride, and often presumption, if there is not a good will to correct the influence of these on the mind, and with this also to rectify the whole principle of acting, and adapt it to its end. The sight of a being who is not adorned with a single feature of a pure and good will, enjoying unbroken prosperity, can never give pleasure to an impartial rational spectator. Thus a good will appears to constitute the indispensable condition even of being worthy of happiness.

There are even some qualities which are of service to this good will itself, and may facilitate its action, yet which have no intrinsic unconditional value, but always presuppose a good will, and this qualifies the esteem that we justly have for them, and does not permit us to regard them as absolutely good. Moderation in the affections and passions, self-control, and calm deliberation are not only good in many respects, but even seem to constitute part of the intrinsic worth of the person; but they are far from deserving to be called good without qualification, although they have been so unconditionally praised by the ancients. For without the principles of a good will, they may become extremely bad; and the coolness of a villain not only makes him far more dangerous, but also directly makes him more abominable in our eyes than he would have been without it.

A good will is good not because of what it performs or effects, not by its aptness for the attainment of some proposed end, but simply by virtue of the volition, that is, it is good in itself, and considered by itself is to be esteemed much higher than all that can be brought about by it in favor of any inclination, nay, even of the sum-total of all inclinations. Even if it should happen that, owing to special disfavor of fortune, or the niggardly provision of a step-motherly nature, this will should wholly lack power to accomplish its purpose, if with its greatest efforts it should yet achieve nothing, and there should remain only the good will (not, to be sure, a mere wish, but the summoning of all means in our power), then, like a jewel, it would still shine by its own light, as a thing which has its whole value in itself. Its usefulness or fruitlessness can neither add to nor take away anything from this value. . . .

. . . Thus the moral worth of an action does not lie in the effect expected from it, nor in any principle of action which requires to borrow its motive from this expected effect. For all these effects—agreeableness of one's condition, and even the promotion of the happiness of others—could have been also brought about by other causes, so that for this there would have been no need of the will of a rational being; whereas it is in this alone that the supreme and unconditional good can be found. The pre-eminent good which we call moral can therefore consist in nothing else than *the conception of law* in itself, *which certainly is only possible in a rational being,* in so far as this conception, and not the expected effect, determines the will. This is a good which is already present in the person who acts accordingly, and we have not to wait for it to appear first in the result.

The Supreme Principle of Morality: The Categorical Imperative

But what sort of law can that be, the conception of which must determine the will, even without paying any regard to the effect expected from it, in order that this will may be called good absolutely and without qualification? As I have deprived the will of every impulse which could arise to it from obedience to any law, there remains nothing but the universal conformity of its actions to law in general, which alone is to serve the will as a principle, *i.e.* I am never to act otherwise than *so that I could also will that my maxim should become a universal law.* Here, now, it is the simple conformity to law in general, without assuming any particular law applicable to certain actions, that serves the will as its principle, and must so serve it, if duty is not to be a vain delusion and a chimerical notion. The common reason of men in its practical judgments perfectly coincides with this, and always has in view the principle here suggested. Let the question be, for example: May I when in distress make a promise with the intention not to keep it? I readily distinguish here between the two significations which the question may have: Whether it is prudent, or whether it is right, to make a false promise? The former may undoubtedly often be the case. I see clearly indeed that it is not enough to extricate myself from a present difficulty by means of this subterfuge, but it must be well considered whether there may not hereafter spring from this lie much greater inconvenience than that from which I now free myself, and as, with all my supposed *cunning,* the consequences cannot be so easily foreseen but that credit once lost may be much more injurious to me than any mischief which I seek to avoid at present, it should be considered whether it would not be more *prudent* to act herein according to a universal maxim, and to make it a habit to promise nothing except with the intention of keeping it. But it is soon clear to me that such a maxim will still only be based on the fear of consequences. Now it is a wholly different thing to be truthful from duty, and to be so from apprehension of injurious consequences. In the first case, the very notion of the action already implies a law for me; in the second case, I must first look about elsewhere to see what results may be combined with it which would affect myself. For to deviate from the principle of duty is beyond all doubt wicked; but to be unfaithful to my maxim of prudence may often be very advantageous to me, although to abide by it is certainly safer. The shortest way, however, and an unerring one, to discover the answer to this question whether a lying promise is consistent with duty, is to ask myself, Should I be content that my maxim (to extricate myself from difficulty by a false promise) should hold good as a universal law, for myself as well as for others? and should I be able to say to myself, "Every one may make a deceitful promise when he finds himself in a difficulty from which he cannot otherwise extricate himself"? Then I presently become aware that while I can will the lie, I can by no means will that lying should be a universal law. For with such a law there would be no promises at all, since it would be in vain to allege my intention in regard to my future actions to those who would not believe this allegation, or if they over-hastily did so, would pay me back in my own coin. Hence my maxim, as soon as it should be made a universal law, would necessarily destroy itself. . . .

Imperatives: Hypothetical and Categorical

Everything in nature works according to laws. Rational beings alone have the faculty of acting according *to the conception of laws,* that is according to principles, *i.e.,* have a *will.* Since the deduction of actions from principles requires *reason,* the will is nothing but practical reason. If reason infallibly determines the will, then the actions of such a being which are recognized as objectively necessary are subjectively necessary also, *i.e.,* the will is a faculty to choose *that only* which reason independent of inclination recognizes as practically necessary, *i.e.,* as good. But if reason of itself does not sufficiently determine the will, if the latter is subject also to subjective conditions (particular impulses) which do not always coincide with the objective conditions; in a word, if the will does not *in itself* completely accord with reason (which is actually the case with men), then the actions which objectively are recognized as necessary are subjectively contingent, and the determination of such a will according to objective laws is *obligation,* that is to say, the relation of the objective laws to a will that is not thoroughly good is conceived as the determination of the will of a rational being by principles of reason, but which the will from its nature does not of necessity follow.

The conception of an objective principle, in so far as it is obligatory for a will, is called a command (of reason), and the formula of the command is called an Imperative.

All imperatives are expressed by the word *ought* [or *shall*], and thereby indicate the relation of an objective law of reason to a will, which from its subjective constitution is not necessarily determined by it (an obligation). They say that something would be good to do or to forbear, but they say it to a will which does not always do a thing because it is conceived to be good to do it. That is practically *good*, however, which determines the will by means of the conceptions of reason, and consequently not from subjective causes, but objectively, that is on principles which are valid for every rational being as such. It is distinguished from the *pleasant,* as that which influences the will only by means of sensation from merely subjective causes, valid only for the sense of this or that one, and not as a principle of reason, which holds for every one.

A perfectly good will would therefore be equally subject to objective laws (viz., laws of good), but could not be conceived as *obliged* thereby to act lawfully, because of itself from its subjective constitution it can only be determined by the conception of good. Therefore no imperatives hold for the Divine will, or in general for a *holy* will; *ought* is here out of place, because the volition is already of itself necessarily in unison with the law. Therefore imperatives are only formulae to express the relation of objective laws of all volition to the subjective imperfection of the will of this or that rational being, *e.g.,* the human will.

Now all *imperatives* command either *hypothetically* or *categorically.* The former represent the practical necessity of a possible action as means to something else that is willed (or at least which one might possibly will). The categorical imperative would be that which represented an action as necessary of itself without reference to another end, *i.e.,* as objectively necessary. . . .

First Formulation of
the Categorical Imperative: Universal Law

There is therefore but one categorical imperative, namely, this: *Act only on that maxim whereby thou canst at the same time will that it should become a universal law.*

Now if all imperatives of duty can be deduced from this one imperative as from their principle, then, although it should remain undecided whether what is called duty is not merely a vain notion, yet at least we shall be able to show what we understand by it and what this notion means.

Since the universality of the law according to which effects are produced constitutes what is properly called *nature* in the most general sense (as to form), that is the existence of things so far as it is determined by general laws, the imperative of duty may be expressed thus: *Act as if the maxim of thy action were to become by thy will a universal law of nature.*

Four Illustrations

We will now enumerate a few duties, adopting the usual division of them into duties to ourselves and to others, and into perfect and imperfect duties.

1. A man reduced to despair by a series of misfortunes feels wearied of life, but is still so far in possession of his reason that he can ask himself whether it would not be contrary to his duty to himself to take his own life. Now he inquires whether the maxim of his action could become a universal law of nature. His maxim is: From self-love I adopt it as a principle to shorten my life when its longer duration is likely to bring more evil than satisfaction. It is asked then simply whether this principle founded on self-love can become a universal law of nature. Now we see at once that a system of nature of which it should be a law to destroy life by means of the very feeling whose special nature it is to impel to the improvement of life would contradict itself, and therefore could not exist as a system of nature; hence that maxim cannot possibly exist as a universal law of nature, and consequently would be wholly inconsistent with the supreme principle of all duty.

2. Another finds himself forced by necessity to borrow money. He knows that he will not be able to repay it, but sees also that nothing will be lent to him, unless he promises stoutly to repay it in a definite time. He desires to make this promise, but he has still so much conscience as to ask himself: Is it not unlawful and inconsistent with duty to get out of a difficulty in this way? Suppose, however, that he resolves to do so, then the maxim of his action would be expressed thus: When I think myself in want of money, I will borrow money and promise to repay it, although I know that I never can do so. Now this principle of self-love or of one's own advantage may perhaps be consistent with my whole future welfare; but the question now is, Is it right? I change then the suggestion of self-love into a universal law, and state the question thus: How would it be if my maxim were a universal law? Then I see at once that it could never hold as a universal law of nature, but would necessarily contradict itself. For supposing it to be a universal law that everyone when he thinks himself in a difficulty should be able to promise whatever he pleases, with the purpose of not keeping his promise, the promise itself would become impossible, as well as the end that one might have in view in it, since no one would consider that anything was promised to him, but would ridicule all such statements as vain pretenses.

3. A third finds in himself a talent which with the help of some culture might make him a useful man in many respects. But he finds himself in

comfortable circumstances, and prefers to indulge in pleasure rather than to take pains in enlarging and improving his happy natural capacities. He asks, however, whether his maxim of neglect of his natural gifts, besides agreeing with his inclination to indulgence, agrees also with what is called duty. He sees then that a system of nature could indeed subsist with such a universal law although men (like the South Sea islanders) should let their talents rust, and resolve to devote their lives merely to idleness, amusement, and propagation of their species—in a word, to enjoyment; but he cannot possibly *will* that this should be a universal law of nature, or be implanted in us as such by a natural instinct. For, as a rational being, he necessarily wills that his faculties be developed, since they serve him, and have been given him, for all sorts of possible purposes.

4. A fourth, who is in prosperity, while he sees that others have to contend with great wretchedness and that he could help them, thinks: What concern is it of mine? Let everyone be as happy as Heaven pleases, or as he can make himself; I will take nothing from him nor even envy him, only I do not wish to contribute anything to his welfare or to his assistance in distress! Now no doubt if such a mode of thinking were a universal law, the human race might very well subsist, and doubtless even better than in a state in which everyone talks of sympathy and good-will, or even takes care occasionally to put it into practice, but, on the other side, also cheats when he can, betrays the rights of men, or otherwise violates them. But although it is possible that a universal law of nature might exist in accordance with that maxim, it is impossible to *will* that such a principle should have the universal validity of a law of nature. For a will which resolved this would contradict itself, inasmuch as many cases might occur in which one would have need of the love and sympathy of others, and in which, by such a law of nature, sprung from his own will, he would deprive himself of all hope of the aid he desires. . . .

Second Formulation of the Categorical Imperative:
Humanity as an End in Itself

. . . Now I say: man and generally any rational being *exists* as an end in himself, *not merely as a means* to be arbitrarily used by this or that will, but in all his actions, whether they concern himself or other rational beings, must be always regarded at the same time as an end. All objects of the inclinations have only a conditional worth; for if the inclinations and the wants founded on them did not exist, then their object would be without value. But the inclinations themselves being sources of want are so far from having an absolute worth for which they should be desired, that, on the contrary, it must be the universal wish of every rational being to be wholly free from them. Thus the worth of any object which is *to be acquired* by our action is always conditional. Beings whose existence depends not on our will but on nature's, have nevertheless, if they are nonrational beings, only a relative value as means, and are therefore called *things;* rational beings, on the contrary, are called *persons,* because their very nature points them out as ends in themselves, that is as something which must not be used merely as means, and so far therefore restricts freedom of action (and is an object of respect). These, therefore, are not merely subjective ends whose existence has a worth *for us* as an effect of our action, but *objective ends,* that is things whose existence is an end in itself: an end moreover for which no other can be substituted, which they should subserve *merely* as means, for otherwise nothing whatever would possess *absolute worth;* but if all worth were conditioned and therefore contingent, then there would be no supreme practical principle of reason whatever.

If then there is a supreme practical principle or, in respect of the human will, a categorical imperative, it must be one which, being drawn from the conception of that which is necessarily an end for everyone because it is *an end in itself,* constitutes an *objective* principle of will, and can therefore serve as a universal practical law. The foundation of this principle is: *rational nature exists as an end in itself.* Man necessarily conceives his own existence as being so: so far then this is a *subjective* principle of human actions. But every other rational being regards its existence similarly, just on the same rational principle that holds for me: so that it is at the same time an objective principle from which as a supreme practical law all laws of the will must be capable of being deduced. Accordingly the practical imperative will be as follows: *So act as to treat humanity, whether in thine own person or in that of any other, in every case as an end withal, never as means only. . . .*

. . . Looking back now on all previous attempts to discover the principle of morality, we need not wonder why they all failed. It was seen that man was bound to laws by duty, but it was not observed that the laws to which he is subject are *only those of his own giving,* though at the same time they are *universal,* and that he is only bound to act in conformity with his own will; a will, however, which is designed by nature to give universal laws. For when one has conceived man only as subject to a law (no matter what), then this law required some interest, either by way of attraction or constraint, since it did not originate as a law from *his own* will, but this will was according to a law obliged by *something else* to act in a certain manner. Now by this necessary consequence all the labor spent in finding a supreme principle of *duty* was irrevocably lost. For men never elicited duty, but only a necessity of acting from a certain interest. Whether this interest was private or otherwise, in any case the imperative must be conditional, and could not by any means be capable of being a moral command. I will therefore call this the principle of *Autonomy* of the will, in contrast with every other which I accordingly reckon as *Heteronomy.*

The Kingdom of Ends

The conception of every rational being as one which must consider itself as giving in all the maxims of its will universal laws, so as to judge itself and its actions from this point of view—this conception leads to another which depends on it and is very fruitful, namely, that of a *kingdom of ends*.

By a *kingdom* I understand the union of different rational beings in a system by common laws. Now since it is by laws that ends are determined as regards their universal validity, hence, if we abstract from the personal differences of rational beings, and likewise from all the content of their private ends, we shall be able to conceive all ends combined in a systematic whole (including both rational beings as ends in themselves, and also the special ends which each may propose to himself), that is to say, we can conceive a kingdom of ends, which on the preceding principles is possible.

For all rational beings come under the *law* that each of them must treat itself and all others *never merely as means,* but in every case *at the same time as ends in themselves*. Hence results a systematic union of rational beings by common objective laws, *i.e.,* a kingdom which may be called a kingdom of ends, since what these laws have in view is just the relation of these beings to one another as ends and means. . . .

KANTIANISM
Robert L. Holmes

Robert L. Holmes is professor of philosophy at the University of Rochester, and author of On War and Morality *(1989) and* Basic Moral Philosophy *(1993), from which this excerpt is taken. Holmes provides an overview of some of the basic ideas in Kant's Universal Law formulation of the categorical imperative and then proceeds to raise two objections to Kant's theory. (Holmes classifies Kant's theory as a version of "moral legalism" by which he means that the rightness and wrongness of actions is determined solely by rules or principles.)*

Immanuel Kant . . . stresses consistency. Indeed, he says that "[c]onsistency is the highest obligation of a philosopher and yet the most rarely

From *Basic Moral Philosophy* (Wadsworth, 1993). Reprinted by permission of the publisher.

found."[1] And he insisted that moral judgments could not be derived from external authority, not even God's. His theory is complex and difficult, however, and there is little agreement about how precisely to interpret it. In what follows, I shall present a way of understanding it that I believe renders it as plausible as possible; an interpretation that is Kantian in spirit rather than in exact detail. . . .

The Concept of Duty

In our ordinary thinking about morality, Kant thinks, we regard the notion of moral duty as having an absoluteness about it. If I have a genuine moral duty to do something, it is binding on me whether I like it or not. It is not merely a matter of preference, or how I feel about things. I cannot justifiably avoid doing my duty simply by deciding it would be inconvenient. Nor can anyone. What is a duty for me must be a moral duty for anyone like me in relevant respects and similarly situated; it is not variable from person to person, as the extreme relativist thinks.

If this is how we think of moral duty, then moral principles must have an absoluteness about them as well, and must apply to everyone alike. This does not mean they apply only to human beings. Moral principles are not merely universal. If all people desire happiness, then the ethical egoist's principle would be universal, because it would apply to all people. But morality is not limited in principle to human beings. Why not?

Those aspects of our nature that bring us within the scope of morality are the facts that we are capable of following rules, drawing inferences, generalizing, and making free choices. We are capable of altering our conduct because we recognize the truth of some propositions and the importance of certain interconnections among them. These are the capacities that make us rational beings.

Rationality, Kant thinks, is central to the whole idea of morality, and human beings may not be the only rational beings. If there is a God, God is rational, and if there are angels, they are rational, too. If, as many astronomers believe today, there is extraterrestrial life, it may be rational. But such life, if it exists, will not be human (the typical science fiction account of aliens from outer space represents them as intelligent but very different from us in nature and appearance).

Now, any being that is capable of deliberating, following rules, and making free choices is subject to the moral law. If you can freely and reflectively choose to do one thing rather than another, then it always makes sense to ask whether what you choose is morally right. It is this, not your physical appearance or your particular desires—much less your background or history—that establishes the relevance of morality to your conduct. Even if you were so constituted as not to desire your own happiness, it would still make sense to assess the rightness or wrongness of what you do.

Objective Principles and Hypothetical Imperatives

Given that morality applies to all rational beings, we still need to ask what morality requires of us as human beings. Kant answers, in effect, that morality requires that we act as fully rational beings would act. Moral conduct is rational conduct.

We do not know whether there are in fact other rational beings besides ourselves, but if there are, we know that by virtue of being rational they will be capable of making decisions and choices, and they will have ends, purposes, and desires (although these may be for quite different objects from those we desire).

Now, to be rational is perhaps above all to be consistent. For example, if you are rational you will do what is necessary to achieve your aim or desire (other things being equal), since it is consistent to do what is necessary to achieve that aim. It is a principle of rationality that to desire an end is to desire the indispensable means to its attainment. Knowing that, we can formulate various objective principles, which are simply principles expressing how a fully rational being would act given certain aims or desires.

From our own experience, we can readily formulate such principles for rational beings who have the same sorts of desires we do. Some of these concern everyday affairs:

1. A fully rational being who wants a car to run will put gas in it.

2. A fully rational being who wants to get from New York to San Francisco in the fastest way possible will fly.

3. A fully rational being who wants to make an early class on time will set the alarm.

Kant would call these "objective principles of skill." They cover a range of practical situations. Others relate specifically to the desire for happiness:

4. A fully rational being who wants to be happy will not smoke cigarettes or use drugs.

5. A fully rational being who wants to be happy will be considerate of others.

6. A fully rational being who wants to be happy will not drive at excessive speeds.

The assumptions in principles 4 through 6 are, of course, that to risk lung cancer, drug addiction, alienating others, or auto accidents is likely to be counterproductive to the pursuit of happiness. Principles of this sort Kant would call "objective principles of prudence."

What is the relevance of such principles to our conduct? The answer is that how a fully rational being would act is normative for how we, as imperfectly rational beings, *ought* to act.

If a fully rational being who wanted to get from New York to San Francisco in the fastest way would fly, then if I want to get there in the fastest way, I ought to fly. That judgment—

If I want to get to San Francisco from New York in the fastest way possible, I ought to fly

—is what Kant calls an imperative. It consists of two parts. The antecedent (the "if" clause) refers to the desire in question, the consequent (the "then" clause) refers to what ought to be done to satisfy that desire.

Notice, however, that the "ought" in the consequent is binding on me only if I have the desire mentioned in the antecedent. If I am in no hurry to get to San Francisco, there is no reason why I should fly; it is not incumbent on me as a rational being to do so. I could just as well drive or take a train. And if I want to enjoy the countryside, that is what I should do. For this reason, Kant speaks of such imperatives as *hypothetical*. The validity of the "ought" depends on my having the appropriate desire.

Hypothetical imperatives, we can see, can be derived from the corresponding objective principles; they depend on verifiable truths about means to ends. Where the desire is variable among people (and for the same person at different times)—as in this case (and in the corresponding hypothetical imperatives derivable from objective principles 1 through 3)—Kant speaks of the imperative as a problematical imperative (or sometimes a technical imperative or imperative of skill). The various "oughts" derivable from principles 4 through 6 likewise presuppose that one has the appropriate desire. The difference in these cases is that we know all human beings desire happiness, so the antecedent of the resultant hypothetical can always be assumed to be true. This means that in principle we can just as easily say,

If you want to be happy, you ought not to take drugs.

or

Given that you want to be happy, you ought not to take drugs.

Either way, the validity of the "ought" still presupposes the desire. If there are beings who are indifferent to their happiness, these considerations would give them no reason to do or refrain from doing the acts in question. Because in our case we can always affirm the desire, Kant calls these hypothetical imperatives "assertorical" (or "pragmatic" or "prudential").

Ethical egoism, in his view, reduces morality to hypothetical imperatives of this sort. It tells us what we ought to do only on the assumption that we want to be happy. And it is for this reason that it is inadequate as a moral principle. Recall that Kant takes it to be part of our commonsense understanding of duty that duty be absolute; that is, unconditional. This requires that moral principles be absolute; they must apply alike to all conceivable rational beings. But the assertorical imperative applies only to beings who, like us, desire happiness. And its implementation in particular cases depends always on an estimate of consequences. Because we can never be altogether certain what the consequences of our acts will be, ethical egoism would mean that we could never be certain what is right.

For example, if you live in New York and have a job interview in San Francisco, you might judge that it is in your best interest—that is, most conducive to your happiness—to fly rather than postpone the interview. But if you fly and the plane crashes, you were wrong, and would have done better to postpone the interview. Or if, thinking the plane might crash, you drive and instead the car crashes, then you were wrong about that. For morality to apply to all conceivable rational beings, and for us to know for certain what is right and wrong, morality cannot be grounded in either human nature or estimates of empirical consequences. It must be grounded in reason.

To see how this can be, let us distinguish a third type of objective principle. In addition to the objective principles of skill and prudence, there are also objective principles of morality. But whereas the principles of skill and prudence express how a fully rational being would act who had certain desires, the objective principles of morality formulate how a fully rational being would act irrespective of desires or preferences. Thus we can say,

7. A fully rational being would tell the truth.

8. A fully rational being would keep promises.

9. A fully rational being would not cheat.

10. A fully rational being would act benevolently toward others.

No mention need be made here of such a being's having any particular desires, not even the desire for happiness. A fully rational being will do certain things and refrain from others simply by virtue of being rational.

If, now, these are things that a fully rational being would do categorically (that is, unconditionally—irrespective of desires or preferences), then they prescribe what we, as imperfectly rational beings, categorically *ought* to do, irrespective of our desires or preferences. Each of us, in other words, can reason as follows:

1. A fully rational being would keep promises.

2. An imperfectly rational being ought to keep promises.

3. I am an imperfectly rational being.

4. Therefore, I ought to keep promises.

Imperative 4 is for Kant a categorical imperative. It does not require the specification of a desire in the antecedent. The validity of the "ought" does not depend on any empirical condition, either subjective (my desires or preferences) or external (the consequences of promise keeping for my or anyone else's happiness).

So moral imperatives (or moral judgments, as we would say) are for Kant categorical imperatives. They cannot be merely hypothetical. We cannot avoid their normative force by disavowing any interest or desire in doing as they prescribe.

But how do we know precisely which judgments, if any, are categorical in this sense? To find out, we need to ask how a perfectly rational being would go about making choices among actions and here we need to introduce a new concept.

Subjective Principles or Maxims

Whenever we choose to perform an action, we are, as it were, choosing a type of action. We are committing ourselves to doing this *type* of act in this *type* of circumstance. We are acting for a reason, and if we encounter another situation that is similar, the same reason applies to it. Otherwise our conduct overall would be fragmented and disconnected; there would be no continuity to what we do and no consistency in our lives. The living out of rational life plans would be impossible.

Another way of putting this is to say that we commit ourselves to a kind of rule whenever we perform a voluntary action, one that might be stated something like this: "In circumstances of this sort, I will perform this sort of act." This does not mean that we invariably adhere to such rules. Sometimes we are inconsistent, and at other times we change our minds and deliberately redirect our lives through new commitments. Nor does it mean we always (or even most of the time) have such a rule expressly in mind when we act. It is rather that, if we reflect on what we are doing, or considering doing, we can in principle always specify some such rule for every act. It states what we propose to do, and perhaps why.

Kant calls rules of this sort "subjective principles," or more often, "maxims." They are subjective in that they claim no validity for ourselves or others and have no applicability beyond our own conduct. But every voluntary action has one. It is part of the very idea of rationality that actions be constrained by such rules of consistency. This would be true even of perfectly rational beings. They would act on maxims as well. . . .

Now insofar as they are rational, there is no difference among perfectly rational beings. Rationality is the same in all of them. This means that, *as* rational beings, they cannot consistently choose to perform actions whose maxims could not be accepted by other rational beings. Otherwise, they would be committing themselves to rules of action that would conflict with the very rationality they themselves embody.

We may put this by saying that a perfectly rational being would act only according to those maxims that could at the same time be universal laws—that could, in other words, be acted on by all conceivable rational beings in relevantly similar circumstances.

The Categorical Imperative

Now, if that is how a perfectly rational being would act, then it is normative of how we, as imperfectly rational beings, *ought* to act. This yields what for Kant is *the* categorical imperative, the basic principle of morality:

Categorical imperative 1 (CI_1):   Act only according to that maxim by which you can at the same time will that it should become a universal law.

I say that this is *the* categorical imperative. Kant sometimes uses the notion of categorical imperative to stand for particular categorical moral judgments, as in "You ought to tell the truth" or "You ought to keep promises." But he also uses it to stand for the basic moral principle from which these particular judgments are derived (how, we will consider in a moment). . . .

Let us pause for a moment to take account of the significance of the CI_1. In the CI_1, we have arrived at Kant's fundamental principle of morality. It is his holding to such a principle that makes him a moral legalist. Our moral judgments (particular categorical imperatives) must be derivable from the CI_1.

Notice furthermore that the CI_1 makes no reference to goodness. It does not tell us to promote the good of anyone—not of ourselves, or of people generally, or of the world as a whole. If we are motivated to follow this principle, we will in fact be cultivating the only thing that is good in itself, namely, a good will, because we will be trying to do what is right because it is right.[2] But the CI_1 does not tell us to estimate the good that will result in order to decide what our duty is. It is not concerned with consequences or with goodness. So in addition to being legalist, Kant's position is nonconsequentialist and deontological.

Applying the Categorical Imperative

What exactly does the CI_1 mean, and how does one apply it to particular situations to determine what is morally right? Or, in Kantian terminology, how does one apply *the* categorical imperative to derive *particular* categorical imperatives?

This is the most vexing part of Kant's ethical theory, and to critics and admirers alike the least satisfactory. Let us try to understand the thinking that underlies it.

Remember that all the preceding is by way of trying to explain how moral conduct is essentially rational. If we do what is morally right, we are acting as a fully rational being would act; if we knowingly do wrong, we are acting irrationally.

Now, how can an act be irrational? Although we often speak of acts as irrational, strictly speaking an action cannot be irrational by itself. Considered in one light, an act is just another event along with all the others that take place in the world. As such, it is neither rational nor irrational. Only if we view an act in a broader context does it make sense to speak of the act as either rational or irrational. This broader context must include the act's interconnections with other actions, and specifically its connection with the concept of a rational being. In other words, it makes sense to speak of acts as rational only in a sense that presupposes an understanding of what it is for beings to be rational.

Thus (to take an example of a verbal act), if we simply reflect on the words "I promise to give you your money back next week," we cannot say whether the act of uttering those words is rational or not. We need to know something about the context: who has spoken the words, to whom they were spoken, what was communicated thereby, and so on (it makes a difference, for example, whether they are uttered in a play, or spoken solemnly from one friend to another). We need, that is, a context that involves rational beings, purposes, and desires.

Suppose the context is the following: You need money quickly, and the only way you can get it is to borrow it. You know someone who is trusting, so you ask her for a loan. Unknown to her, however, you plan to leave town within the next few days and don't intend to repay it. In this context, your uttering the words in question constitutes the making of a promise—a deceitful one, however—and as such represents a transaction between two rational persons (nonrational creatures do not have a concept of promising). What takes place can fully be understood only in terms of the idea of rationality. In this situation, you are using the rational practice of promising, and the other person's rationality as well, to further your own ends. The very effectiveness of the transaction for your purposes presupposes this rationality.

To show why it is wrong to make such a deceitful promise, we must show it is irrational. But the act of speaking those words just by itself, I have said, is neither rational nor irrational, so something must link that act with other possible acts and with the relevant features of rationality embodied in those involved in the transaction.

Here is where the notion of a maxim comes in. First we must state what the maxim of such an act would be, something like this: "If I find myself in need of money, I will borrow it and promise to repay it, knowing that I will never do so." This is a kind of rule to which you would be committing yourself by performing the act in question in the context we have imagined. You would, in other words, be committing yourself to acts of a certain *kind* in situations of a certain *kind*. The maxim shows that beyond the particularity of the act there is a generality provided by the rule. This makes it possible to begin to consider the act rationally.

Now because a fully rational being would act only on maxims that could be made universal laws for all rational beings, the CI directs us, as imperfectly rational beings, to do likewise. That is what we *ought* to do.

What does that mean in this case? We have specified the maxim of the act. We must now consider what it would be like if it were a universal law—that is, if it were adopted by all rational beings, so that *everyone* made it a rule, when in need of money, to borrow it and promise to repay it, intending not to do so. What would that be like?

Clearly, if everyone acted on that maxim no one would lend money. Everyone would know in advance that it would never be repaid. If we take the notion of "promising" to extend to all kinds of financial transactions that might not involve the actual uttering of just those words, the institutions of banking, finance and investing would collapse, because all such institutions presuppose trust that certain agreements and commitments will be honored.

That might be disastrous or even catastrophic, you might say. But why would it be irrational?

Here we need to specify one additional factor, the purpose for which you made the deceitful promise in the first place. That purpose, obviously, was to get money. But now we can see that there is a kind of contradiction here. It is between your purpose and the universal acceptance of the maxim by which you would be acting in trying to achieve that purpose. If the maxim were universally accepted, you could not achieve your purpose, for no one would lend money. In performing the act, you would be using a means (a deceitful promise) to an end (getting money), which would be undercut by the universal acceptance of the very maxim to which the act would commit you. You would at one and the same time be doing one thing (committing yourself to the universal acceptance of the maxim) that if universally done would conflict with another thing you are also doing (trying to borrow money).

Here is the inconsistency (Kant speaks of it as a "contradiction"). As consistency is a requirement of rationality, you would in this case be acting irrationally. Because the act is irrational, it is contrary to duty and wrong.[3]

The example of the deceitful promise illustrates what Kant calls a "perfect duty." But he recognizes also what he calls "imperfect duties," such as a duty to develop one's talents. Let us consider briefly how these differ.

Suppose a person decides to quit school at an early age, concluding that it is not worth his while learning to read and write well, or to do math, or to use a computer. His maxim, if he gives it any thought, might be something like "I'll neglect developing my abilities, skills, and talents if I feel like it." Could one universalize this maxim? In one sense yes. One can imagine a world in which everyone acted on that maxim; it would simply be a world in which people were uneducated and lazy. Unlike the case of the maxim involved in the deceitful promise, there is no "contradiction" involved in trying to conceive of such a world. It is relatively easy to do, in fact. But what Kant says we cannot consistently do is will that such a world actually come about. Why not? Because we all have various aims and objectives in life (ultimately we all want to be happy, and our other aims and objectives are connected with this desire), such as for a home, a car, money for vacations and travel, leisure time to pursue our interests, and so on. Many, more specifically, want to practice medicine or law, or to pursue careers in music or acting or business. However, if we do not develop certain abilities and talents, the attainment of these other objectives will be impossible. We will not be able to compete in the job market, or if we do get a job we will be unlikely to gain advancement; as a consequence we will be unlikely ever to have the wherewithal to do the things we want. Or if our aims require a college degree or beyond, we will never even get into college. Moreover, if everyone acted on the same maxim, there would not even be the opportunities there in the first place. Quite apart from one's own inclinations and initiative, the opportunities to achieve many objectives are possible only because most other people have developed their abilities and talents (the company with which you could get a job if you qualified might not exist if the management and other workers had not worked hard to make it a going concern). There could be such a world. But given the aims virtually every one of us has, it is not one we can consistently will to come about. . . .

Kant Not a Consequentialist

We have seen the essentials of what Kant thinks lies behind our common-sense notion of duty. It is a complex conceptual apparatus that represents the most formidable attempt in the history of ethics to show how morality is thoroughly rational. Although Kant's theory is sometimes contrasted with theories of virtue, note that it has no necessary incompatibility with such theories; in fact, although we have not considered it, Kant himself has a theory of virtue, stressing the importance of developing character, and virtues such as conscientiousness and beneficence.[4] It is just that overall his theory is best considered an ethics of conduct because of the importance it assigns to conduct as well as to rules and principles.

It has also seemed to some that despite its apparent deontological orientation, Kant's theory is in fact ultimately consequentialist, because it requires that we consider the consequences of universalizing our maxims. This, however, is mistaken. Kant does not say that rightness is determined either by the consequences of acts, or by the consequences of our universalizing them. What he says is that we must reflect on what the world would be like if our maxims *were* universally accepted, and must consider whether such a world would be rationally conceivable, and such that we could consistently will that it come about. But considering what the consequences would be if our maxims were universally accepted does not itself have consequences in the actual world. This considering is done by reason alone. What *does* have consequences in the actual world, of course, are actions we perform as a result of determining what our duty is. But these are not themselves the consequences of our universalizing our maxims (though they are consequences of our choosing to perform the actions after assessing their rightness by rational means). What the actual consequences would be if we performed certain actions does not enter into the process by which we determine rightness at all. For that reason, Kant is not a consequentialist. Nor, in that case, does consideration of what the value of the consequences of our actions would be enter into that determination either, so he is not an axiologist either.

But if it is not a sustainable objection against Kant that he was a consequentialist despite himself, there are other problems for his theory, only two of which we have space to mention here.

The first problem is that his whole theory founders unless we can make sense of saying that every voluntary action has a correctly specifiable maxim. As we have seen, the notion of a maxim is pivotal in the whole rational process by which we determine rightness.

The categorical imperative purports to govern all conduct. And it is presumed not to be difficult to determine what it prescribes. But it requires that we specify correctly the maxim of proposed actions. The problem is that prospective actions do not come with one and only one maxim unmistakably attached to them. Whether I describe the maxim of my action as "moving my arm in situations of this sort" or as "paying a bribe in situations of this sort" may make a difference to whether I can universalize it. Every act seems to admit of having many different maxims associated with it, and which of these we take to be the correct one can make a difference to the ultimate determination of the rightness of the act.

Even before that, whatever we do admits of being characterized as any one of an indefinite number of actions. In some circumstances, the action that a person performs might be characterized either as that of moving his arm, swinging a racket, hitting a tennis ball, or returning a serve. And all these might be correct characterizations. In more serious circumstances, what someone does might be characterized as moving his finger, pushing a button, following orders, or launching a nuclear missile—again, each with equal correctness. So what is the "act" that is our proper concern when it comes to determining rightness, and what is its maxim? Is it "If I want this system to operate, I will press this button"? Or "When given orders in situations of this sort, I will comply"? Or "When ordered to initiate a nuclear attack, I will do so"? Whether you could consistently will that all rational beings act on your maxim might well depend on precisely which of these you take to be the maxim. The first might lead you only to consider an efficient world in which people make things run in the intended way by starting them properly. The third might lead you to consider a world in which everyone is willing to initiate the destruction of civilization if ordered to do so.

But even if this problem were surmounted, there is a second that is more fundamental. It lies in Kant's assumption that how fully rational beings would act is normative for how we, as imperfectly rational beings, ought to act. . . . What is presupposed by Kant's reasoning is a principle on the order of "One ought to act as a perfectly rational being would act." This would then enable one to conclude that we ought to act in this way.

In other words, to get from

1. A fully rational being would do X.

to

2. An imperfectly rational being ought to do X.

we need a premise such as

1'. One ought to act as a fully rational being would act.

But once we formulate an assumed premise of this sort, we see it has problems. Many people would question whether focusing on fully rational conduct is at all the way to approach morality. Some, like Hume (who wrote before Kant), would say that reason by itself is utterly incapable of guiding conduct, since it can only deal with relations among things. It can show us the way to selecting correct means to our ends, but it cannot select our ends for us. For that we need our "passional" nature (feelings, emotions, desires). It is how we feel about ends that leads us to adopt or reject them. And some feminists would maintain that this whole Kantian conception of reason, as objective and free of historical and social contexts, is essentially a male conception, one that fails to do justice to women's experience, which is rooted in feeling, connectedness, and caring.

These problems are not necessarily fatal to Kant's theory, but they need to be reckoned with. In any event, Kant's is a powerful theory and represents perhaps the paradigm of moral legalism.

Notes

1. Immanuel Kant, *Critique of Practical Reason and Other Writings in Moral Philosophy*, ed. and tr. Lewis White Beck (Chicago: University of Chicago Press, 1949), p. 135.
2. Meaning now by "right" what is mandatory or required, not merely what is permissible.
3. Note that this shows only that it is wrong to act on this particular maxim, associated with a false promise. This does not show that breaking a promise for another reason, such as to save someone's life, is necessarily wrong. To determine that, you would need to consider the nature of the maxim in that case, and whether it could be successfully universalized. Also note that, although Kant thinks that a pure moral philosophy is free of anything empirical, to derive specific duties from the categorical imperative requires some empirical knowledge— in this case, for example, about what must be the case for human beings to make promises successfully.
4. This has tempted some to view his theory as primarily an ethics of virtue. See, for example, Onora O'Neill, *Constructions of Reason: Explorations of Kant's Practical Philosophy* (Cambridge, England: Cambridge University Press, 1989), p. 161.

KANT ON TREATING PEOPLE AS ENDS IN THEMSELVES
Onora O'Neill

Onora O'Neill is professor of philosophy at Newnham College, Cambridge University. She is author of The Faces of Hunger *(1985),* Constructions of Reason *(1989), and* Towards Justice and Virtue *(1996). O'Neill provides an explication of the ideas and implications of Kant's formula of the End-in-Itself formulation of the categorical imperative.*

Kant's moral theory has acquired the reputation of being forbiddingly difficult to understand and, once understood, excessively demanding in its requirements. I don't believe that this reputation has been wholly earned, and I am going to try to undermine it. . . .

The main method by which I propose to avoid some of the difficulties of Kant's moral theory is by explaining only one part of the theory. This does not seem to me to be an irresponsible approach in this case. One of the things that makes Kant's moral theory hard to understand is that he gives a number of different versions of the principle that he calls the Supreme Principle of Morality, and these different versions don't look at all like one another. They also don't look at all like the utilitarians' Greatest Happiness Principle. But the Kantian principle is supposed to play a similar role in arguments about what to do.

Kant calls his Supreme Principle the *Categorical Imperative;* its various versions also have sonorous names. One is called the Formula of Universal Law; another is the Formula of the Kingdom of Ends. The one on which I shall concentrate is known as the *Formula of the End in Itself.* To understand why Kant thinks that these picturesquely named principles are equivalent to one another takes quite a lot of close and detailed analysis of Kant's philosophy. I shall avoid this and concentrate on showing the implications of this version of the Categorical Imperative.

The Formula of the End in Itself

Kant states the Formula of the End in Itself as follows:

Act in such a way that you always treat humanity, whether in your own person or in the person of any other, never simply as a means but always at the same time as an end.

From *Matters of Life and Death,* edited by Tom Regan (New York: McGraw-Hill, 1986). Reprinted by permission of the publisher.

To understand this we need to know what it is to treat a person as a means or as an end. According to Kant, each of our acts reflects one or more *maxims*. The maxim of the act is the principle on which one sees oneself as acting. A maxim expresses a person's policy, or if he or she has no settled policy, the principle underlying the particular intention or decision on which he or she acts. Thus, a person who decides "This year I'll give 10 percent of my income to famine relief" has as a maxim the principle of tithing his or her income for famine relief. In practice, the difference between intentions and maxims is of little importance, for given any intention, we can formulate the corresponding maxim by deleting references to particular times, places, and persons. In what follows I shall take the terms "maxim" and "intention" as equivalent.

Whenever we act intentionally, we have at least one maxim and can, if we reflect, state what it is. (There is of course room for self-deception here— "I'm only keeping the wolf from the door" we may claim as we wolf down enough to keep ourselves overweight, or, more to the point, enough to feed someone else who hasn't enough food.)

When we want to work out whether an act we propose to do is right or wrong, according to Kant, we should look at our maxims and not at how much misery or happiness the act is likely to produce, and whether it does better at increasing happiness than other available acts. We just have to check that the act we have in mind will not use anyone as a mere means, and, if possible, that it will treat other persons as ends in themselves.

Using Persons as Mere Means

To use someone as a *mere means* is to involve them in a scheme of action *to which they could not in principle consent*. Kant does not say that there is anything wrong about using someone as a means. Evidently we have to do so in any cooperative scheme of action. If I cash a check I use the teller as a means, without whom I could not lay my hands on the cash; the teller in turn uses me as a means to earn his or her living. But in this case, each party consents to her or his part in the transaction. Kant would say that though they use one another as means, they do not use one another as *mere* means. Each person assumes that the other has maxims of his or her own and is not just a thing or a prop to be manipulated.

But there are other situations where one person uses another in a way to which the other could not in principle consent. For example, one person may make a promise to another with every intention of breaking it. If the promise is accepted, then the person to whom it was given must be ignorant of what the promisor's intention (maxim) really is. If one knew that the promisor did not intend to do what he or she was promising, one would, after all, not accept or rely on the promise. It would be as though there had been no promise made. Successful false promising depends on deceiving the person to whom the promise is made about what one's real maxim is. And since the person who is deceived doesn't know that real maxim, he or she can't in principle consent to his or her part in the proposed scheme of action. The person who is deceived is, as it were, a prop or a tool—a mere means—in the false promisor's scheme. A person who promises falsely treats the acceptor of the promise as a prop or a thing and not as a person. In Kant's view, it is this that makes false promising wrong.

One standard way of using others as mere means is by deceiving them. By getting someone involved in a business scheme or a criminal activity on false pretenses, or by giving a misleading account of what one is about, or by making a false promise or a fraudulent contract, one involves another in something to which he or she in principle cannot consent, since the scheme requires that he or she doesn't know what is going on. Another standard way of using others as mere means is by coercing them. If a rich or powerful person threatens a debtor with bankruptcy unless he or she joins in some scheme, then the creditor's intention is to coerce; and the debtor, if coerced, cannot consent to his or her part in the creditor's scheme. To make the example more specific: If a moneylender in an Indian village threatens not to renew a vital loan unless he is given the debtor's land, then he uses the debtor as a mere means. He coerces the debtor, who cannot truly consent to this "offer he can't refuse." (Of course the outward form of such transactions may look like ordinary commercial dealings, but we know very well that some offers and demands couched in that form are coercive.)

In Kant's view, acts that are done on maxims that require deception or coercion of others, and so cannot have the consent of those others (for consent precludes both deception and coercion), are wrong. When we act on such maxims, we treat others as mere means, as things rather than as ends in themselves. If we act on such maxims, our acts are not only wrong but unjust: such acts wrong the particular others who are deceived or coerced.

Treating Persons as Ends in Themselves

Duties of justice are, in Kant's view (as in many others'), the most important of our duties. When we fail in these duties, we have used some other or others as mere means. But there are also cases where, though we do not use others as mere means, still we fail to use them as ends in themselves in the fullest possible way. To treat someone as an end in him or herself requires in the first place that one not use him or her as mere means, that one respect each as a rational person with his or her own maxims. But beyond that, one may also seek to foster others' plans and maxims by sharing some of their ends. To act beneficently is to seek others' happiness, therefore to intend to achieve some of the things that those others aim at with their maxims. If I want to make others happy, I will adopt maxims that not merely do not manipulate them but that foster some of their plans and activities. Beneficent acts try to achieve what others want. However, we cannot seek everything that others want; their wants are too numerous and diverse, and, of course, sometimes incompatible. It follows that beneficence has to be selective.

There is then quite a sharp distinction between the requirements of justice and of beneficence in Kantian ethics. Justice requires that we act on *no* maxims that use others as mere means. Beneficence requires that we act on *some* maxims that foster others' ends, though it is a matter for judgment and discretion which of their ends we foster. Some maxims no doubt ought not to be fostered because it would be unjust to do so. Kantians are not committed to working interminably through a list of happiness-producing and misery-reducing acts; but there are some acts whose obligatoriness utilitarians may need to debate as they try to compare total outcomes of different choices, to which Kantians are stringently bound. Kantians will claim that they have done nothing wrong if none of their acts is unjust, and that their duty is complete if in addition their life plans have in the circumstances been reasonably beneficent.

In making sure that they meet all the demands of justice, Kantians do not try to compare all available acts and see which has the best effects. They consider only the proposals for action that occur to them and check that these proposals use no other as mere means. If they do not, the act is permissible; if omitting the act would use another as mere means, the act is obligatory. Kant's theory has less scope than utilitarianism. Kantians do not claim to discover whether acts whose maxims they don't know fully are just. They may be reluctant to judge others' acts or policies that cannot be regarded as the maxim of any person or institution. They cannot rank acts in order of merit. Yet, the theory offers more precision than utilitarianism when data are scarce. One can usually tell whether one's act would use others as mere means, even when its impact on human happiness is thoroughly obscure.

The Limits of Kantian Ethics:
Intentions and Results

Kantian ethics differs from utilitarian ethics both in its scope and in the precision with which it guides action. Every action, whether of a person or of an agency, can be assessed by utilitarian methods, provided only that information is available about all the consequences of the act. The theory has unlimited scope, but, owing to lack of data, often lacks precision. Kantian ethics has a more restricted scope. Since it assesses actions by looking at the maxims of agents, it can only assess intentional acts. This means that it is most at home in assessing individuals' acts; but it can be extended to assess acts of agencies that (like corporations and governments and student unions) have decision-making procedures. It can do nothing to assess patterns of action that reflect no intention or policy, hence it cannot assess the acts of groups lacking decision-making procedures, such as the student movement, the women's movement, or the consumer movement.

It may seem a great limitation of Kantian ethics that it concentrates on intentions to the neglect of results. It might seem that all conscientious Kantians have to do is to make sure that they never intend to use others as mere means, and that they sometimes intend to foster others' ends. And, as we all know, good intentions sometimes lead to bad results, and correspondingly, bad intentions sometimes do no harm, or even produce good. . . . If some traditional arguments in favor of capitalism are right, the greed and selfishness of the profit motive have produced unparalleled prosperity for many.

But such discrepancies between intentions and results are the exception and not the rule. For we cannot just *claim* that our intentions are good and do what we will. Our intentions reflect what we expect the immediate results of our action to be. Nobody credits the "intentions" of a couple who practice neither celibacy nor contraception but still insist "we never meant to have (more) children." Conception is likely (and known to be likely) in such cases. Where people's expressed intentions ignore the normal and predictable results of what they do, we infer that (if they are not amazingly ignorant) their words do not express their true intentions. The Formula of the End in Itself applies to the intentions on which one acts—not to some prettified version that one may avow. Provided this intention—the agent's real intention— uses no other as mere means, he or she does nothing unjust. If some of his or her intentions foster others' ends, then he or she is sometimes beneficent. It is therefore possible for people to test their proposals by Kantian arguments even when they lack the comprehensive causal knowledge that utilitarianism requires. Conscientious Kantians can work out whether they will be doing wrong by some act even though they know that their foresight is limited and that they may cause some harm or fail to cause some benefit. But they will not cause harms that they can foresee without this being reflected in their intentions.

Kant and Respect for Persons

Kantians reach different conclusions about human life. Human life is valuable because humans (and conceivably other beings, e.g., angels or apes) are the bearers of rational life. Humans are able to choose and to plan. This capacity and its exercise are of such value that they ought not to be sacrificed for anything of lesser value. Therefore, no one rational or autonomous creature should be treated as mere means for the enjoyment or even the happiness of another. We may in Kant's view justifiably—even nobly—risk or sacrifice our lives for others. For in doing so we follow our own maxim and nobody uses us as mere means. But no others may use either our lives or our bodies for a scheme that they have either coerced or deceived us into joining. For in doing so they would fail to treat us as rational beings; they would use us as mere means and not as ends in ourselves.

It is conceivable that a society of Kantians, all of whom took pains to use no other as mere means, would end up with less happiness or with fewer persons alive than would some societies of complying utilitarians. For since the Kantians would be strictly bound only to justice, they might without wrongdoing be quite selective in their beneficence and fail to maximize either survival rates or happiness, or even to achieve as much of either as a strenuous group of utilitarians, who somehow make the right calculations. On the other hand, nobody will have been made an instrument of others' survival or happiness in the society of complying Kantians.

ON TREATING PEOPLE AS ENDS IN THEMSELVES: A CRITIQUE OF KANT
Fred Feldman

Fred Feldman is professor of philosophy at the University of Massachusetts, Amherst. His books include Doing the Best We Can *(1986),* Confrontations With the Reaper *(1991), and* Utilitarianism, Hedonism and Desert: Essays in Moral Philosophy *(1997). Feldman argues that the main problem with Kant's End-in-Itself formula of the categorical imperative is that the meaning of* treating someone as a mere means *is never made adequately clear and so cannot function as a criterion of right action.*

The Formula of the End in Itself

We can draw a broad distinction between things that are good as means, and things that are good as ends. The distinction emerges clearly enough if

From *Introductory Ethics* by Fred Feldman, © 1978. Reprinted by permission of Prentice Hall, Inc.

we select some good thing and ask why it is good. Take sunlight. Sunlight is surely a good thing. But why is it good? Some would say that sunlight is good because, among other things, it makes plants grow, and it is a good thing that plants grow. But why is it good that plants grow? It is good that plants grow, it could be maintained, because without plants there would be no life on the earth, and it is good that there is life. But why is it good that there is life? Life, many would say, is good in itself. Its goodness does not arise as a result of what it leads to, or contributes to. It is good not because of its results, but because of itself. If these reflections about life are correct, then we can say that sunlight is good as a *means,* whereas life is good as an *end.* Another way to put this would be to say that sunlight is extrinsically good, whereas life is intrinsically good. Still another way to put it would be to say that sunlight is a means, whereas life is an end in itself.

We can define "means" in terms of "end in itself":

D_1: *x is a means = df. there is something, y, that is an end in itself, and x contributes, directly or indirectly, to the existence of y.*

Thus, according to D_1, sunlight is a means, since it contributes to the existence of life, which we are assuming to be an end in itself. If life is an end in itself, then money, health, education, and abundant natural resources may be taken to be good as means. Each of these things contribute to life, something that may be good in itself.

Kant claims that "rational nature exists as an end in itself."[1] By this, he seems to mean that all rational beings, including people, are ends in themselves. In other words, every person is intrinsically good. From this, Kant infers that it can never be morally right to treat any person merely as a means. That is, it is never morally right to treat a person as if he were simply a useful object for your own purposes. This view, which is the second version of the categorical imperative, is stated by Kant in a variety of ways:

Act in such a way that you always treat humanity, whether in your own person or in the person of any other, never simply as a means, but always at the same time as an end.[2]

A rational being, by his very nature an end and consequently an end in himself, must serve for every maxim as a condition limiting all merely relative and arbitrary ends.[3]

So act in relation to every rational being (both to yourself and to others) that he may at the same time count in your maxim as an end in himself.[4]

Let us understand Kant to be saying in these passages that one ought never to act in such a way as to treat anyone merely as a means. In other words:

CI₂: An act is morally right if and only if the agent, in performing it, refrains from treating any person merely as a means.

According to CI_2, there is a moral prohibition against treating anyone merely as a means. We should recognize that CI_2 does not rule out treating a person as a means. That is, CI_2 must not be confused with this rather implausible view:

CI₂′: An act is morally right if and only if, in performing it, the agent refrains from treating any person as a means.

CI_2' rules out any act in which the agent treats anyone as a means. But this is absurd, since we use other people as means to our ends all the time, and we cannot avoid doing so. A student uses his teacher as a means to gaining an education; a teacher uses her students as a means to gaining a livelihood; a customer in a restaurant uses his waiter as a means to gaining his dinner. None of these acts is ruled out by CI_2. For in each of these cases the agent of the act may also treat the others involved, *at least in part,* as ends in themselves. Thus, although these acts would violate a preposterous principle such as CI_2', it is not clear that they would have to violate the more plausible principle, CI_2. For as we are understanding it, this second version of the categorical imperative only rules out treating persons *merely* as means.

CI_2 embodies an important moral insight, one that many would find plausible. It is the idea that it is wrong to "use" people. People are not mere objects, to be manipulated to serve our purpose. We cannot treat people as we treat wrecked cars, or wilted flowers, or old tin cans. Such things can be thrown out or destroyed when we no longer have any use for them. People, on the other hand, have dignity and worth, and must be treated accordingly.

Thus, what CI_2 says seems fairly plausible. Nevertheless, many moral philosophers would be uneasy about the claim that CI_2 is a formulation of "the supreme principle of morality." Can it really be the case that *all* wrong action is action in which people are used merely as means? Can all of our moral obligations be seen as obligations to treat people as ends? Some philosophers, admitting that it is important to treat people with respect, will deny that CI_2 captures the whole of our moral obligation. Others may even have their doubts about the acceptability of the insight embodied in CI_2, even if that insight were interpreted rather generously.

Problems for CI₂

The greatest problem for CI_2 is not, however, the lack of a convincing proof. Nor is it that CI_2 is subject to obvious counterexamples. Rather, the main difficulty with CI$_2$ is that its meaning is never made sufficiently clear. The most troublesome concept in this version of the categorical imperative is the concept of "treating someone merely as a means." It is pretty clear that if you own and mistreat slaves, then you treat them as means. But what about some more typical cases? What about a patron in a diner who grunts out his order to the waitress without even looking at her? What about a "freeloader" who lives with relatives? What about a factory owner who pays minimum wages and refuses to install safety equipment? Are these people treating others merely as means? Suppose the patron smiles and leaves a tip. Suppose the freeloader offers to do some work around the house. Suppose the factory owner gives a bonus at Christmas. Would they still be treating others merely as means? Would they be treating them, in part, as ends in themselves? It is very hard to tell.

When a concept is left unclear, one way to gain some clarification is by looking closely at the author's examples. Often, the examples will shed light on the more important general concept. Fortunately, Kant has given several examples of the application of CI$_2$. Close consideration of these may help to clarify the intent of the principle. . . .

The first example is the man who contemplates committing suicide. As we saw previously, Kant's view is that suicide in this particular case would be wrong. Hence, he tries to show that the contemplated act would violate CI$_2$:

If he does away with himself in order to escape from a painful situation, he is making use of a person merely as a means to maintain a tolerable state of affairs till the end of his life. But man is not a thing—not something to be used merely as a means: he must always in all his actions be regarded as an end in himself. Hence I cannot dispose of man in my person by maiming, spoiling, or killing.[5]

Kant's point here seems to be that if the man were to commit suicide, then he would be using himself merely as a means to the end of making his life tolerable until its end. If this is Kant's point, it certainly seems quite strained. Surely, the man could claim that in order to treat himself as an end, he must commit suicide. For if he does not commit suicide, he will suffer. And, he could insist, it is not appropriate for a person who is an end in himself to suffer.

So Kant's comments on this example are not very helpful. He does not say anything that gives us a new insight into the concept of treating someone merely as a means. Hence, we turn to the second example.

Kant's comments on the second example are more revealing. This is the case of the lying promise. Kant suggests that the man who makes the lying promise is "intending to make use of another man merely as a means to an end he does not share."[6] Kant goes on to point out the other man "cannot possibly agree with my way of behaving to him."[7] Kant's point here seems to be this: The man to whom the lie is told does not want to be used in the way the liar uses him. If he knew what was going on, he would refuse to lend the money. Thus, the liar is using him merely as a means. For this reason, his act is in violation of CI_2, and so is wrong.

Understood in this way, Kant's comments suggest a definition of what is meant by saying that a person, A, treats a person, B, merely as a means:

D_2: *A treats B merely as a means = df. A treats B in such a way that if B knew all about it, B would not want A to treat him in that way.*

Thus, if you do not agree to being treated in a certain way, then if I treat you in that way I use you merely as a means. I use you for my purposes, but not for your own. Hence, according to CI_2, I act wrongly.

This line of reasoning may be plausible, but it leads to unacceptable results in a wide variety of cases. A large group of these cases have a similar pattern: B wants to do something morally wrong. A prevents B from doing this wrong act. According to D_2, A is then using B merely as a means, since B would not agree to A treating him that way. According to CI_2, then, A is acting wrongly. This seems absurd.

Let us consider an example. Suppose B is planning to steal A's motorcycle. A learns of B's plans and decides to chain his motorcycle to a lamppost, thereby making it impossible for B to achieve his goal. Surely, if B knew what A was doing, B would not agree to it. B would not want A to chain up the motorcycle. For if A's motorcycle is chained, B cannot steal it. According to D_2, therefore, in chaining the motorcycle A is using B merely as a means. This, together with CI_2, entails that A's act of chaining the motorcycle is morally wrong. This result is surely incorrect.

As long as we interpret "treating a person merely as a means" according to D_2, it will not be clear how this problem can be avoided. It appears, then, that we should not accept this second account of the crucial concept. It does not provide us with a plausible view about what Kant might have meant. Let us consider the next example to see if we can find a more helpful suggestion. . . .

Since the third example is rather questionable anyway, let us move on and try to find some illumination in the final example. This is the example of the man who refuses to give to charity. Kant's comments here are more helpful. He apparently holds that the man who refuses to give to charity thereby acts wrongly. His error is that he fails to "agree positively with humanity as an end in itself."[8] If the man were to have done this, Kant suggests, he would have had to try, as much as he could have, to "further the ends of others."[9]

Kant claims that since other people are ends in themselves, we act rightly only if we make their ends our own. This is an interesting idea, so let us examine it more closely.

Kant's comments on the final example suggest another interpretation of what is meant by "A treats B merely as a means." Kant explicitly says that we must further the ends of others. By this he seems to mean that unless we try, as much as we can, to see to it that others achieve their goals, we are not treating them as ends in themselves. We are treating them merely as means. Thus, if another person is trying to be happy, we must not only refrain from making him unhappy, we must try to help him become happy. The man who gives nothing to charity obviously violates this requirement. He treats those who need aid merely as means. We can define this concept as follows:

D_3: A treats B merely as a means = df. B has some goal, and A could help B achieve that goal, but A refrains from doing so.

When we combine CI_2 with D_3, we seem to get the correct result in the charity case. Those who need charity have a certain goal—happiness. The agent can help them to achieve that goal, but he decides to refrain from doing so. Hence, according to D_3, he treats them merely as means. But CI_2 says that one acts rightly only if he treats no one merely as a means. So, in this case CI_2 entails that the man who refuses to give charity does not act rightly. His selfish act is morally wrong. This result seems acceptable.

However, the problem with D_3 should be obvious. It is, in effect, the same as the problem with D_2. If other people want, for example, to destroy the environment, then according to D_3, we must help them to achieve their misguided goal; otherwise, we are treating them merely as means. Thus, CI_2 and D_3 entail that if we refrain from helping such people to destroy the environment, we are acting wrongly. This seems preposterous.

So the trouble with D_3 is that, together with CI_2, it requires us to help others to achieve their goals, whatever those goals may be. If the others have morally acceptable goals, this may seem to be a reasonable doctrine. But if the goals of the others are morally wrong, then it is absurd to insist that we should try to help them to achieve these goals. Yet this is just what D_3 and CI_2 require.

Before we leave CI_2, we may find it worthwhile to consider one final proposal. Kant does not make this proposal himself, but some sympathetic readers may find hints of it in the *Groundwork*. The basic idea is that there are some goals that it is rational for a person to have, and others that it is irrational for a person to have. For example, it might be said that it is rational for a person to have happiness as his goal, whereas it is irrational of him to have the destruction of the environment as his goal. Perhaps Kant would say that we are under no moral obligation to help others achieve irrational goals, but if another person is attempting to achieve a rational goal, then we should "make his end our own."

One way to develop this idea would be as follows. First, we must introduce a new definition:

D_4: *A treats B merely as a means* = df. *B has some rational goal, and A can help B achieve that goal, but A refrains from doing so.*

The difference between D_3 and D_4 is small, but significant. According to D_3, we treat another person merely as a means if we fail to help him achieve his goal, whatever that goal may be. According to D_4, we treat him merely as a means if we fail to help him achieve a rational, or reasonable, goal. Thus, the concept defined in D_4 may be more promising.

When we combine D_4 with CI_2, we get what may seem to be a more plausible moral doctrine. For under this interpretation, CI_2 requires us only to help others to achieve their *rational* goals. So there would be no need to help another person to destroy the environment, or commit a crime. On the other hand, there would be a need to help another to become happy—assuming that it is rational for that person to want to become happy.

Although the use of D_4 helps to make this version of the categorical imperative somewhat more successful, very great problems remain. For one, it often happens that there are several different persons who might benefit from one person's action. For example, suppose a man has an unbreakable piece of candy that he can give to either of two twins, Jean and Joan. If he gives the candy to Jean, he will make her happy. This will help Jean to achieve a rational goal she has. However, if he gives the candy to Jean, he will not be helping Joan to achieve a rational goal she has, for he will fail to help her to become happy. Similarly, if he gives it to Joan, he will fail to help Jean achieve a rational goal. Thus, according to D_4, whichever twin the man helps, he treats the other merely as a means. CI_2, then, implies that his act of giving the candy is morally wrong.

The general point should be clear. I can help each of many different persons achieve his rational goals. However, I cannot simultaneously help *all* of these individuals achieve their rational goals. I must choose some to help and some to ignore. According to D_4, it would follow that I have to treat some of them merely as means. CI_2 then yields the inevitable result that I act wrongly. This seems much too severe.

The second main problem with D_4 is that it makes use of a rather obscure concept—the concept of a "rational goal." If you think about it for a minute, you will see that where ultimate goals are concerned, it is hard to distinguish the rational from the irrational. Normally, we would say that a person who aims to collect a large amount of money is pursuing a rational goal, whereas a person who aims to collect a large number of bent nails is pursuing an irrational goal. But what is the difference? If each can gain happiness from his collection, why is one more rational than the other? Perhaps the only rational goal is happiness itself.

It is interesting to note that if we assume that happiness is the only rational goal, and if we also assume that Kant's view is the more moderate view that we should do the most we can to help other people achieve their rational goals, then Kant's view becomes indistinguishable from act utilitarianism. Of course, there is nothing in Kant's writing to suggest that he ever made either of these assumptions. With these reflections, we have strayed quite far from Kant's text. Perhaps it would be better to avoid such speculations.

It appears, then, that CI_2 is not a very successful principle. The insight behind it is vague, although plausible. There surely is something morally objectionable about using people. However, Kant's discussion of this view does not do enough to clarify this vague insight. Whether we interpret "A treats B merely as a means" according to D_2, D_3, or D_4, CI_2 yields obviously incorrect results in many cases. Until some more plausible account of the meaning of CI_2 is proposed, we must conclude that it is not an acceptable moral doctrine.

Notes

1. Immanuel Kant, *Groundwork of the Metaphysic of Morals*, translated and analyzed by H. J. Paton (New York: Harper & Row, 1964), p. 96.
2. *Ibid.*
3. *Ibid.*, p. 104.
4. *Ibid.*, p. 105.
5. *Ibid.*, p. 97.
6. *Ibid.*
7. *Ibid.*
8. *Ibid.*, p. 98.
9. *Ibid.*

CHAPTER 7

The Ethics of Care

MORAL ORIENTATION AND MORAL DEVELOPMENT
Carol Gilligan

Carol Gilligan is professor of education at the Harvard Graduate School of Education. Her books include In a Different Voice *(1982), and* Mapping the Moral Domain *coedited with Janie Victoria Ward, Jill McLean Taylor, and Betty Bardige (1988). In her 1982 book, Gilligan cited empirical evidence for the hypothesis that there is, in addition to the so-called justice perspective, a moral perspective focused on care. Her work has been the basis for the articulation of an ethic of care by such theorists as Nel Noddings (see the next selection). In this article, Gilligan compares the justice and care perspectives. The justice perspective finds articulation in the moral theories of Aquinas, Mill, and Kant, in which morality is conceived to be a matter of autonomous individuals settling conflicting claims against standards of equal and impartial respect. By contrast, the care perspective conceives morality to be a matter of creating and maintaining relationships in which agents respond to the perceived needs of others.*

The difference of focus between justice and care approaches to morality is illustrated in connection with abortion decisions and other situations calling for a moral response. The existence of two moral perspectives raises various questions that Gilligan considers about whether people tend, in their moral thinking, to focus on those concerns associated with one moral perspective at the expense of those concerns associated with the alternative perspective, and the extent to which this focus might be related to gender.

From *Women and Moral Theory,* edited by Eva F. Kittay and Diana T. Meyers. © 1987 by Rowman & Little-field Publishers, Lanham, MD. Reprinted by permission of the publisher.

When one looks at an ambiguous figure like the drawing that can be seen as a young or old woman, or the image of the vase and the faces, one initially sees it in only one way. Yet even after seeing it in both ways, one way often seems more compelling. This phenomenon reflects the laws of perceptual organization that favor certain modes of visual grouping. But it also suggests a tendency to view reality as unequivocal and thus to argue that there is one right or better way of seeing.

The experiments of the Gestalt psychologists on perceptual organization provide a series of demonstrations that the same proximal pattern can be organized in different ways so that, for example, the same figure can be seen as a square or a diamond, depending on its orientation in relation to a surrounding frame. Subsequent studies show that the context influencing which of two possible organizations will be chosen may depend not only on the features of the array presented but also on the perceiver's past experience or expectation. Thus, a bird-watcher and a rabbit-keeper are likely to see the duck-rabbit figure in different ways; yet this difference does not imply that one way is better or a higher form of perceptual organization. It does, however, call attention to the fact that the rabbit-keeper, perceiving the rabbit, may not see the ambiguity of the figure until someone points out that it can also be seen as a duck.

This paper presents a similar phenomenon with respect to moral judgment, describing two moral perspectives that organize thinking in different ways. The analogy to ambiguous figure perception arises from the observation that although people are aware of both perspectives, they tend to adopt one or the other in defining and resolving moral conflict. Since moral judgments organize thinking about choice in difficult situations, the adoption of a single perspective may facilitate clarity of decision. But the wish for clarity may also imply a compelling human need for resolution or closure, especially in the face of decisions that give rise to discomfort or unease. Thus, the search for clarity in seeing may blend with a search for justification, encouraging the position that there is one right or better way to think about moral problems. This question, which has been the subject of intense theological and philosophical debate, becomes of interest to the psychologist not only because of its psychological dimensions—the tendency to focus on one perspective and the wish for justification—but also because one moral perspective currently dominates psychological thinking and is embedded in the most widely used measure for assessing the maturity of moral reasoning.

In describing an alternative standpoint, I will reconstruct the account of moral development around two moral perspectives, grounded in different dimensions of relationship that give rise to moral concern. The justice perspective, often equated with moral reasoning, is recast as one way of seeing moral problems and a care perspective is brought forward as an alternate vision or frame. The distinction between justice and care as alternative perspectives or moral orientations is based empirically on the observation that a shift in the focus of attention from concerns about justice to concerns about care changes the definition of what constitutes a moral problem, and leads the same situation to be seen in different ways. Theoretically, the distinction between justice and care cuts across the familiar divisions between thinking and feeling, egoism and altruism, theoretical and practical reasoning. It calls attention to the fact that all human relationships, public and private, can be characterized *both* in terms of equality and in terms of attachment, and that both inequality and detachment constitute grounds for moral concern. Since everyone is vulnerable both to oppression and to abandonment, two moral visions—one of justice and one of care—recur in human experience. The moral injunctions, not to act unfairly toward others, and not to turn away from someone in need, capture these different concerns.

The conception of the moral domain as comprised of at least two moral orientations raises new questions about observed differences in moral judgment and the disagreements to which they give rise. Key to this revision is the distinction between differences in developmental stage (more or less adequate positions within a single orientation) and differences in orientation (alternative perspectives or frameworks). The findings reported in this paper of an association between moral orientation and gender speak directly to the continuing controversy over sex differences in moral reasoning. In doing so, however, they also offer an empirical explanation for why previous thinking about moral development has been organized largely within the justice framework.

My research on moral orientation derives from an observation made in the course of studying the relationship between moral judgment and action. Two studies, one of college students describing their experiences of moral conflict and choice, and one of pregnant women who were considering abortion, shifted the focus of attention from the ways people reason about hypothetical dilemmas to the ways people construct moral conflicts and choices in their lives. This change in approach made it possible to see what experiences people define in moral terms, and to explore the relationship between the understanding of moral problems and the reasoning strategies used and the actions taken in attempting to resolve them. In this context, I observed that women, especially when speaking about their own experiences of moral conflict and choice, often define moral problems in a way that eludes the categories of moral theory and is at odds with the assumptions that shape psychological thinking about morality and about the self.[1]

This discovery, that a different voice often guides the moral judgments and the actions of women, called attention to a major design problem in previous moral judgment research: namely, the use of all-male samples as the empirical basis for theory construction.

The selection of an all-male sample as the basis for generalizations that are applied to both males and females is logically inconsistent. As a research strategy, the decision to begin with a single-sex sample is inherently problematic, since the categories of analysis will tend to be defined on the basis of the initial data gathered and subsequent studies will tend to be restricted to these categories. Piaget's work on the moral judgment of the child illustrates these problems since he defined the evolution of children's consciousness and practice of rules on the basis of his study of boys playing marbles, and then undertook a study of girls to assess the generality of his findings. Observing a series of differences both in the structure of girls' games and "in the actual mentality of little girls," he deemed these differences not of interest because "it was not this contrast which we proposed to study." Girls, Piaget found, "rather complicated our interrogatory in relation to what we know about boys," since the changes in their conception of rules, although following the same sequence observed in boys, did not stand in the same relation to social experience. Nevertheless, he concluded that "in spite of these differences in the structure of the game and apparently in the players' mentality, we find the same process at work as in the evolution of the game of marbles."[2]

Thus, girls were of interest insofar as they were similar to boys and confirmed the generality of Piaget's findings. The differences noted, which included greater tolerance, a greater tendency toward innovation in solving conflicts, a greater willingness to make exceptions to rules, and a lesser concern with legal elaboration, were not seen as germane to "the psychology of rules," and therefore were regarded as insignificant for the study of children's moral judgment. Given the confusion that currently surrounds the discussion of sex differences in moral judgment, it is important to emphasize that the differences observed by Piaget did not pertain to girls' understanding of rules *per se* or to the development of the idea of justice in their thinking, but rather to the way girls structured their games and their approach to conflict resolution—that is, to their use rather than their understanding of the logic of rules and justice.

Kohlberg, in his research on moral development, did not encounter these problems since he equated moral development with the development of justice reasoning and initially used an all-male sample as the basis for theory and test construction. In response to his critics, Kohlberg has recently modified his claims, renaming his test a measure of "justice reasoning" rather than of "moral maturity" and acknowledging the presence of a care perspective in people's moral thinking.[3] But the widespread use of Kohlberg's measure as a measure of moral development together with his own continuing tendency to equate justice reasoning with moral judgment leaves the problem of orientation differences unsolved. More specifically, Kohlberg's efforts to assimilate thinking about care to the six-stage developmental sequence he derived and refined by analyzing changes in justice reasoning (relying centrally on his all-male longitudinal sample) underscores the continuing importance of the points raised in this paper concerning (1) the distinction between differences in developmental stage within a single orientation and differences in orientation, and (2) the fact that the moral thinking of girls and women was not examined in establishing either the meaning or the measurement of moral judgment within contemporary psychology.

An analysis of the language and logic of men's and women's moral reasoning about a range of hypothetical and real dilemmas underlies the distinction elaborated in this paper between a justice and a care perspective. The empirical association of care reasoning with women suggests that discrepancies observed between moral theory and the moral judgments of girls and women may reflect a shift in perspective, a change in moral orientation. Like the figure-ground shift in ambiguous figure perception, justice and care as moral perspectives are not opposites or mirror-images of one another, with justice uncaring and care unjust. Instead, these perspectives denote different ways of organizing the basic elements of moral judgment: self, others, and the relationship between them. With the shift in perspective from justice to care, the organizing dimension of relationship changes from inequality/equality to attachment/detachment, reorganizing thoughts, feelings, and language so that words connoting relationship like "dependence" or "responsibility" or even moral terms such as "fairness" and "care" take on different meanings. To organize relationships in terms of attachment rather than in terms of equality changes the way human connection is imagined, so that the images or metaphors of relationship shift from hierarchy or balance to network or web. In addition, each organizing framework leads to a different way of imagining the self as a moral agent.

From a justice perspective, the self as moral agent stands as the figure against a ground of social relationships, judging the conflicting claims of self and others against a standard of equality or equal respect (the Categorical Imperative, the Golden Rule). From a care perspective, the relationship becomes the figure, defining self and others. Within the context of relationship, the self as a moral agent perceives and responds to the perception of need. The shift in moral perspective is manifest by a change in the moral question from "What is just?" to "How to respond?"

For example, adolescents asked to describe a moral dilemma often speak about peer or family pressure in which case the moral question becomes how to maintain moral principles or standards and resist the influence of one's parents or friends. "I have a right to my religious opinions," one teenager explains, referring to a religious difference with his parents. Yet, he adds, "I respect their views." The same dilemma, however, is also construed by adolescents as a problem of attachment, in which case the moral question becomes: how to respond both to oneself and to one's friends or one's parents, how to maintain or strengthen connection in the face of differences in belief. "I understand their fear of my new religious ideas," one teenager explains, referring to her religious disagreement with her parents, "but they really ought to listen to me and try to understand my beliefs."

One can see these two statements as two versions of essentially the same thing. Both teenagers present self-justifying arguments about religious disagreement; both address the claims of self and of others in a way that honors both. Yet each frames the problem in different terms, and the use of moral language points to different concerns. The first speaker casts the problem in terms of individual rights that must be respected within the relationship. In other words, the figure of the considering is the self looking on the disagreeing selves in relationship, and the aim is to get the other selves to acknowledge the right to disagree. In the case of the second speaker, figure and ground shift. The relationship becomes the figure of the considering, and relationships are seen to require listening and efforts at understanding differences in belief. Rather than the right to disagree, the speaker focuses on caring to hear and to be heard. Attention shifts from the grounds for agreement (rights and respect) to the grounds for understanding (listening and speaking, hearing and being heard). This shift is marked by a change in moral language from the stating of separate claims to rights and respect ("I have a right . . . I respect their views.") to the activities of relationship—the injunction to listen and try to understand ("I understand . . . they ought to listen . . . and try to understand."). The metaphor of moral voice itself carries the terms of the care perspective and reveals how the language chosen for moral theory is not orientation neutral.

The language of the public abortion debate, for example, reveals a justice perspective. Whether the abortion dilemma is cast as a conflict of rights or in terms of respect for human life, the claims of the fetus and of the pregnant woman are balanced or placed in opposition. The morality of abortion decisions thus construed hinges on the scholastic or metaphysical question as to whether the fetus is a life or a person, and whether its claims take precedence over those of the pregnant woman. Framed as a problem of care, the dilemma posed by abortion shifts. The connection between the fetus and the pregnant woman becomes the focus of attention and the question becomes whether it is responsible or irresponsible, caring or careless, to extend or to end this connection. In this construction, the abortion dilemma arises because there is no way not to act, and no way of acting that does not alter the connection between self and others. To ask what actions constitute care or are more caring directs attention to the parameters of connection and the costs of detachment, which become subjects of moral concern.

Finally, two medical students, each reporting a decision not to turn in someone who has violated the school rules against drinking, cast their decision in different terms. One student constructs the decision as an act of mercy, a decision to override justice in light of the fact that the violator has shown "the proper degrees of contrition." In addition, this student raises the question as to whether or not the alcohol policy is just, i.e., whether the school has the right to prohibit drinking. The other student explains the decision not to turn in a proctor who was drinking on the basis that turning him in is not a good way to respond to this problem, since it would dissolve the relationship between them and thus cut off an avenue for help. In addition, this student raises the question as to whether the proctor sees his drinking as a problem.

This example points to an important distinction, between care as understood or construed within a justice framework and care as a framework or a perspective on moral decision. Within a justice construction, care becomes the mercy that tempers justice; or connotes the special obligations or supererogatory duties that arise in personal relationships; or signifies altruism freely chosen—a decision to modulate the strict demands of justice by considering equity or showing forgiveness; or characterizes a choice to sacrifice the claims of the self. All of these interpretations of care leave the basic assumptions of a justice framework intact: the division between the self and others, the logic of reciprocity or equal respect.

As a moral perspective, care is less well elaborated, and there is no ready vocabulary in moral theory to describe its terms. As a framework for moral decision, care is grounded in the assumption that self and other are interdependent, an assumption reflected in a view of action as responsive and, therefore, as arising in relationship rather than the view of action as emanating from within the self and, therefore, "self governed." Seen as responsive, the self is by definition connected to others, responding to perceptions, interpreting events, and governed by the organizing tendencies of human interaction and human language. Within this framework, detachment, whether from self or from others, is morally problematic, since it breeds moral blindness or indifference—a failure to discern or respond to need. The question of what responses constitute care and what responses lead to hurt draws attention to the fact that one's own terms may differ from those of others. Justice in this context becomes understood as respect for people in their own terms.

The medical student's decision not to turn in the proctor for drinking reflects a judgment that turning him in is not the best way to respond to the drinking problem, itself seen as a sign of detachment or lack of concern. Caring for the proctor thus raises the question of what actions are most likely to ameliorate this problem, a decision that leads to the question of what are the proctor's terms.

The shift in organizing perspective here is marked by the fact that the first student does not consider the terms of the other as potentially different but instead assumes one set of terms. Thus the student alone becomes the arbiter of what is *the* proper degree of contrition. The second student, in turn, does not attend to the question of whether the alcohol policy itself is just or fair. Thus each student discusses an aspect of the problem that the other does not mention.

These examples are intended to illustrate two cross-cutting perspectives that do not negate one another but focus attention on different dimensions of the situation, creating a sense of ambiguity around the question of what is the problem to be solved. Systematic research on moral orientation as a dimension of moral judgment and action initially addressed three questions: (1) Do people articulate concerns about justice and concerns about care in discussing a moral dilemma? (2) Do people tend to focus their attention on one set of concerns and minimally represent the other? and (3) Is there an association between moral orientation and gender? Evidence from studies that included a common set of questions about actual experiences of moral conflict and matched samples of males and females provides affirmative answers to all three questions.

When asked to describe a moral conflict they had faced, 55 out of 80 (69 percent) educationally advantaged North American adolescents and adults raised considerations of both justice and care. Two-thirds (54 out of 80) however, focused their attention on one set of concerns, with focus defined as 75 percent or more of the considerations raised pertaining either to justice or to care. Thus the person who presented, say, two care considerations in discussing a moral conflict was more likely to give a third, fourth, and fifth than to balance care and justice concerns—a finding consonant with the assumption that justice and care constitute organizing frameworks for moral decision. The men and the women involved in this study (high school students, college students, medical students, and adult professionals) were equally likely to demonstrate the focus phenomenon (two-thirds of both sexes fell into the outlying focus categories). There were, however, sex differences in the direction of focus. With one exception, all of the men who focused, focused on justice. The women divided, with roughly one third focusing on justice and one third on care.[4]

These findings clarify the different voice phenomenon and its implications for moral theory and for women. First, it is notable that if women were eliminated from the research sample, care focus in moral reasoning would virtually disappear. Although care focus was by no means character-istic of all women, it was almost exclusively a female phenomenon in this sample of educationally advantaged North Americans. Second, the fact that the women were advantaged means that the focus on care cannot readily be attributed to educational deficit or occupational disadvantage—the expla-nation Kohlberg and others have given for findings of lower levels of justice reasoning in women.[5] Instead, the focus on care in women's moral reason-ing draws attention to the limitations of a justice-focused moral theory and highlights the presence of care concerns in the moral thinking of both women and men. In this light, the Care/Justice group composed of one third of the women and one third of the men becomes of particular interest, pointing to the need for further research that attends to the way people organize justice and care in relation to one another—whether, for example, people alternate perspectives, like seeing the rabbit and the duck in the rabbit-duck figure, or integrate the two perspectives in a way that resolves or sustains ambiguity.

Third, if the moral domain is comprised of at least two moral orienta-tions, the focus phenomenon suggests that people have a tendency to lose sight of one moral perspective in arriving at moral decision—a liability equally shared by both sexes. The present findings further suggest that men and women tend to lose sight of different perspectives. The most striking result is the virtual absence of care-focused reasoning among men. Since the men raised concerns about care in discussing moral conflicts and thus pre-sented care concerns as morally relevant, a question is why they did not elaborate these concerns to a greater extent.

In summary, it becomes clear why attention to women's moral thinking led to the identification of a different voice and raised questions about the place of justice and care within a comprehensive moral theory. It also is clear how the selection of an all-male sample for research on moral judgment fos-ters an equation of morality with justice, providing little data discrepant with this view. In the present study, data discrepant with a justice-focused moral theory comes from a third of the women. Previously, such women were seen as having a problem understanding "morality." Yet these women may also be seen as exposing the problem in a justice-focused moral theory. This may ex-plain the decision of researchers to exclude girls and women at the initial stage of moral judgment research. If one begins with the premise that "all morality consists in respect for rules,"[6] or "virtue is one and its name is jus-tice,"[7] then women are likely to appear problematic within moral theory. If one begins with women's moral judgments, the problem becomes how to construct a theory that encompasses care as a focus of moral attention rather than as a subsidiary moral concern.

Notes

1. C. Gilligan, "In a Different Voice: Women's Conceptions of Self and of Morality." *Harvard Educational Review* (1982) 47: 481–517; *In a Different Voice: Psychological Theory and Women's Development* (Cambridge, Mass.: Harvard University Press, 1977).
2. J. Piaget, *The Moral Judgment of the Child* (New York, N.Y.: The Free Press Paperback Edition, 1965), pp. 76–84.
3. L. Kohlberg, *The Psychology of Moral Development* (San Francisco, Calif.: Harper & Row, 1984).
4. C. Gilligan and J. Attanucci, *Two Moral Orientations* (Harvard University, unpublished manuscript, 1986).
5. L. Kohlberg, *Moral Development;* also L. Walker, "Sex Differences in the Development of Moral Reasoning: A Critical Review of the Literature," *Child Development* (1984) 55(3): 677–691.
6. J. Piaget, *Moral Judgment.*
7. L. Kohlberg, *Moral Development.*

AN ETHIC OF CARING
Nel Noddings

Nel Noddings is professor of education at Stanford University. Her books include Caring: A Feminine Approach to Ethics and Moral Education *(1984),* Awakening the Inner Eye: Intuition and Education *(with Paul J. Shore, 1984), and* Women and Evil *(1989). According to Noddings, moral obligation is rooted in a sentiment or feeling of "natural care"—a sentiment typified by the care a woman has for her infant. Natural caring together with one's reflective evaluation of the caring relation as good gives rise to a second, specifically moral, sentiment experienced as an obligation to respond to anyone in need with whom we come into contact in concrete, real-life situations. Furthermore, two criteria govern our obligation to care: (1) the existence of or potential for presently being related to another, and (2) the potentiality of the cared-for individual to reciprocate the care of the one caring. After examining the implications of this ethic of care for the case of making an abortion decision, Noddings considers the role of judgments of right and wrong in an ethic of care and what sort of justification one can provide for such an ethic.*

From Natural to Ethical Caring

David Hume long ago contended that morality is founded upon and rooted in feeling—that the "final sentence" on matters of morality, "that which renders morality an active virtue—. . . this final sentence depends on some internal sense or feeling, which nature has made universal in the whole species. For what else can have an influence of this nature?"[1]

What is the nature of this feeling that is "universal in the whole species"? I want to suggest that morality as an "active virtue" requires two feelings and not just one. The first is the sentiment of natural caring. There can be no ethical sentiment without the initial, enabling sentiment. In situations where we act on behalf of the other because we want to do so, we are acting in accord with natural caring. A mother's caretaking efforts in behalf of her child are not usually considered ethical but natural. Even maternal animals take care of their offspring, and we do not credit them with ethical behavior.

The second sentiment occurs in response to a remembrance of the first. Neitzsche speaks of love and memory in the context of Christian love and Eros, but what he says may safely be taken out of context to illustrate the point I wish to make here:

There is something so ambiguous and suggestive about the word love, something that speaks to memory and to hope, that even the lowest intelligence and the coldest heart still feel something of the glimmer of this word. The cleverest woman and the most vulgar man recall the relatively least selfish moments of their whole life, even if Eros has taken only a low flight with them.[2]

This memory of our own best moments of caring and being cared for sweeps over us as a feeling—as an "I must"—in response to the plight of the other and our conflicting desire to serve our own interests. There is a transfer of feeling analogous to transfer of learning. In the intellectual domain, when I read a certain kind of mathematical puzzle, I may react by thinking, "That is like the sailors, monkey, and coconuts problem," and then, "Diophantine equations" or "modulo arithmetic" or "congruences." Similarly, when I encounter an other and feel the natural pang conflicted with my own desires—"I must—I do not want to"—I recognize the feeling and remember what has followed it in my own best moments. I have a picture of those moments in which I was cared for and in which I cared, and I may reach toward this memory and guide my conduct by it if I wish to do so.

Recognizing that ethical caring requires an effort that is not needed in natural caring does not commit us to a position that elevates ethical caring over natural caring. Kant has identified the ethical with that which is done out of duty and not out of love, and that distinction in itself seems right. But an ethic built on caring strives to maintain the caring attitude and is thus dependent upon, and not superior to, natural caring. The source of ethical behavior is, then, in twin sentiments—one that feels directly for the other and one that feels for and with that best self, who may accept and sustain the initial feeling rather than reject it.

We shall discuss the ethical ideal, that vision of best self, in some depth. When we commit ourselves to obey the "I must" even at its weakest and most fleeting, we are under the guidance of this ideal. It is not just any picture. Rather, it is our best picture of ourselves caring and being cared for. It may even be colored by acquaintance with one superior to us in caring, but, as I shall describe it, it is both constrained and attainable. It is limited by what we have already done and by what we are capable of, and it does not idealize the impossible so that we may escape into ideal abstraction. . . .

Obligation

There are moments for all of us when we care quite naturally. We just do care; no ethical effort is required. "Want" and "ought" are indistinguishable in such cases. I want to do what I or others might judge I ought to do. But can there be a "demand" to care? There can be, surely, no demand for the initial impulse that arises as a feeling, an inner voice saying "I must do something," in response to the need of the cared-for. This impulse arises naturally, at least occasionally, in the absence of pathology. We cannot demand that one have this impulse, but we shrink from one who never has it. One who never feels the pain of another, who never confesses the internal "I must" that is so familiar to most of us, is beyond our normal pattern of understanding. Her case is pathological, and we avoid her.

But even if I feel the initial "I must," I may reject it. I may reject it instantaneously by shifting from "I must do something" to "Something must be done," and removing myself from the set of possible agents through whom the action should be accomplished. I may reject it because I feel that there is nothing I can do. If I do either of these things without reflection upon what I might do in behalf of the cared-for, then I do not care. Caring requires me to respond to the initial impulse with an act of commitment: I commit myself either to overt action on behalf of the cared-for (I pick up my crying infant) or I commit myself to thinking about what I might do. In the latter case, as we have seen, I may or may not act overtly in behalf of the cared-for. I may abstain from action if I believe that anything I might do would tend to work against the best interests of the cared-for. But the test of my caring is not wholly in how things turn out; the primary test lies in an examination of what I considered, how fully I received the other, and whether the free pursuit of his projects is partly a result of the completion of my caring in him.

But am I obliged to embrace the "I must"? In this form, the question is a bit odd, for the "I must" carries obligation with it. It comes to us as obligation. But accepting and affirming the "I must" are different from feeling it, and these responses are what I am pointing to when I ask whether I am obliged to embrace the "I must." The question nags at us; it is a question that has been asked, in a variety of forms, over and over by moralists and moral theorists. Usually, the question arises as part of the broader question of justification. We ask something of the sort: Why must I (or should I) do what suggests itself to reason as "right" or as needing to be done for the sake of some other? We might prefer to supplement "reason" with "and/or feeling." This question is, of course, not the only thorny question in moral theory, but it is one that has plagued theorists who see clearly that there is no way to derive an "I ought" statement from a chain of facts. I may agree readily that "things would be better"—that is, that a certain state of affairs commonly agreed to be desirable might be attained—if a certain chain of events were to take place. But there is still nothing in this intellectual chain that can produce the "I ought." I may choose to remain an observer on the scene.

Now I am suggesting that the "I must" arises directly and prior to consideration of what it is that I might do. The initial feeling is the "I must." When it comes to me indistinguishable from the "I want," I proceed easily as one-caring. But often it comes to me conflicted. It may be barely perceptible, and it may be followed almost simultaneously by resistance. When someone asks me to get something for him or merely asks for my attention, the "I must" may be lost in a clamor of resistance. Now a second sentiment is required if I am to behave as one-caring. I care about myself as one-caring and, although I do not care naturally for the person who has asked something of me—at least not at this moment—I feel the genuine moral sentiment, the "I ought," that sensibility to which I have committed myself.

Let me try to make plausible my contention that the moral imperative arises directly. And, of course, I must try to explain how caring and what I am calling the "moral imperative" are related. When my infant cries in the night, I not only feel that I must do something but I want to do something. Because I love this child, because I am bonded to him, I want to remove his pain as I would want to remove my own. The "I must" is not a dutiful imperative but one that accompanies the "I want." If I were tied to a chair, for example, and wanted desperately to get free, I might say as I struggled, "I must do something; I must get out of these bonds." But this "must" is not yet the moral or ethical "ought." It is a "must" born of desire.

The most intimate situations of caring are, thus, natural. I do not feel that taking care of my own child is "moral" but, rather, natural. A woman who allows her own child to die of neglect is often considered sick rather than immoral; that is, we feel that either she or the situation into which she has been thrust must be pathological. Otherwise, the impulse to respond, to nurture the living infant, is overwhelming. We share the impulse with other creatures in the animal kingdom. Whether we want to consider this response as "instinctive" is problematic, because certain patterns of response may be implied by the term and because suspension of reflective consciousness seems also to be implied (and I am not suggesting that we have no choice), but I have no difficulty in considering it as innate. Indeed, I am claiming that the impulse to act in behalf of the present other is itself innate. It lies latent in each of us, awaiting gradual development in a succession of caring relations. I am suggesting that our inclination toward and interest in morality derives from caring. In caring, we accept the natural impulse to act on behalf of the present other. We are engrossed in the other. We have received him and feel his pain or happiness, but we are not compelled by this impulse. We have a choice; we may accept what we feel, or we may reject it. If we have a strong desire to be moral, we will not reject it, and this strong desire to be moral is derived, reflectively, from the more fundamental and natural desire to be and to remain related. To reject the feeling when it arises is either to be in an internal state of imbalance or to contribute willfully to the diminution of the ethical ideal.

But suppose in a particular case that the "I must" does not arise, or that it whispers faintly and disappears, leaving distrust, repugnance, or hate. Why, then, should I behave morally toward the object of my dislike? Why should I not accept feelings other than those characteristic of caring and, thus, achieve an internal state of balance through hate, anger, or malice?

The answer to this is, I think, that the genuine moral sentiment (our second sentiment) arises from an evaluation of the caring relation as good, as better than, superior to, other forms of relatedness. I feel the moral "I must" when I recognize that my response will either enhance or diminish my ethical ideal. It will serve either to increase or decrease the likelihood of genuine caring. My response affects me as one-caring. In a given situation with someone I am not fond of, I may be able to find all sorts of reasons why I should not respond to his need. I may be too busy. He may be undiscerning. The matter may be, on objective analysis, unimportant. But, before I decide, I must turn away from this analytic chain of thought and back to the concrete situation. Here is this person with this perceived need to which is attached this importance. I must put justification aside temporarily. Shall I respond? How do I feel as a duality about the "I" who will not respond?

I am obliged, then, to accept the initial "I must" when it occurs and even to fetch it out of recalcitrant slumber when it fails to awake spontaneously.

The source of my obligation is the value I place on the relatedness of caring. This value itself arises as a product of actual caring and being cared-for and my reflection on the goodness of these concrete caring situations.

Now, what sort of "goodness" is it that attaches to the caring relation? It cannot be a fully moral goodness, for we have already described forms of caring that are natural and require no moral effort. But it cannot be a fully nonmoral goodness either, for it would then join a class of goods many of which are widely separated from the moral good. It is, perhaps, properly described as a "premoral good," one that lies in a region with the moral good and shades over into it. We cannot always decide with certainty whether our caring response is natural or ethical. Indeed, the decision to respond ethically as one-caring may cause the lowering of barriers that previously prevented reception of the other, and natural caring may follow.

I have identified the source of our obligation and have said that we are obligated to accept, and even to call forth, the feeling "I must." But what exactly must I do? Can my obligation be set forth in a list or hierarchy of principles? So far, it seems that I am obligated to maintain an attitude and, thus, to meet the other as one-caring and, at the same time, to increase my own virtue as one-caring. If I am advocating an ethic of virtue, do not all the usual dangers lie in wait: hypocrisy, self-righteousness, withdrawal from the public domain? We shall discuss these dangers as the idea of an ethical ideal is developed more fully.

Let me say here, however, why it seems preferable to place an ethical ideal above principle as a guide to moral action. It has been traditional in moral philosophy to insist that moral principles must be, by their very nature as moral principles, universifiable. If I am obligated to do X under certain conditions, then under sufficiently similar conditions you also are obligated to do X. But the principle of universifiability seems to depend, as Nietzsche pointed out, on a concept of "sameness."[3] In order to accept the principle, we should have to establish that human predicaments exhibit sufficient sameness, and this we cannot do without abstracting away from concrete situations those qualities that seem to reveal the sameness. In doing this, we often lose the very qualities or factors that gave rise to the moral question in the situation. That condition which makes the situation different and thereby induces genuine moral puzzlement cannot be satisfied by the application of principles developed in situations of sameness.

This does not mean that we cannot receive any guidance from an attempt to discover principles that seem to be universifiable. We can, under this sort of plan, arrive at the doctrine of "prima facie duty" described by W. D. Ross.[4] Ross himself, however, admits that this doctrine yields no real guidance for moral conduct in concrete situations. It guides us in abstract moral thinking; it tells us, theoretically, what to do, "all other things being equal." But other things are rarely if ever equal. A and B, struggling with a moral decision, are two different persons with different factual histories, different projects and aspirations, and different ideals. It may indeed be right, morally right, for A to do X and B to do not-X. We may, that is, connect "right" and "wrong" to faithfulness to the ethical ideal. This does not cast us into relativism, because the ideal contains at its heart a component that is universal: Maintenance of the caring relation. . . .

Our obligation is limited and delimited by relation. We are never free, in the human domain, to abandon our preparedness to care; but practically, if we are meeting those in our inner circles adequately as ones-caring and receiving those linked to our inner circles by formal chains of relation, we shall limit the calls upon our obligation quite naturally. We are not obliged to summon the "I must" if there is no possibility of completion in the other. I am not obliged to care for starving children in Africa, because there is no way for this caring to be completed in the other unless I abandon the caring to which I am obligated. I may still choose to do something in the direction of caring, but I am not obliged to do so. . . .

Now, this is very important, and we should try to say clearly what governs our obligation. On the basis of what has been developed so far, there seem to be two criteria: the existence of or potential for present relation, and the dynamic potential for growth in relation, including the potential for increased reciprocity and, perhaps, mutuality. The first criterion establishes an absolute obligation and the second serves to put our obligations into an order of priority.

If the other toward whom we shall act is capable of responding as cared-for and there are no objective conditions that prevent our receiving this response—if, that is, our caring can be completed in the other—then we must meet that other as one-caring. If we do not care naturally, we must call upon our capacity for ethical caring. When we are in relation or when the other has addressed us, we must respond as one-caring. The imperative in relation is categorical. When relation has not yet been established, or when it may properly be refused (when no formal chain or natural circle is present), the imperative is more like that of the hypothetical: I must if I wish to (or am able to) move into relation.

The second criterion asks us to look at the nature of potential relation and, especially, at the capacity of the cared-for to respond. The potential for response in animals, for example, is nearly static; they cannot respond in mutuality, nor can the nature of their response change substantially. But a child's potential for increased response is enormous. If the possibility of relation is dynamic—if the relation may clearly grow with respect to reciprocity—then the possibility and degree of my obligation also grows. If response is imminent, so also is my obligation. This criterion will help us to distinguish between our obligation to members of the nonhuman animal world and, say, the human fetus. We must keep in mind, however, that the second criterion binds us in proportion to the probability of increased response and to the imminence of that response. Relation itself is fundamental in obligation.

I shall give an example of thinking guided by these criteria, but let us pause for a moment and ask what it is we are trying to accomplish. I am working deliberately toward criteria that will preserve our deepest and most tender human feelings. The caring of mother for child, of human adult for human infant, elicits the tenderest feelings in most of us. Indeed, for many women, this feeling of nurturance lies at the very heart of what we assess as good. A philosophical position that has difficulty distinguishing between our obligation to human infants and, say, pigs is in some difficulty straight off. It violates our most deeply cherished feeling about human goodness. This violation does not, of course, make the position logically wrong, but it suggests that especially strong grounds will be needed to support it. . . .

Now, let's consider an example: the problem of abortion. Operating under the guidance of an ethic of caring, we are not likely to find abortion in general either right or wrong. We shall have to inquire into individual cases. An incipient embryo is an information speck—a set of controlling instructions for a future human being. Many of these specks are created and flushed away without their creators' awareness. From the view developed here, the information speck is an information speck; it has no given sanctity. There should be no concern over the waste of "human tissue," since nature herself is wildly prolific, even profligate. The one-caring is concerned not with human tissue but with human consciousness—with pain, delight, hope, fear, entreaty, and response.

But suppose the information speck is mine, and I am aware of it. This child-to-be is the product of love between a man deeply cared-for and me. Will the child have his eyes or mine? His stature or mine? Our joint love of mathematics or his love of mechanics or my love of language? This is not just an information speck; it is endowed with prior love and current knowledge. It is sacred, but I—humbly, not presumptuously—confer sacredness upon it. I cannot, will not destroy it. It is joined to loved others through formal chains of caring. It is linked to the inner circle in a clearly defined way. I might wish that I were not pregnant, but I cannot destroy this known and potentially loved person-to-be. There is already relation albeit indirect and formal. My decision is an ethical one born of natural caring.

But suppose, now, that my beloved child has grown up; it is she who is pregnant and considering abortion. She is not sure of the love between herself and the man. She is miserably worried about her economic and emotional future. I might like to convey sanctity on this information speck; but I am not

God—only mother to this suffering cared-for. It is she who is conscious and in pain, and I as one-caring move to relieve the pain. This information speck is an information speck and that is all. There is no formal relation, given the breakdown between husband and wife, and with the embryo, there is no present relation; the possibility of future relation—while not absent, surely—is uncertain. But what of this possibility for growing response? Must we not consider it? We must indeed. As the embryo becomes a fetus and, growing daily, becomes more nearly capable of response as cared-for, our obligation grows from a nagging uncertainty—an "I must if I wish"—to an utter conviction that we must meet this small other as one-caring.

If we try to formalize what has been expressed in the concrete situation described so far, we arrive at a legal approach to abortion very like that of the Supreme Court: abortions should be freely available in the first trimester, subject to medical determination in the second trimester, and banned in the third, when the fetus is viable. A woman under the guidance of our ethic would be likely to recognize the growing possibility of relation; the potential is clearly dynamic. Further many women recognize the relation as established when the fetus begins to move about. It is not a question of when life begins but of when relation begins.

But what if relation is never established? Suppose the child is born and the mother admits no sense of relatedness. May she commit infanticide? One who asks such questions misinterprets the concept of relatedness that I have been struggling to describe. Since the infant, even the near-natal fetus, is capable of relation—of the sweetest and most unselfconscious reciprocity—one who encounters the infant is obligated to meet it as one-caring. Both parts of this claim are essential; it is not only the child's capability to respond but also the encounter that induces obligation. There must exist the possibility for our caring to be completed in the other. If the mother does not care naturally, then she must summon ethical caring to support her as one-caring. She may not ethically ignore the child's cry to live. . . .

Our ethic of caring—which we might have called a "feminine ethic"— begins to look a bit mean in contrast to the masculine ethics of universal love or universal justice. But universal love is illusion. Under the illusion, some young people retreat to the church to worship that which they cannot actualize; some write lovely poetry extolling universal love; and some, in terrible disillusion, kill to establish the very principles which should have entreated them not to kill. Thus are lost both principles and persons.

Right and Wrong

How are we to make judgments of right and wrong under this ethic? First, it is important to understand that we are not primarily interested in judging but, rather, in heightening moral perception and sensitivity. But "right" and "wrong" can be useful.

Suppose a mother observes her young child pulling the kitten's tail or picking it up by the ears. She may claim, "Oh, no, it is not nice to hurt the kitty," or, "You must not hurt the kitty." Or she may simply say, "Stop. See—you are hurting the kitty," and she may then take the kitten in her own hands and show the child how to handle it. She holds the kitten gently, stroking it, and saying, "See? Ah, ah, kitty, nice kitty. . . ." What the mother is supposing in this interaction is that the realization that his act is hurting the kitten supplemented by the knowledge of how to avoid inflicting hurt, will suffice to change the child's behavior. If she believes this, she has no need for the statement, "It is wrong to hurt the kitty." She is not threatening sanctions but drawing dual attention to a matter of fact (the hurting) and her own commitment (I will not hurt). Beyond this, she is supposing that her child, well-cared-for-himself, does not want to inflict pain. . . .

The one-caring, clearly, applies "right" and "wrong" most confidently to her own decisions. This does not, as we have insisted before, make her a relativist. The caring attitude that lies at the heart of all ethical behavior is universal. . . .

. . . [I]n general the one-caring evaluates her own acts with respect to how faithfully they conform to what is known and felt through the receptivity of caring. But she also uses "right" and "wrong" instructively and respectfully to refer to the judgments of significant others. If she agrees because the matter at hand can be assessed in light of caring, she adds her personal commitment and example; if she has doubts—because the rule appealed to seems irrelevant or ambiguous in the light of caring—she still acknowledges the judgment but adds her own dissent or demurrer. Her eye is on the ethical development of the cared-for and, as she herself withholds judgment until she has heard the "whole story," she wants the cared-for to encounter others, receive them, and reflect on what he has received. Principles and rules are among the beliefs he will receive, and she wants him to consider these in the light of caring.

But is this all we can say about right and wrong? Is there not a firm foundation in morality for our legal judgments? Surely, we must be allowed to say, for example, that stealing is wrong and is, therefore, properly forbidden by law. Because it is so often wrong—and so easily demonstrated to be wrong—under an ethic of caring, we may accede that such a law has its roots *partly* in morality. We may legally punish one who has stolen, but we may not pass moral judgment on him until we know why he stole. An ethic of caring is likely to be stricter in its judgment, but more supportive and corrective in following up its judgment, than ethics otherwise grounded. For the one-caring, stealing is almost always wrong:

Ms. A talks with her young son. *But, Mother,* the boy pleads, *suppose I want to make you happy and I steal something you want from a big chain store. I haven't hurt anyone, have I? Yes, you have,* responds his mother, and she points to the predicament of the store managers who may be accused of poor stewardship and to the higher prices suffered by their neighbors. *Well, suppose I steal from a rich, rich person? He can replace what I take easily, and . . . Wait,* says Ms. A. *Is someone suffering? Are you stealing to relieve that suffering, and will you make certain that what you steal is used to relieve it? . . . But can't I steal to make someone happy?* her son persists. Slowly, patiently, Ms. A explains the position of one-caring. *Each one* who comes under our gaze must be met as one-caring. When I want to please X and I turn toward Y as a means for satisfying my desire to please X, I must now meet Y as one-caring. I do not judge him for being rich—for treasuring what I, perhaps, regard with indifference. I may not cause him pain by taking or destroying what he possesses. *But what if I steal from a bad guy—someone who stole to get what he has?* Ms. A smiles at her young son, struggling to avoid his ethical responsibility: *Unless he is an immediate threat to you or someone else, you must meet him, too, as one-caring.*

The lessons in "right" and "wrong" are hard lessons—not swiftly accomplished by setting up as an objective the learning of some principle. We do not say: It is wrong to steal. Rather, we consider why it was wrong or may be wrong in this case to steal. We do not say: It is wrong to kill. By setting up such a principle, we also imply its exceptions, and then we may too easily act on authorized exceptions. The one-caring wants to consider, and wants her child to consider, the act itself in full context. She will send him into the world skeptical, vulnerable, courageous, disobedient, and tenderly receptive, The "world" may not depend upon him to obey its rules or fulfill its wishes, but you, the individual he encounters, may depend upon him to meet you as one-caring.

The Problem of Justification

. . . Why should I be committed to not causing pain? Now, clearly, in one sense, I cannot answer this better than we already have. When the "Why?" refers to motivation, we have seen that the one-caring receives the other and acts in the other's behalf as she would for herself; that is, she acts with a similar motive energy. Further, I have claimed that, when natural caring fails, the motive energy in behalf of the other can be summoned out of caring for the ethical self. We have discussed both natural caring and ethical caring. Ethical caring, as I have described it, depends not upon rule or principle but upon the development of an ideal self. It does not depend upon just any ideal of self, but the ideal developed in congruence with one's best remembrance of caring and being cared-for.

So far, in recommending the ethical ideal as a guide to ethical conduct, I have suggested that traditional approaches to the problem of justification are mistaken. When the ethical theorist asks, "Why should I behave thus-and-so?" his question is likely to be aimed at justification rather than motivation and at a logic that resides outside the person. He is asking for reasons of the sort we expect to find in logical demonstration. He may expect us to claim that moral judgments can be tested as claims to facts can be tested, or that moral judgments are derived from divine commandment, or that moral truths are intuitively apprehended. Once started on this line of discussion, we may find ourselves arguing abstractly about the status of relativism and absolutism, egoism and altruism, and a host of other positions that, I shall claim, are largely irrelevant to moral conduct. They are matters of considerable intellectual interest, but they are distractions if our primary interest is in ethical conduct.

Moral statements cannot be justified in the way that statements of fact can be justified. They are not truths. They are derived not from facts or principles but from the caring attitude. Indeed, we might say that moral statements come out of the moral view or attitude, which, as I have described it, is the rational attitude built upon natural caring. When we put it this way, we see that there can be no justification for taking the moral viewpoint—that in truth, the moral viewpoint is prior to any notion of justification.

Notes

1. David Hume, "An Enquiry Concerning the Principles of Morals," in *Ethical Theories,* ed. A. I. Melden (Englewood Cliffs, N.J.: Prentice-Hall, Inc., 1967), p. 275.
2. Friedrich Nietzsche, "Mixed Opinions and Maxims," in *The Portable Nietzsche,* ed. Walter Kaufmann (New York: The Viking Press, Inc., 1954), p. 65.
3. Friedrich Nietzsche, *The Will to Power,* trans. Walter Kaufmann (New York: Random House, 1967), pp. 476, 670. For a contemporary argument against strict application of universalizability, see Peter Winch, *Ethics and Action* (London: Routledge & Kegan Paul, 1972).
4. W. D. Ross, *The Right and the Good* (Oxford: Clarendon Press, 1930).

CARING AND EVIL
Claudia Card

Claudia Card is professor of philosophy at the University of Wisconsin, Madison and faculty affiliate in women's studies and environmental studies. Her publications include Adventures in Lesbian Philosophy *(1994),* Lesbian Choices *(1995) and* The Unnatural Lottery *(1996). Card raises two related objections to Noddings' ethic of care. First, it does not seem that an ethic of care without justice can make good sense of our ethical responsibilities to strangers and, second, it runs the danger of "valorizing" exploitative relationships. These problems indicate, according to Card, the importance of supplementing and limiting care with considerations of justice.*

N el Noddings' "feminine approach to ethics"[1] is something like Carol Gilligan's "care perspective" in ethics. . . . Gilligan has recognized the need for both justice and care in a fully mature ethic.[2] Nel Noddings apparently disagrees. She presents her ethic of care as an *alternative* to an ethic of principle, rejecting universalizability except in the universal accessibility of the caring attitude. This rejection of justice as a fundamental ethical concept raises issues so important that I focus on it, rather than on topics where I find more with which to agree.

My question is: Can an ethic of care without justice enable us adequately to resist evil? By resisting evil, I have in mind something relatively modest: resisting complicity in evil-doing. I have long since abandoned ambitions of reducing evil in the world at large (leaving it a better place than I found it); such ambitions are usually dangerous as well as arrogant. Still, we can and ought to resist complicity in the evils around us. I have in mind evils of two kinds: the evils strangers do to strangers and the evils intimates do to intimates. Each raises different problems. Issues of racism and sexism can illustrate the two.

On the one hand, resting all of ethics on caring threatens to exclude as ethically insignificant our relationships with most people in the world, because we do not know them individually and never will. Regarding as ethically insignificant our relationships with people remote from ourselves is a constituent of racism and zenophobia. On the other hand, resting all of ethics on caring also seems in danger of valorizing relationships that are sheerly exploitative of our distinctively human capacity to take another's

Reprinted from *Hypatia* 5, 1990 by permission of the author.

point of view. It thereby threatens to exacerbate the positions of women and other care-takers in a sexist society. By "sheer exploitation" I mean valuing others and their capacities sheerly for what they contribute to ourselves or our projects, by contrast with valuing them for themselves, apart from our own development and projects.

Our Relations with Strangers

Consider the first problem, our ethical relations with most people in the world. Nel Noddings grants (even insists) that no one has the responsibility even to try to care for everyone, in the full-blown sense of "caring" that her book develops. I agree. But that leaves the question of what ethical notions *are* relevant to our relationships with strangers, persons whose lives we may significantly affect although we will never know them as individuals, never encounter them. Where we have no responsibility to care *for* others, I should think that we still have responsibilities to refrain from doing them harm—to be *careful,* in a sense that does *not* require encounters with those for whose sakes we ought to take care.

On Nel Noddings' analysis caring requires real encounters with individuals. My ethical responsibility is to meet those whom I encounter as one-caring. The ideal, apparently, is to reproduce the quality of caring experienced in infancy, an experience lacking what most of us would recognize as reciprocity. (I will say more about that shortly). She is concerned not to dilute caring to include just any positive concern we can have for another. Her "caring for" is not just "being concerned about"; it has three elements: (1) motivational engrossment—or "displacement"—in another, a regard for or inclination toward the other (she speaks of "being present to" them), and an action component, *care-taking,* such as protection or maintenance. Ideally, the reception of caring involves a responsiveness of spontaneously sharing with the carer one's aspirations, appraisals, and accomplishments, in particular, sharing the development that caring made possible.

The strengths of this analysis, which distinguishes caring from other ways of being concerned, also suggest certain limitations of caring as the basis for an ethic. Technology has made it possible for the effects of our actions to extend far beyond the range of our personal encounters. We can affect drastically, even fatally, people we will never know as individuals. What does a caring ethic say about our relations with them?

By means of what she calls "chains" of connection, Nel Noddings holds that we can be *prepared to care* for others who are presently outside our "circles" of connection—for outsiders such as our children's spouses-to-be. "Chains" are defined as "personal or formal relationships." The latter, however, are not defined, and the "chains" offered as examples suggest differing interpretations. The example of the spouse of one's child, suggests that a "chain" has as a connecting link an individual whom one *has* encountered. This is also suggested by the idea of a preparedness to care because of others for whom we already care. This example makes sense of the metaphor of a "chain": individuals known to us are the links. However, to restrict ethics to such connections in a nuclear age would be preposterous.

A different example, one's future students who are simply potential place-holders in a formal relationship of teacher-student, extends our connections further but does not make sense of the chain metaphor. On this model, I as a teacher am apparently connected ("chainwise?") to my potential students. But what are the "links"? My present students may be connected with future students through me. But what links *me* with future students? To avoid circularity, my present students need *another* connection with future ones in order to link me to those future students. Still, if nearly anyone might enter into a relationship with me that I presently have to others, perhaps we have an answer to the question about our ethical relationships to strangers: they are "potentially" not strangers. Is that answer satisfactory? I have several questions.

First, what if the potentiality is never realized, as it never will be with regard to most people in the world? Does the existence of a potential relationship mean that *potentially* I have an ethical relationship with those who are presently strangers? Or does it mean that because of the potentiality, I have such a relationship now?

If the latter, how can caring in the sense requiring encounter apply? Are we to *imagine* an encounter? If an imagined encounter can substitute for a real one, what does the so-called "motivational displacement" of caring really have to do with the particularities of others? Nel Noddings has objected to the abstractness of an ethic of principle. It seems that here, however, ethical relationships are being defined by abstract potentialities, or even speculations, and if by such abstractions, why not by those in the idea of justice? And if the present potentiality for future encounters makes my relationship with strangers ethically significant now, how has universality been rejected?

On the other hand, if the existence of a potential relationship means only that *potentially* I have an ethical relationship with those who are presently strangers, am I free to act in ways that will veritably insure the unrealizability of that potentiality? Just what are the implications of a potential ethical relationship for one's actual responsibilities?

Second, *which* relationships linking us to strangers count as ethically significant? Are formal relationships *kinds* of relationship, as opposed to particular relationships? If so, *which* kinds of relationship? The examples suggest *institutionally* defined relationships, such as marriages and the relationships defined by educational institutions. However, if "formal relationships" are institutionally defined, we need justice to evaluate them. Some institutions unjustly exclude whole groups of people. If my formal relationships to others were defined by such institutions, it would seem to follow that I had no formal relationships to those excluded and therefore no ethical relationships to them, unless I were connected by personal relationships. But that is not plausible. If "formal relationships" are not institutionally defined, then how are they defined? What is the "form"?

The notion of "chains" is left at too intuitive a level. I have no intuitive sense of these "chains" that explains the examples. Why, for example, is the embryo a woman carries not connected with her by indefinitely *many* "chains," independently of her relationship with its father? It has indefinitely many potentialities for entering into relationships with her. Yet, in the case of an embryo carried by a woman not sure of the love between herself and the man, Nel Noddings says (referring to the embryo as an "information speck"), "This information speck is an information speck and that is all. There is no formal relation, given the breakdown between husband and wife, and with the embryo, there is no present relation. . . ," but that there is a "growing possibility of relation."[3] Why is there no formal relation? (Is it not, for example, potentially its mother's student?) How does a connection by "formal relation" differ from "the possibility of relation"? Is the difference significant? . . .

Part of the point of justice is to make possible cooperative relationships with more people than one can or should even try to care for. It applies to interactions among many who are not bound by ties of affection but who have a stake in securing certain common advantages by mutual cooperation. This is especially important in a society plagued by racism, ethnocentrism, and zenophobia. In a poorly integrated multicultural society dominated by phobic stereotypes, opportunities for interracial caring relationships are not what they should be. In such a context, if one's ethical repertoire is exhausted by caring, there is nothing left to operate with respect to many of the interracial consequences of one's conduct. Normally, this is one place for justice and respect for others. . . .

Personal Relationships and Problems of Abuse

If the care ethic threatens to exclude too much, it also threatens to include too much by valorizing relationships that sheerly exploit carers. Elevating caring into an ethical ideal threatens to valorize the maintenance by carers of relationships that ought to be dissolved or those from which a carer should be able to withdraw without being in any way "ethically diminished." Consider the problem of intimate partner abuse. . . .

The care ethic seems to lack a basis for objecting to an abused carer's remaining in the relationship when leaving becomes possible. Referring to a famous burning bed case, Nel Noddings holds that if we must exclude from our caring someone for whom we have cared, we thereby act under a "diminished ethical ideal."[4] I should have thought the richness of our ethical ideals *enabled* us to reject bad relationships and freed us up for ethically fuller ones. After all, it is by contrasting abusive relationships with such ideals that we are finally able to see the abuse for what it is.

Getting stuck in the "pre-act" consciousness of the attitude of one-caring can be ethically disastrous. Caring has the consequence of supporting people in their projects. Caring unrestrained by other values is not necessarily a good thing. It can be better to cease caring than to allow one's caring to be exploited in the service of immoral ends.

Perhaps the case of abusive relationships also points to a gap in Professor Noddings' account of caring itself. That account does not explicitly include the idea of *valuing* individuals for themselves. Motivational displacement is not the same. We can take up the perspectives of others out of sheer necessity for survival, the necessity to anticipate others' needs in order to be a good servant or slave, for example. Women learn well to do this with men; slaves have learned well to do it with masters. To be the valuers that ethical caring requires we need to preserve in ourselves, as well as value in others, a certain spiritual integrity. Otherwise, we risk becoming simply tools or extensions of others. With a capacity for "motivational displacement"—receiving others into oneself—but lacking integrity as a self who chooses and rejects relationships, one is in danger of dissolving into a variety of personalities, changing one's colors (or values) like a chameleon in changing environments. Women know this danger intimately, as does anyone whose personal safety has regularly depended upon how well they were able to "receive others into themselves."

This last is not so much a disagreement as a suggestion for further development in analyzing caring as an ethical ideal. Where I disagree is on the need to both supplement and limit care with justice. In one sense caring *is* more basic to human life than justice: we can *survive* without justice more easily than without caring. However, this is part of the human tragedy because, in another sense, justice is also basic: life can be *worth* living despite the absence of caring from most people in the world, but in a densely populated high-tech world, life is not apt to be *worth* living without justice from a great many people, including many whom we will never know.

NOTES

1.   Nel Noddings, *Caring: A Feminine Approach to Ethics and Moral Education.* (Berkeley, CA: University of California Press, 1984).

2. At least, she did in *In a Different Voice* (Cambridge, MA: Harvard University Press, 1982), but it is no longer clear that she holds this view. In her essay, "Moral Orientation and Moral Development" (*Women and Moral Theory,* Eva Kittay and Diana T. Meyers, eds, Totawa, NJ: Rowman and Littlefield, 1987), she develops the idea that the justice and care orientations are related to one another as alternative gestalts. It is not clear from the account of these gestalts whether each has a place for the basic concept in the other or not, nor if so, what place it has.
3. *Caring,* p. 88.
4. *Ibid.,* p. 114.

CHAPTER 8

Pluralism and Particularism

MORAL CHOICE WITHOUT PRINCIPLES
Jean-Paul Sartre

*Jean-Paul Sartre (1905–1980) was a leading figure in the existentialist move-
ment in this century. His philosophical writings included* Being and Nothing-
ness *(1943) and his novels and plays included* The Age of Reason *(1945) and*
No Exit *(1945). In the following selection, Sartre denies that there are moral
principles of the sort sought by Aquinas, Bentham, and Kant that can provide
guidance in a great many real-life situations. He illustrates this claim with his
famous story about the young man torn between staying with his mother who
needed him and joining the Free French Forces.*

I shall cite the case of one of my students who came to see me under the
following circumstances: his father was on bad terms with his mother, and,
moreover, was inclined to be a collaborationist; his older brother had been
killed in the German offensive of 1940, and the young man, with somewhat
immature but generous feelings, wanted to avenge him. His mother lived
alone with him, very much upset by the half-treason of her husband and the
death of her older son; the boy was her only consolation.

The boy was faced with the choice of leaving for England and joining the
Free French Forces—that is, leaving his mother behind—or remaining with
his mother and helping her to carry on. He was fully aware that the woman
lived only for him and that his going-off—and perhaps his death—would
plunge her into despair. He was also aware that every act that he did for his

From *Essays in Existentialism* by Jean-Paul Sarte (New York: Philosophical Library, 1965). Reprinted by permission of the publisher.

mother's sake was a sure thing, in the sense that it was helping her to carry on, whereas every effort he made toward going off and fighting was an uncertain move which might run aground and prove completely useless; for example, on his way to England he might, while passing through Spain, be detained indefinitely in a Spanish camp; he might reach England or Algiers and be stuck in an office at a desk job. As a result, he was faced with two very different kinds of action: one, concrete, immediate, but concerning only one individual; the other concerned an incomparably vaster group, a national collectivity, but for that very reason was dubious, and might be interrupted en route. And, at the same time, he was wavering between two kinds of ethics. On the one hand, an ethics of sympathy, of personal devotion; on the other, a broader ethics, but one whose efficacy was more dubious. He had to choose between the two.

Who could help him choose? Christian doctrine? No. Christian doctrine says, "Be charitable, love your neighbor, take the more rugged path, etc., etc." But which is the more rugged path? Whom should he love as a brother? The fighting man or his mother? Which does the greater good, the vague act of fighting in a group, or the concrete one of helping a particular human being to go on living? Who can decide *a priori*? Nobody. No book of ethics can tell him. The Kantian ethics says, "Never treat any person as a means, but as an end." Very well, if I stay with mother, I'll treat her as an end and not as a means; but by virtue of this very fact, I'm running the risk of treating the people around me who are fighting, as means; and, conversely, if I go to join those who are fighting, I'll be treating them as an end, and, by doing that, I run the risk of treating my mother as a means.

If values are vague, and if they are always too broad for the concrete and specific case that we are considering, the only thing left for us is to trust our instincts. That's what this young man tried to do; and when I saw him, he said, "In the end, feeling is what counts. I ought to choose whichever pushes me in one direction. If I feel that I love my mother enough to sacrifice everything else for her—my desire for vengeance, for action, for adventure—then I'll stay with her. If, on the contrary, I feel that my love for my mother isn't enough, I'll leave."

But how is the value of a feeling determined? What gives his feeling for his mother value? Precisely the fact that he remained with her. I may say that I like so-and-so well enough to sacrifice a certain amount of money for him, but I may say so only if I've done it. I may say "I love my mother well enough to remain with her" if I have remained with her. The only way to determine the value of this affection is, precisely, to perform an act which confirms and defines it. But, since I require this affection to justify my act, I find myself caught in a vicious circle. . . .

. . . In other words, the feeling is formed by the acts one performs; so, I can not refer to it in order to act upon it. Which means that I can neither seek within myself the true condition which will impel me to act, nor apply to a system of ethics for concepts which will permit me to act. You will say, "At least, he did go to a teacher for advice." But if you seek advice from a priest, for example, you have chosen this priest; you already knew, more or less, just about what advice he was going to give you. In other words, choosing your adviser is involving yourself. The proof of this is that if you are a Christian, you will say, "Consult a priest." But some priests are collaborating, some are just marking time, some are resisting. Which to choose? If the young man chooses a priest who is resisting or collaborating, he has already decided on the kind of advice he's going to get. Therefore, in coming to see me he knew the answer I was going to give him, and I had only one answer to give: "You're free, choose, that is, invent." No general ethics can show you what is to be done; there are no omens in the world. . . .

. . . [The] objection: "You're able to do anything, no matter what" is not to the point. In one sense choice is possible, but what is not possible is not to choose. I can always choose, but I ought to know that if I do not choose, I am still choosing. Though this may seem purely formal, it is highly important for keeping fantasy and caprice within bounds. If it is true that in facing a situation, for example, one in which, as a person capable of having sexual relations, of having children, I am obliged to choose an attitude, and if I in any way assume responsibility for a choice which, in involving myself, also involves all mankind, this has nothing to do with caprice, even if no *a priori* value determines my choice. . . .

. . . [M]an is in an organized situation in which he himself is involved. Through his choice, he involves all mankind, and he can not avoid making a choice: either he will remain chaste, or he will marry without having children, or he will marry and have children; anyhow, whatever he may do, it is impossible for him not to take full responsibility for the way he handles this problem. Doubtless, he chooses without referring to preestablished values, but it is unfair to accuse him of caprice. Instead, let us say that moral choice is to be compared to the making of a work of art. And before going any further, let it be said at once that we are not dealing here with an aesthetic ethics, because our opponents are so dishonest that they even accuse us of that. The example I've chosen is a comparison only.

Having said that, may I ask whether anyone has ever accused an artist who has painted a picture of not having drawn his inspiration from rules set up *a priori*? Has any one ever asked, "What painting ought he to make?" It is clearly understood that there is no definite painting to be made, that the artist is engaged in the making of his painting, and that the painting to be made is precisely the painting he will have made. It is clearly understood that there are no *a priori* aesthetic values, but that there are values which appear subsequently in the coherence of the painting, in the correspondence between what the artist intended and the result. Nobody can tell what the painting of tomorrow will be like. Painting can be judged only after it has once been made. What connection does that have with ethics? We are in the same creative situation. We never say that a work of art is arbitrary. When we speak of a canvas of Picasso, we never say that it is arbitrary; we understand quite well that he was making himself what he is at the very time he was painting, that the ensemble of his work is embodied in his life.

The same holds on the ethical plane. What art and ethics have in common is that we have creation and invention in both cases. We can not decide *a priori* what there is to be done. I think that I pointed that out quite sufficiently when I mentioned the case of the student who came to see me, and who might have applied to all the ethical systems, Kantian or otherwise, without getting any sort of guidance. He was obliged to devise his law himself. Never let it be said by us that this man—who, taking affection, individual action, and kind-heartedness toward a specific person as his ethical principle, chooses to remain with his mother, or who, preferring to make a sacrifice, chooses to go to England—has made an arbitrary choice. Man makes himself. He isn't ready made at the start. In choosing his ethics, he makes himself, and force of circumstances is such that he can not abstain from choosing one. We define man only in relationship to involvement. It is therefore absurd to charge us with arbitrariness of choice.

WHAT MAKES RIGHT ACTS RIGHT?
W. D. Ross

Sir William David Ross (1877–1971) was provost of Oriel College, Oxford University. His books include two important works in ethics, The Right and the Good *(1930) and* The Foundations of Ethics *(1939). Contrary to many moral theorists, Ross denies that there is some single moral principle that can be used to derive more specific moral obligations. Rather he defends a version of ethical*

From *The Right and the Good* by W. D. Ross (Oxford: Oxford University Press, 1930). Reprinted by permission of the publisher.

pluralism, *according to which there are a number of irreducible moral rules that are basic in moral thought. These rules express what Ross calls* prima facie *duties—duties such as keeping promises and avoiding injury to others—which may conflict in specific circumstances. When such duties do conflict, what is demanded is that we use moral judgment in order to determine which* prima facie *duty is (in that circumstance) weightiest and should be obeyed. Because he thought that the truth of the moral rules (he lists seven in all) could be grasped by intuition in the manner in which we grasp basic mathematical truths, Ross's view is sometimes called* intuitionism.

W hen a plain man fulfills a promise because he thinks he ought to do so, it seems clear that he does so with no thought of its total consequences, still less with any opinion that these are likely to be the best possible. He thinks in fact much more of the past than of the future. What makes him think it right to act in a certain way is that fact that he has promised to do so—that and, usually, nothing more. That his act will produce the best possible consequences is not his reason for calling it right. What lends color to the theory we are examining, then, is not the actions (which form probably a great majority of our actions) in which some such reflection as "I have promised" is the only reason we give ourselves for thinking a certain action right, but the exceptional cases in which the consequences of fulfilling a promise (for instance) would be so disastrous to others that we judge it right not to do so. It must of course be admitted that such cases exist. If I have promised to meet a friend at a particular time for some trivial purpose, I should certainly think myself justified in breaking my engagement if by doing so I could prevent a serious accident or bring relief to the victims of one. And the supporters of the view we are examining hold that my thinking so is due to my thinking that I shall bring more good into existence by the one action than by the other. A different account may, however, be given of the matter, an account which will, I believe, show itself to be the true one. It may be said that besides the duty of fulfilling promises I have and recognize a duty of relieving distress, and that when I think it right to do the latter at the cost of not doing the former, it is not because I think I shall produce more good thereby but because I think it the duty which is in the circumstances more of a duty. This account surely corresponds much more closely with what we really think in such a situation. If, so far as I can see, I could bring equal amounts of good into being by fulfilling my promise and by helping someone to whom I had made no promise, I should not hesitate to regard the former as my duty. Yet on the view that what is right is right because it is productive of the most good I should not so regard it. . . .

In fact the theory of . . . utilitarianism . . . seems to simplify unduly our relations to our fellows. It says, in effect, that the only morally significant relation in which my neighbors stand to me is that of being possible beneficiaries by my action. They do stand in this relation to me, and this relation is morally significant. But they may also stand to me in the relation of promisee to promiser, of creditor to debtor, of wife to husband, of child to parent, of friend to friend, of fellow countryman to fellow countryman, and the like; and each of these relations is the foundation of a *prima facie* duty, which is more or less incumbent on me according to the circumstances of the case. When I am in a situation, as perhaps I always am, in which more than one of these *prima facie* duties is incumbent on me, what I have to do is to study the situation as fully as I can until I form the considered opinion (it is never more) that in the circumstances one of them is more incumbent than any other; then I am bound to think that to do this *prima facie* duty is my duty *sans phrase* in the situation.

I suggest "*prima facie* duty" or "conditional duty" as a brief way of referring to the characteristic (quite distinct from that of being a duty proper) which an act has, in virtue of being of a certain kind (e.g., the keeping of a promise), of being an act which would be a duty proper if it were not at the same time of another kind which is morally significant. Whether an act is a duty proper or actual duty depends on *all* the morally significant kinds it is an instance of. . . .

There is nothing arbitrary about these *prima facie* duties. Each rests on a definite circumstance which cannot seriously be held to be without moral significance. Of *prima facie* duties I suggest, without claiming completeness or finality for it, the following division.

(1) Some duties rest on previous acts of my own. These duties seem to include two kinds, (*a*) those resting on a promise or what may fairly be called an implicit promise, such as the implicit undertaking not to tell lies which seems to be implied in the act of entering into conversation (at any rate by civilized men), or of writing books that purport to be history and not fiction. These may be called the duties of fidelity. (*b*) Those resting on a previous wrongful act. These may be called the duties of reparation. (2) Some rest on previous acts of other men, i.e., services done by them to me. These my be loosely described as the duties of gratitude. (3) Some rest on the fact or possibility of a distribution of pleasure or happiness (or of the means thereto) which is not in accordance with the merit of the persons concerned; in such cases there arises a duty to upset or prevent such a distribution. These are the duties of justice. (4) Some rest on the mere fact that there are other beings in the world whose condition we can make better in respect of virtue, or of intelligence, or of pleasure. These are the duties of beneficence. (5) Some rest on the fact that we can improve our own condition in respect of virtue

or of intelligence. These are the duties of self-improvement. (6) I think that we should distinguish from (4) the duties that may be summed up under the title of "not injuring others." No doubt to injure others is incidentally to fail to do them good; but it seems to me clear that non-maleficence is apprehended as a duty distinct from that of beneficence, and as a duty of a more stringent character. It will be noticed that this alone among the types of duty has been stated in a negative way. An attempt might no doubt be made to state this duty, like the others, in a positive way. It might be said that it is really the duty to prevent ourselves from acting either from an inclination to harm others or from an inclination to seek our own pleasure, in doing which we should incidentally harm them. But on reflection it seems clear that the primary duty here is the duty not to harm others, this being a duty whether or not we have an inclination that if followed would lead to our harming them; and that when we have such an inclination the primary duty not to harm others gives rise to a consequential duty to resist the inclination. The recognition of this duty of non-maleficence is the first step on the way to the recognition of the duty of beneficence; and that accounts for the prominence of the commands "thou shalt not kill," "thou shalt not commit adultery," "thou shalt not steal," "thou shalt not bear false witness," in so early a code as the Decalogue. But even when we have come to recognize the duty of beneficence, it appears to me that the duty of non-maleficence is recognized as a distinct one, and as *prima facie* more binding. We should not in general consider it justifiable to kill one person in order to keep another alive, or to steal from one in order to give alms to another. . . .

The essential defect of the . . . utilitarian theory is that it ignores, or at least does not do full justice to, the highly personal character of duty. If the only duty is to produce the maximum of good, the question who is to have the good—whether it is myself, or my benefactor, or a person to whom I have made a promise to confer that good on him, or a mere fellow man to whom I stand in no such special relation—should make no difference to my having a duty to produce that good. But we are all in fact sure that it makes a vast difference. . . .

. . . That an act, *qua* fulfilling a promise, or *qua* effecting a just distribution of good, or *qua* returning services rendered, or *qua* promoting the good of others, or *qua* promoting the virtue or insight of the agent, is *prima facie* right, is self-evident; not in the sense that it is evident from the beginning of our lives, or as soon as we attend to the proposition for the first time, but in the sense that when we have reached sufficient mental maturity and have given sufficient attention to the proposition it is evident without any need of proof, or of evidence beyond itself. It is self-evident just as a mathematical axiom, or the validity of a form of inference, is evident. The moral order expressed in these propositions is just as much part of the fundamental nature of the universe (and, we may add, of any possible universe in which there were moral agents at all) as is the spatial or numerical structure expressed in the axioms of geometry or arithmetic. In our confidence that these propositions are true there is involved the same trust in our reason that is involved in our confidence in mathematics; and we should have no justification for trusting it in the latter sphere and distrusting it in the former. In both cases we are dealing with propositions that cannot be proved, but that just as certainly need no proof. . . .

Our judgments about our actual duty in concrete situations have none of the certainty that attaches to our recognition of the general principles of duty. A statement is certain, i.e., is an expression of knowledge, only in one or other of two cases: when it is either self-evident, or a valid conclusion from self-evident premises. And our judgments about our particular duties have neither of these characters. (1) They are not self-evident. Where a possible act is seen to have two characteristics, in virtue of one of which it is *prima facie* right, and in virtue of the other *prima facie* wrong, we are (I think) well aware that we are not certain whether we ought or ought not to do it; that whether we do it or not, we are taking a moral risk. We come in the long run, after consideration, to think one duty more pressing than the other, but we do not feel certain that it is so. And though we do not always recognize that a possible act has two such characteristics, and though there *may* be cases in which it has not, we are never certain that any particular possible act has not, and therefore never certain that it is right, nor certain that it is wrong. For, to go no further in the analysis, it is enough to point out that any particular act will in all probability in the course of time contribute to the bringing about of good or of evil for many human beings, and thus have a *prima facie* rightness or wrongness of which we know nothing. (2) Again, our judgments about our particular duties are not logical conclusions from self-evident premises. The only possible premises would be the general principles stating their *prima facie* rightness or wrongness *qua* having the different characteristics they do have; and even if we could (as we cannot) apprehend the extent to which an act will tend on the one hand, for example, to bring about advantages for our benefactors, and on the other hand to bring about disadvantages for fellow men who are not our benefactors, there is no principle by which we can draw the conclusion that it is on the whole right or on the whole wrong. In this respect the judgment as to the rightness of a particular act is just like the judgment as to the beauty of a particular natural object or work of art. A poem is, for instance, in respect of certain qualities beautiful and in respect of certain others not beautiful; and our judgment as to the degree of beauty it possesses on the whole is never reached by logical reasoning from the apprehension of its particular beauties or particular defects. Both in this and in the moral case we have more or less probable opinions which are not logically justified conclusions from the general principles that are recognized as self-evident.

There is therefore much truth in the description of the right act as a fortunate act. If we cannot be certain that it is right, it is our good fortune if the act we do is the right act. This consideration does not, however, make the doing of our duty a mere matter of chance. There is a parallel here between the doing of duty and the doing of what will be to our personal advantage. We never *know* what act will in the long run be to our advantage. Yet it is certain that we are more likely in general to secure our advantage if we estimate to the best of our ability the probable tendencies of our actions in this respect, than if we act on caprice. And similarly we are more likely to do our duty if we reflect to the best of our ability on the *prima facie* rightness or wrongness of various possible acts in virtue of the characteristics we perceive them to have, than if we act without reflection. With this greater likelihood we must be content. . . .

In what has preceded, a good deal of use has been made of "what we really think" about moral questions. . . .

. . . It might be said that this is in principle wrong; that we should not be content to expound what our present moral consciousness tells us but should aim at a criticism of our existing moral consciousness in the light of theory. Now I do not doubt that the moral consciousness of men has in detail undergone a good deal of modification as regards the things we think right, at the hands of moral theory. But . . . we have to ask ourselves whether we really, when we reflect, *are* convinced that this is self-evident, and whether we really *can* get rid of our view that promise-keeping has a bindingness independent of productiveness of maximum good. In my own experience I find that I cannot, in spite of a very genuine attempt to do so. . . .

I would maintain, in fact, that what we are apt to describe as "what we think" about moral questions contains a considerable amount that we do not think but know, and that this forms the standard by reference to which the truth of any moral theory has to be tested, instead of having itself to be tested by reference to any theory. I hope that I have in what precedes indicated what in my view these elements of knowledge are that are involved in our ordinary moral consciousness.

It would be a mistake to found a natural science on "what we really think," i.e., on what reasonably thoughtful and well-educated people think about the subjects of the science before they have studied them scientifically. For such opinions are interpretations, and often misinterpretations, of sense-experience; and the man of science must appeal from these to sense-experience itself, which furnishes his real data. In ethics no such appeal is possible. We have no more direct way of access to the facts about rightness and goodness and about what things are right or good, than by thinking about them; the moral convictions of thoughtful and well-educated people are the data of ethics just as sense-perceptions are the data of a natural science. Just as some of the latter have to be rejected as illusory, so have some of the former; but as the latter are rejected only when they are in conflict with other more accurate sense-perceptions, the former are rejected only when they are in conflict with other convictions which stand better the test of reflection. The existing body of moral convictions of the best people is the cumulative product of the moral reflection of many generations, which has developed an extremely delicate power of appreciation of moral distinctions; and this the theorist cannot afford to treat with anything other than the greatest respect. The verdicts of the moral consciousness of the best people are the foundation on which he must build; though he must first compare them with one another and eliminate any contradictions they may contain.

PRINCIPLES OR PARTICULARISM?
David McNaughton

David McNaughton is lecturer in philosophy at the University of Keele and author of Moral Vision *(1988). Ethical particularism takes a skeptical view of the role and importance of moral principles in moral thinking. The particularist claims that we must judge each moral situation individually without the secure guidance of moral principles that many philosophers have sought. The particularist is united with the pluralist in rejecting the claim (by monists) that there is some overarching single moral principle that can effectively guide moral thinking and decision making. But the particularist also rejects the pluralist's claim that certain features of actions and situations are always relevant to the moral assessment of actions. According to the particularist, then, making moral judgments about specific cases requires that we carefully examine the details of the situation and assess the various morally relevant features of that situation in deciding what is right and wrong to do.*

From *Moral Vision* by David McNaughton (Oxford: Blackwell Publishers, 1988). Reprinted by permission of the publisher.

The Role of Moral Principles

. . . [T]he particularist is skeptical about the role of moral principles in moral reasoning. . . .

. . . He believes that we have to judge each particular moral decision on its individual merits; we cannot appeal to general rules to make that decision for us. Moral particularism takes the view that moral principles are at best useless, and at worst a hindrance, in trying to find out which is the right action. What is required is the correct conception of the particular case in hand, with its unique set of properties. There is thus no substitute for a sensitive and detailed examination of each individual case.

Skepticism about the utility of moral principles may seem to strike at the very heart of our conception of morality. The concept of a moral principle appears to play a central, and apparently impregnable, role in our moral thought. To be virtuous is to have acquired, and to live by, a set of good moral principles. Moral education is viewed as the inculcation of the right principles in the young. The suggestion that we can do without moral principles is thus likely to appear unworthy of serious attention. This is certainly the opinion of most of the philosophers who have even bothered to consider the possibility of moral particularism.

The conviction that we cannot manage without moral principles finds its main expression in a concern about how we are to cope when we find ourselves in a new, and perhaps puzzling, situation. We require guidance to help us to do the right thing. What would meet that need for guidance would be a set of tried and tested rules that would enable us to apply what we have learned in the old familiar cases to the new and unfamiliar one. Moral principles appear to fit the bill; they tell us which of the nonmoral features of any situation are morally significant and so enable us to reach the right decision. . . .

The . . . source of this conviction . . . is found in a strangely compelling picture of what it is to make a reasoned decision. In giving reasons for any decision, I am implicitly appealing to something general, to something that could be applied to other cases. If something is a reason in this case it cannot just be a reason in this case; it must be a reason elsewhere. Since we give reasons for our moral opinions we must, explicitly or implicitly, be appealing to general rules or moral principles. A moral principle is, if you like, a moral reason which has had its generality made explicit. Thus, if the reason this action is wrong is that it would involve telling a lie, then the wrongness of acting like that must somehow carry over into other cases which involve the telling of lies.

When I give reasons for my claim that an action is, say, morally wrong, I appeal to other properties of the action which make it wrong. I may appeal to some of its nonmoral properties—that it caused pain or that it involved the deliberate telling of an untruth—or to some of its "thick" moral properties—that it was ungenerous or cowardly. The latter kind of answer appears, however, only to offer a partial justification of my moral opinion. For I may properly be asked to give reasons for believing that it is ungenerous or cowardly and I shall then have to refer to the nonmoral properties which make it so. So, in giving the full reasons for my belief that the action was wrong, I shall have to give a list of the nonmoral properties that make it wrong. A full justification of my moral views as a whole would thus eventually involve the articulation of all my moral principles, that is, a list of all the nonmoral properties of actions which I believe to be generally morally relevant.

The search for the perfect moral theory might thus be seen as a quest for the best set of moral principles which, if followed, would enable the agent to reach the right decision in any case he may encounter. Such a system would provide a complete, finite, check-list of nonmoral properties which are morally relevant to the rightness or to the wrongness of an action. With the aid of such a check-list the agent could examine any actual or possible action and determine its rightness or wrongness by consulting his list. How long the list should be, just how many moral principles there are, is a matter for debate. The simplest system is, of course, a monistic one, in which only one property is morally relevant and all others may safely be ignored.

A PARTICULARIST RESPONSE

The particularist's objection to this conception of moral reasoning is that what we may want to say about the moral character of a particular action may always outrun any such attempt at codification. We have to be sensitive to the way the features of this individual case come together to determine its moral nature. . . .

He also rejects the conception of reason to which the argument appealed. On that picture, whether or not some nonmoral feature of an action is a reason for its being morally wrong is quite unaffected by the presence or absence of other properties. If the presence of a nonmoral property is a reason for an action's being wrong then, since its being a reason will not be altered one whit by other properties the action may have, whenever an action has that property it will provide a reason for the action's being wrong. The particularist regards this account of reasons as unduly atomistic. It supposes that each reason is insulated from its surroundings so that the effect of each on the rightness or wrongness of the action as a whole can be judged separately. The particularist prefers a holistic account. We cannot judge the effect of the presence of any one feature in isolation from the effect of the others. Whether or not one particular property is morally relevant, and in what way, may depend on the precise nature of the other properties of the action.

To illustrate: I take my nephews and nieces to the circus for a treat. They enjoy it. I have done the right thing. Why? Because I succeeded in giving them pleasure. Because the fact that my action gave pleasure was here the reason for its being right, does it follow that, whenever an action gives pleasure, we shall have reason for thinking it right? No. Consider the following. A government is considering reintroducing hanging, drawing and quartering in public for terrorist murders. If reactions to public hangings in the past are anything to go by a lot of people may enjoy the spectacle. Does that constitute a reason in favor of reintroduction? Is the fact that people would enjoy it here a reason for its being right? It would be perfectly possible to take just the opposite view. The fact that spectators might get a sadistic thrill from the brutal spectacle could be thought to constitute an objection to reintroduction. Whether the fact that an action causes pleasure is a reason for or against doing it is not something that can be settled in isolation from other features of the action. It is only when we know the context in which the pleasure will occur that we are in a position to judge.

In short, the particularist claims that we cannot know, in advance, what contribution any particular nonmoral property will make to the moral nature of an action. We cannot know, in advance, whether it will be morally relevant at all and, if so, whether its presence will count for or against doing the action. The contribution that each property makes will depend on the other properties that go along with it in this case. It follows that there is no way of ruling out, in advance, some nonmoral properties as being morally irrelevant. Any property may be morally relevant. Whether it is so will depend, once again, on the surrounding properties.

Where does the particularist stand in the debate between monism and pluralism? Sometimes that debate is presented as being between those who hold that there is only one fundamental moral principle and those who hold that there is an irreducible plurality of principles. . . .

. . . [T]he particularist rejects the terms of this debate. The issue is sometimes expressed in terms of morally relevant properties; is there one, or more than one, morally relevant property? In this debate the particularist takes an extreme pluralist position for no property can be ruled out, in advance, as never being relevant to the rightness or wrongness of an action. . . .

. . . It would provide additional support for particularism if it could be shown that no ideal system of moral principles could deliver what it aspires to: a systematically organized set of moral principles that will tell the agent what to do in any particular case. The crucial test here is the problem of moral conflict.

Moral Conflict

. . . [O]ur ordinary moral thought appears to be pluralist rather than monist in character. We appeal to a variety of values and moral principles in our moral reasoning, and utilitarian attempts to show that there is just one ultimate value or one basic moral principle were unconvincing. The obvious difficulty facing a pluralist system is the problem of moral conflict. Where there is a plurality of moral principles there is the possibility that more than one might apply to a particular situation and suggest conflicting answers to the question: Which action is the right one?

In Sartre's famous example, a young man in occupied France during the Second World War was torn between loyalty to his sick and widowed mother and loyalty to his country. He felt that he ought to stay at home and look after her but he also believed that he should join the Free French Army. It is characteristic of such a painful conflict that the person facing it takes himself to be under two obligations, which conflict in this particular case, so that he cannot honor both. The problem that faces a pluralist moral theory is to find a method by which such conflicts can be resolved.

The problem of resolving moral conflicts is certainly a difficulty for a pluralist theory but it is not in itself an objection to pluralism. Indeed, since we do experience moral conflicts, it is a strength of pluralism that it makes room for them. For just that reason, a sophisticated monism will not rule them out either, for it will allow that there can be a plurality of subsidiary moral principles between which conflict can occur. It is a strength of monism that it offers a clear method of resolving such disputes; since there is one basic principle from which all the others derive it must be to it that appeal is made in such cases. The weakness of monism is that it cannot explain the anguish that such conflicts often cause. If the clashing principles are merely secondary ones then it is unclear why the agent should be torn between them. He must regard such a conflict as merely an indication that the system of secondary principles, which he has found it useful to construct, does not always deliver a decisive verdict so that he must resort to his basic principle. For him, conflicts should not even be a cause for unease, let alone anguish.

The pluralist, however, should be in a better position to account for that anguish. The agent is under two distinct obligations, each of which has its own claim on him and each of which, perhaps, represents a distinct value which he is called on to foster. In choosing between them he will necessarily fail to honor one moral claim on him and this is what makes the choice painful.

Stressing the difficulty of such choices on a pluralist view serves to emphasize the problem with which we started: How are such conflicts to be resolved? More particularly, what form will such a resolution take? If, in a particular case, there are two independent but conflicting obligations then one of them will have to give if the conflict is to be resolved. Yet how can one of them give if both genuinely apply in this situation? . . .

MORAL PRINCIPLES AND *PRIMA FACIE* DUTIES

Ross . . . distinguishes between a *prima facie* duty and a duty proper or an actual duty. . . An agent has a *prima facie* duty to do or to forbear doing *x* in a particular situation if a moral principle enjoining or forbidding *x* applies to that situation. Thus I have a *prima facie* duty not to tell my neighbor that I like her hat, since to do so would be to tell a lie, and there is a moral principle against lying. Where more than one moral principle applies then I will have more than one *prima facie* duty; in cases of moral conflict I will not be able to fulfill all my *prima facie* duties at once. In our example I also have a *prima facie* duty not to offend my neighbor, and I shall necessarily be in breach of one of these *prima facie* duties.

Where only one moral principle applies to my situation then my actual duty—the action that would be the right one in this particular case—is determined by that moral principle. In other words, where I only have one *prima facie* duty, that duty is also my actual duty. In cases where I am under conflicting *prima facie* duties then there is not set rule by which I can determine my actual duty. In each such case I have to examine that particular situation and determine which *prima facie* duty is the most stringent, or carries the greatest weight, in these circumstances. Deciding what to do in a moral conflict is a matter of judgment which cannot be codified. In wondering what to say in response to my neighbor's query I have to weigh the *prima facie* duty not to lie against the *prima facie* duty not to be rude. . . .

. . . My mastery of a set of moral principles will serve to alert me to the fact that a moral conflict exists in cases such as that of my neighbor's hat, but that is as far as it will carry me. No appeal to moral principles can serve to resolve that conflict—at this point I am on my own.

Ross's theory also makes sense of the thought that, in a moral conflict, the agent is actually under two obligations both of which, in this case, he cannot fulfill. For both *prima facie* obligations do apply to the agent. Although he can fulfill only one of them, that does not make it any less true that the other applies to him. It can be a source of genuine regret that he has to breach one of them even if he knows his decision to be the correct one. . . .

WEIGHING OBLIGATIONS

We saw that Ross did not believe that there was any set rule by which we could judge, where obligations conflict, which is the weightier. Attempts to codify such decisions only reveal the belief that there is some computational procedure by which competing obligations can be precisely weighed—but that is just what Ross and the particularist deny. Such decisions require judgment, and judgment is only possible for someone who has a real insight into the issues involved; it cannot be replicated by the use of a decision procedure which could be grasped by someone who had no appreciation of what was at stake. Yet that is what the original account of moral principles appeared to offer—a set of rules which could be applied by anyone, whatever their sensitivity or experience, to discover the right answer.

Moreover, it is absurd to suppose that there will be a determinate answer, in each particular case, to the question which of two obligations is the weightier. There may be cases where it is impossible to judge. This should not be taken to mean that, in such cases, the two obligations are of exactly equal weight. Nor should it be supposed that there must be an answer in principle but that it is difficult to arrive at it in practice. That would be to revert to the computational model. What it means is that there may be no correct answer or, perhaps better, that the correct answer is: there is no answer. But that does not mean that it does not matter what you do. That realization may increase rather than diminish the anguish of having to choose. . . .

Particularism and Prima Facie Duties

Ross's understanding of the nature of moral principles is the only one that offers a satisfactory account of moral conflict. In such cases it accords well with what the particularist wishes to maintain. It insists that we can only reach a decision in such cases by looking at the features of the particular case in order to judge which *prima facie* duty is the weightier in these, and only in these, circumstances. It denies that moral conflicts can be settled by any mechanical decision procedure that could be applied by anyone whether or not he had insight into the moral issues. Such decisions require judgment and sensitivity.

What Ross offers is not, of course, particularism, since moral principles do play a role. First, we appeal to them in showing that there is a moral conflict to be resolved, and in determining which features are relevant to its resolution. Second, the appeal to them is decisive in cases where only one principle applies in that situation. How do I discover these principles?

According to Ross . . . we start with the particular case. We realize, say, that this action is wrong and then, perhaps, that it is so because of some particular feature—that it is a case, say, of telling a lie. Through our experience of particular cases of this kind we are enabled to grasp the *general* truth, that lying is what we might call a wrong-making characteristic. As we have already seen, that does not mean that any action which involves lying is actually wrong, for there may by other, right-making, characteristics of the action which outweigh this wrong-making characteristic on this occasion. Lying is a wrong-making characteristic in that the fact that something is a lie is *always* a reason against doing it. The fact that some course of action involved telling a lie could never be a morally neutral characteristic of the action, still less a reason in favor of doing it.

The particularist denies that we can generalize from the particular case. We cannot know, in advance, that some nonmoral characteristic must be relevant in all cases and always in the same way. The particularist can learn from Ross's hostility to a computational approach to solving moral conflicts, but he is unconvinced by his generalism.

It is important to distinguish three different positions here. First, there is Ross's view that if a characteristic matters in one place it must matter everywhere. Second, there is the weaker view that there must be at least some characteristics which always matter, even if there are others which only matter sometimes. The particularist rejects these positions. Third, there is the much weaker view that there *may* be some characteristics which, as a matter of fact, always count in the same way. The particularist need have no quarrel with this position.

Moral Principles in Ordinary Life

At the beginning of this chapter I suggested that skepticism about the utility of moral principles not only undermined a certain kind of moral theory but also appeared at odds with our ordinary moral thinking. Since that skepticism turned out to be almost wholly justified it seems that the particularist has some explaining to do. He needs to show that his theory does not unduly distort our moral thinking.

It turned out, however, that the particularist's skepticism was not about anything that might be called a moral principle, but only about what we might call the check-list conception of what a moral principle is. There may, however, be kinds of moral principle to which the particularist would have no objection. If it turns out that it is to these kinds of principles that people appeal in ordinary life, then particularism can embrace them.

It is, in my view, quite difficult to determine just what moral principles are widely accepted in our society, since the role of moral principles is a good deal more talked about than illustrated. A number of the sayings to which people subscribe, some of them with a biblical basis, are quite general in their purport and themselves require interpretation and moral sensitivity to be applied: "honor your father and mother"; love your neighbor as yourself"; "be true to yourself." The purpose of such remarks appear to be to serve to indicate areas of general moral concern, leaving us to work out how, or if, they may have a bearing on any particular case.

In order to know, for example, whether a child's action is genuinely a case of honoring its parents we need to look at all the details of the case. Take the case of the Eskimos who, it is said, used to leave old people to die on the ice once they had become too old to hunt or to make a contribution to the welfare of the tribes in other ways. At first glance such an action appears callous and uncaring in the extreme. But more knowledge of the context can completely reverse that initial impression. When this practice flourished euthanasia was essential for the survival of the tribe as a whole. This was generally recognized and accepted by everyone, including the aged parents themselves, who would initiate the chain of events leading to their own death. I understand that a father would tell his son that he wished to go on one last hunting trip; they would go out together, kill a seal, and eat it. After they had talked for a while and said their farewells, the father would tell his son to go home, while he would stretch out on the ice and wait for death. The son's part in this ritual appears to be an example of honoring one's parents.

The particularist need find nothing objectionable in an appeal to such principles. In order to see whether they truly apply we have to look at each case in all its lived detail. Nor is appeal to such a principle decisive. For the principle only gestures toward one area of moral concern; there are others.

The need for precise moral principles is most clearly seen, it is said, in the teaching of children. Even this is doubtful. The role of moral principles in the proper education of the young can easily be exaggerated. Moral lessons are not usually taught by instilling a list of principles into the child's mind. Rather, when the child does something, or witnesses some action, the parent draws attention to the morally important features of this particular action. But let it be admitted that we do teach simple moral principles to children, such as "don't steal," and that we often pretend that they are exceptionless. Does this undermine the particularist case? Not in the least. It is often necessary, in matters of prudence as well as morality, to issue blanket rules for the good of the child—"*Never* talk to strangers." It does not follow that, when they grow up, they cannot throw away the leading strings of moral principles and learn to find their own way.

But why, it might be objected, teach them moral principles in the first place if it is better, in the end, if they dispense with them? Because they are useful at the time. When people are learning to write essays they are taught rudimentary rules of style. Later they come to realize that there is no rule of style that has not been broken by some writer to considerable effect. They could not have started without stylistic guidelines of any kind—rules which are, for the most part, acceptable. As their sense of prose rhythm develops they gradually dispense with them. In the end, if they are not discarded, they prove a hindrance to good writing. And so it may be with moral principles.

CHAPTER 9

Virtue and the Ethics of Perfectionism

VIRTUE AND CHARACTER
Aristotle

Aristotle (384–322 B.C.E.) is one of the most important philosophers ever to have lived. The son of a physician, he was a student of Plato and served as tutor to Alexander the Great. He contributed important works on logic, the sciences, and virtually every area of philosophy.

In the following selection from his Nicomachean Ethics, *Aristotle begins by arguing that a happy or good life essentially involves a life of activity in accordance with virtue. He then goes on to define virtue as a disposition to avoid extremes in feeling and action. For example, in matters relating to money, the virtue of generosity stands between the extremes of extravagance and stinginess.*

Characteristics of the Good

1. *The good is the end of action.*

But let us return once again to the good we are looking for, and consider just what it could be, since it is apparently one thing in one action or craft, and another thing in another; for it is one thing in medicine, another in generalship, and so on for the rest.

What, then, is the good in each of these cases? Surely it is that for the sake of which the other things are done; and in medicine this is health, in generalship victory, in house-building a house, in another case something else, but in every action and decision it is the end, since it is for the sake of the end that everyone does the other things.

And so, if there is some end of everything that is pursued in action, this will be the good pursued in action; and if there are more ends than one, these will be the goods pursued in action.

Our argument has progressed, then, to the same conclusion [as before, that the highest end is the good]; but we must try to clarify this still more.

2.   *The good is complete.*

Though apparently there are many ends, we choose some of them, e.g., wealth, flutes and, in general, instruments, because of something else; hence it is clear that not all ends are complete. But the best good is apparently something complete. Hence, if only one end is complete, this will be what we are looking for; and if more than one are complete, the most complete of these will be what we are looking for.

CRITERIA FOR COMPLETENESS

An end pursued in itself, we say, is more complete than an end pursued because of something else; and an end that is never choiceworthy because of something else is more complete than ends that are choiceworthy both in themselves and because of this end; and hence an end that is always [choice-worthy, and also] choiceworthy in itself, never because of something else, is unconditionally complete.

3.   *Happiness meets the criteria for completeness, but other goods do not.*

Now happiness more than anything else seems unconditionally complete, since we always [choose it, and also] choose it because of itself, never because of something else.

Honor, pleasure, understanding and every virtue we certainly choose because of themselves, since we would choose each of them even if it had no further result, but we also choose them for the sake of happiness, supposing that through them we shall be happy. Happiness, by contrast, no one ever chooses for their sake, or for the sake of anything else at all.

4.   *The good is self-sufficient; so is happiness.*

The same conclusion [that happiness is complete] also appears to follow from self-sufficiency, since the complete good seems to be self-sufficient.

Now what we count as self-sufficient is not what suffices for a solitary person by himself, living an isolated life, but what suffices also for parents, children, wife and in general for friends and fellow-citizens, since a human being is a naturally political [animal]. Here, however, we must impose some limit; for if we extend the good to parents' parents and children's children and to friends of friends, we shall go on without limit; but we must examine this another time.

Anyhow, we regard something as self-sufficient when all by itself it makes a life choiceworthy and lacking nothing; and that is what we think happiness does.

5. *The good is most choiceworthy; so is happiness.*

Moreover, [the complete good is most choiceworthy, and] we think happiness is most choiceworthy of all goods, since it is not counted as one good among many. If it were counted as one among many, then, clearly, we think that the addition of the smallest of goods would make it more choiceworthy; for [the smallest good] that is added becomes an extra quantity of goods [so creating a good larger than the original good], and the larger of two goods is always more choiceworthy. [But we do not think any addition can make happiness more choiceworthy; hence it is most choiceworthy.]

Happiness, then, is apparently something complete and self-sufficient, since it is the end of the things pursued in action.

A clearer account of the good: the human soul's activity expressing virtue.

But presumably the remark that the best good is happiness is apparently something [generally] agreed, and what we miss is a clearer statement of what the best good is.

1. *If something has a function, its good depends on its function.*

Well, perhaps we shall find the best good if we first find the function of a human being. For just as the good, i.e., [doing] well, for a flautist, a sculptor, and every craftsman, and, in general, for whatever has a function and [characteristic] action, seems to depend on its function, the same seems to be true for a human being, if a human being has some function.

2. *What sorts of things have functions?*

Then do the carpenter and the leatherworker have their functions and actions, while a human being has none, and is by nature idle, without any function? Or, just as eye, hand, foot and, in general, every [bodily] part apparently has its functions, may we likewise ascribe to a human being some functions besides all of theirs?

3. *The human function.*

What, then, could this be? For living is apparently shared with plants, but what we are looking for is the special function of a human being; hence we should set aside the life of nutrition and growth. The life next in order is some sort of life of sense-perception; but this too is apparently shared, with horse, ox and every animal. The remaining possibility, then, is some sort of life of action of the [part of the soul] that has reason.

Clarification of "has reason" and "life."

Now this [part has two parts, which have reason in different ways], one as obeying the reason [in the other part], the other as itself having reason and thinking. [We intend both.] Moreover, life is also spoken of in two ways [as capacity and as activity], and we must take [a human being's special function to be] life as activity, since this seems to be called life to a fuller extent.

4.   *The human good is activity expressing virtue.*

(a) We have found, then, that the human function is the soul's activity that expresses reason [as itself having reason] or requires reason [as obeying reason]. (b) Now the function of F, e.g., of a harpist, is the same in kind, so we say, as the function of an excellent F, e.g., an excellent harpist. (c) The same is true unconditionally in every case, when we add to the function the superior achievement that expresses the virtue; for a harpist's function, e.g., is to play the harp, and a good harpist's is to do it well. (d) Now we take the human function to be a certain kind of life, and take this life to be the soul's activity and actions that express reason. (e) [Hence by (c) and (d)] the excellent man's function is to do this finely and well. (f) Each function is completed well when its completion expresses the proper virtue. (g) Therefore [by (d), (e) and (f)] the human good turns out to be the soul's activity that expresses virtue.

5.   *The good must also be complete.*

And if there are more virtues than one, the good will express the best and most complete virtue. Moreover, it will be in a complete life. For one swallow does not make a spring, nor does one day; nor, similarly, does one day or a short time make us blessed and happy. . . .

Virtues of Character in General

HOW A VIRTUE OF CHARACTER IS ACQUIRED

Virtue, then, is of two sorts, virtue of thought and virtue of character. Virtue of thought arises and grows mostly from teaching, and hence needs experience and time. Virtue of character [i.e., of *ēthos*] results from habit [*ethos*]; hence its name "ethical," slightly varied from "*ethos.*"

Virtue comes about, not by a process of nature, but by habituation.

Hence it is also clear that none of the virtues of character arises in us naturally.

1.   What is natural cannot be changed by habituation.

For if something is by nature [in one condition], habituation cannot bring it into another condition. A stone, e.g., by nature moves downwards, and habituation could not make it move upwards, not even if you threw it up ten thousand times to habituate it; nor could habituation make fire move downwards, or bring anything that is by nature in one condition into another condition.

Thus the virtues arise in us neither by nature nor against nature, but we are by nature able to acquire them, and reach our complete perfection through habit.

2.   Natural capacities are not acquired by habituation.

Further, if something arises in us by nature, we first have the capacity for it, and later display the activity. This is clear in the case of the senses; for we did not acquire them by frequent seeing or hearing, but already had them when we exercised them, and did not get them by exercising them.

Virtues, by contrast, we acquire, just as we acquire crafts, by having previously activated them. For we learn a craft by producing the same product that we must produce when we have learned it, becoming builders, e.g., by building and harpists by playing the harp; so also, then, we become just by doing just actions, temperate by doing temperate actions, brave by doing brave actions.

3.   Legislators concentrate on habituation.

What goes on in cities is evidence for this also. For the legislator makes the citizens good by habituating them, and this is the wish of every legislator; if he fails to do it well he misses his goal. [The right] habituation is what makes the difference between a good political system and a bad one.

4.   Virtue and vice are formed by good and bad actions.

Further, just as in the case of a craft, the sources and means that develop each virtue also ruin it. For playing the harp makes both good and bad harpists, and it is analogous in the case of builders and all the rest; for building well makes good builders, building badly, bad ones. If it were not so, no teacher would be needed, but everyone would be born a good or a bad craftsman.

It is the same, then, with the virtues. For actions in dealings with [other] human beings make some people just, some unjust; actions in terrifying situations and the acquired habit of fear or confidence make some brave and others cowardly. The same is true of situations involving appetites and anger;

for one or another sort of conduct in these situations makes some people temperate and gentle, others intemperate and irascible.

Conclusion: The importance of habituation.

To sum up, then, in a single account: A state [of character] arises from [the repetition of] similar activities. Hence we must display the right activities, since differences in these imply corresponding differences in the states. It is not unimportant, then, to acquire one sort of habit or another, right from our youth; rather, it is very important, indeed all-important. . . .

But our claims about habituation raise a puzzle: How can we become good without being good already?

However, someone might raise this puzzle: "What do you mean by saying that to become just we must first do just actions and to become temperate we must first do temperate actions? For if we do what is grammatical or musical, we must already be grammarians or musicians. In the same way, then, if we do what is just or temperate, we must already be just or temperate."

First reply: Conformity versus understanding.

But surely this is not so even with the crafts, for it is possible to produce something grammatical by chance or by following someone else's instructions. To be a grammarian, then, we must both produce something grammatical and produce it in the way in which the grammarian produces it, i.e., expressing grammatical knowledge that is in us.

Second reply: Crafts versus virtues.

Moreover, in any case what is true of crafts is not true of virtues. For the products of a craft determine by their own character whether they have been produced well; and so it suffices that they are in the right state when they have been produced. But for actions expressing virtue to be done temperately or justly [and hence well] it does not suffice that they are themselves in the right state. Rather, the agent must also be in the right state when he does them. First, he must know [that he is doing virtuous actions]; second, he must decide on them, and decide on them for themselves; and, third, he must also do them from a firm and unchanging state.

As conditions for having a craft these three do not count, except for the knowing itself. As a condition for having a virtue, however, the knowing counts for nothing, or [rather] for only a little, whereas the other two conditions are very important, indeed all-important. And these other two conditions are achieved by the frequent doing of just and temperate actions.

Hence actions are called just or temperate when they are the sort that a just or temperate person would do. But the just and temperate person is not the one who [merely] does these actions, but the one who also does them in the way in which just or temperate people do them.

It is right, then, to say that a person comes to be just from doing just actions and temperate from doing temperate actions; for no one has even a prospect of becoming good from failing to do them.

Virtue requires habituation, and therefore requires practice, not just theory.

The many, however, do not do these actions but take refuge in arguments, thinking that they are doing philosophy, and that this is the way to become excellent people. In this they are like a sick person who listens attentively to the doctor, but acts on none of his instructions. Such a course of treatment will not improve the state of his body; any more than will the many's way of doing philosophy improve the state of their souls.

A Virtue of Character Is a State Intermediate
Between Two Extremes, and Involving Decision

THE GENUS

Feelings, Capacities, States.   Next we must examine what virtue is. Since there are three conditions arising in the soul—feelings, capacities and states—virtue must be one of these.

By feelings I mean appetite, anger, fear, confidence, envy, joy, love, hate, longing, jealousy, pity, in general whatever implies pleasure or pain.

By capacities I mean what we have when we are said to be capable of these feelings—capable of, e.g., being angry or afraid or feeling pity.

By states I mean what we have when we are well or badly off in relation to feelings. If, e.g., our feeling is too intense or slack, we are badly off in relation to anger, but if it is intermediate, we are well off; and the same is true in the other cases.

Virtue is not a feeling . . .

First, then, neither virtues nor vices are feelings. (a) For we are called excellent or base in so far as we have virtues or vices, not in so far as we have feelings. (b) We are neither praised nor blamed in so far as we have feelings; for we do not praise the angry or the frightened person, and do not blame the person who is simply angry, but only the person who is angry in a particular way. But we are praised or blamed in so far as we have virtues or vices. (c) We are angry and afraid without decision; but the virtues are decisions of some kind, or [rather] require decision. (d) Besides, in so far as we have feelings, we are said to be moved; but in so far as we have virtues or vices, we are said to be in some condition rather than moved.

Or a capacity . . .

For these reasons the virtues are not capacities either; for we are neither called good nor called bad in so far as we are simply capable of feelings. Further, while we have capacities by nature, we do not become good or bad by nature; we have discussed this before.

But a state

If, then, the virtues are neither feelings nor capacities, the remaining possibility is that they are states. And so we have said what the genus of virtue is.

THE DIFFERENTIA

But we must say not only, as we already have, that it is a state, but also what sort of state it is.

Virtue and the Human Function.   It should be said, then, that every virtue causes its possessors to be in a good state and to perform their functions well; the virtue of eyes, e.g., makes the eyes and their functioning excellent, because it makes us see well; and similarly, the virtue of a horse makes the horse excellent, and thereby good at galloping, at carrying its rider and at standing steady in the face of the enemy. If this is true in every case, then the virtue of a human being will likewise be the state that makes a human being good and makes him perform his function well. . . .

The Numerical Mean and the Mean Relative to Us.   In everything continuous and divisible we can take more, less and equal, and each of them either in the object itself or relative to us; and the equal is some intermediate between excess and deficiency.

By the intermediate in the object I mean what is equidistant from each extremity; this is one and the same for everyone. But relative to us the intermediate is what is neither superfluous nor deficient; this is not one, and is not the same for everyone.

If, e.g., ten are many and two are few, we take six as intermediate in the object, since it exceeds [two] and is exceeded [by ten] by an equal amount, [four]; this is what is intermediate by numerical proportion. But that is not how we must take the intermediate that is relative to us. For if, e.g., ten pounds [of food] are a lot for someone to eat, and two pounds a little, it does not follow that the trainer will prescribe six, since this might also be either a little or a lot for the person who is to take it—for Milo [the athlete] a little, but for the beginner in gymnastics a lot; and the same is true for running and wrestling. In this way every scientific expert avoids excess and deficiency and seeks and chooses what is intermediate—but intermediate relative to us, not in the object.

Virtue seeks the mean relative to us: Argument from craft to virtue.

This, then, is how each science produces its product well, by focusing on what is intermediate and making the product conform to that. This, indeed, is why people regularly comment on well-made products that nothing could be added or subtracted, since they assume that excess or deficiency ruins a good [result] while the mean preserves it. Good craftsmen also, we say, focus on what is intermediate when they produce their product. And since virtue, like nature, is better and more exact than any craft, it will also aim at what is intermediate.

Arguments from the Nature of Virtue of Character.   By virtue I mean virtue of character; for this [pursues the mean because] it is concerned with feelings and actions, and these admit of excess, deficiency and an intermediate condition. We can be afraid, e.g., or be confident, or have appetites, or get angry, or feel pity, in general have pleasure or pain, both too much and too little, and in both ways not well; but [having these feelings] at the right times, about the right things, towards the right people, for the right end, and in the right way, is the intermediate and best condition, and this is proper to virtue. Similarly, actions also admit of excess, deficiency and the intermediate condition.

Now virtue is concerned with feelings and actions, in which excess and deficiency are in error and incur blame, while the intermediate condition is correct and wins praise, which are both proper features of virtue. Virtue, then, is a mean, in so far as it aims at what is intermediate.

Moreover, there are many ways to be in error, since badness is proper to what is unlimited, as the Pythagoreans pictured it, and good to what is limited; but there is only one way to be correct. That is why error is easy and correctness hard, since it is easy to miss the target and hard to hit it. And so for this reason also excess and deficiency are proper to vice, the mean to virtue; "for we are noble in only one way, but bad in all sorts of ways."

Definition of Virtue.   Virtue, then, is (a) a state that decides, (b) [consisting] in a mean, (c) the mean relative to us, (d) which is defined by reference to reason, (e) i.e., to the reason by reference to which the intelligent person would define it. It is a mean between two vices, one of excess and one of deficiency.

It is a mean for this reason also: Some vices miss what is right because they are deficient, others because they are excessive, in feelings or in actions, while virtue finds and chooses what is intermediate.

Hence, as far as its substance and the account stating its essence are concerned, virtue is a mean; but as far as the best [condition] and the good [result] are concerned, it is an extremity.

The definition must not be misapplied to cases in which there is no mean.

But not every action or feeling admits of the mean. For the names of some automatically include baseness, e.g., spite, shamelessness, envy [among feelings], and adultery, theft, murder, among actions. All of these and similar things are called by these names because they themselves, not their excesses or deficiencies, are base.

Hence in doing these things we can never be correct, but must invariably be in error. We cannot do them well or not well—e.g., by committing adultery with the right woman at the right time in the right way; on the contrary, it is true unconditionally that to do any of them is to be in error.

[To think these admit of a mean], therefore, is like thinking that unjust or cowardly or intemperate action also admits of a mean, an excess and a deficiency. For then there would be a mean of excess, a mean of deficiency, an excess of excess and a deficiency of deficiency.

Rather, just as there is no excess or deficiency of temperance or of bravery, since the intermediate is a sort of extreme [in achieving the good], so also there is no mean of these [vicious actions] either, but whatever way anyone does them, he is in error. For in general there is no mean of excess or of deficiency, and no excess or deficiency of a mean.

The Definition of Virtue as a Mean Applies to the Individual Virtues

However, we must not only state this general account but also apply it to the particular cases. For among accounts concerning actions, though the general ones are common to more cases, the specific ones are truer, since actions are about particular cases, and our account must accord with these. Let us, then, find these from the chart.

CLASSIFICATION OF VIRTUES OF CHARACTER

Virtues Concerned with Feelings.   1. First, in feelings of fear and confidence the mean is bravery. The excessively fearless person is nameless (and in fact many cases are nameless), while the one who is excessively confident is rash; the one who is excessively afraid and deficient in confidence is cowardly.

2. In pleasures and pains, though not in all types, and in pains less than in pleasures, the mean is temperance and the excess intemperance. People deficient in pleasure are not often found, which is why they also lack even a name; let us call them insensible.

Virtues Concerned with External Goods.   3. In giving and taking money the mean is generosity, the excess wastefulness and the deficiency ungenerosity. Here the vicious people have contrary excesses and defects; for the wasteful person spends to excess and is deficient in taking, whereas the ungenerous person takes to excess and is deficient in spending. At the moment we are speaking in outline and summary. . . .

4. In questions of money there are also other conditions. Another mean is magnificence; for the magnificent person differs from the generous by being concerned with large matters, while the generous person is concerned with small. The excess is ostentation and vulgarity, and the deficiency niggardliness, and these differ from the vices related to generosity. . . .

5. In honor and dishonor the mean is magnanimity, the excess something called a sort of vanity, and the deficiency pusillanimity.

6. And just as we said that generosity differs from magnificence in its concern with small matters, similarly there is a virtue concerned with small honors, differing in the same way from magnanimity, which is concerned with great honors. For honor can be desired either in the right way or more or less than is right. If someone desires it to excess, he is called an honor-lover, and if his desire is deficient he is called indifferent to honor, but if he is intermediate he has no name. The corresponding conditions have no name either, except the condition of the honor-lover, which is called honor-loving.

This is why people at the extremes claim the intermediate area. Indeed, we also sometimes call the intermediate person an honor-lover, and sometimes call him indifferent to honor; and sometimes we praise the honor-lover, sometimes the person indifferent to honor. . . .

Virtues Concerned with Social Life.   7. Anger also admits of an excess, deficiency and mean. These are all practically nameless; but since we call the intermediate person mild, let us call the mean mildness. Among the extreme people let the excessive person be irascible, and the vice be irascibility, and let the deficient person be a sort of inirascible person, and the deficiency be inirascibility.

There are three other means, somewhat similar to one another, but different. For they are all concerned with association in conversations and actions, but differ in so far as one is concerned with truth-telling in these areas, the other two with sources of pleasure, some of which are found in amusement, and the others in daily life in general. Hence we should also discuss these states, so that we can better observe that in every case the mean is praiseworthy, while the extremes are neither praiseworthy nor correct, but blameworthy. Most of these cases are also nameless, and we must try, as in the other cases also, to make names ourselves, to make things clear and easy to follow.

8. In truth-telling, then, let us call the intermediate person truthful, and the mean truthfulness; pretense that overstates will be boastfulness, and the

person who has it boastful; pretense that understates will be self-deprecation, and the person who has it self-deprecating.

9. In sources of pleasure in amusements let us call the intermediate person witty, and the condition wit; the excess buffoonery and the person who has it a buffoon; and the deficient person a sort of boor and the state boorishness.

10. In the other sources of pleasure, those in daily life, let us call the person who is pleasant in the right way friendly, and the mean state friendliness. If someone goes to excess with no [further] aim he will be ingratiating; if he does it for his own advantage, a flatterer. The deficient person, unpleasant in everything, will be a sort of quarrelsome and ill-tempered person.

Mean States That Are Not Virtues.   11. There are also means in feelings and concerned with feelings: shame, e.g., is not a virtue, but the person prone to shame as well as the virtuous person we have described receives praise. For here also one person is called intermediate, and another—the person excessively prone to shame, who is ashamed about everything—is called excessive; the person who is deficient in shame or never feels shame at all is said to have no sense of disgrace; and the intermediate one is called prone to shame.

12. Proper indignation is the mean between envy and spite; these conditions are concerned with pleasure and pain at what happens to our neighbors. For the properly indignant person feels pain when someone does well undeservedly; the envious person exceeds him by feeling pain when anyone does well, while the spiteful person is so deficient in feeling pain that he actually enjoys [other people's misfortunes].

VIRTUE AND MORAL THEORY
Bernard Mayo

Bernard Mayo is author of Ethics and the Moral Life *(1958). In the following selection from that book, he contrasts moral theories that are concerned primarily with questions of* what to do *with those whose main focus is on* how to be. *Mayo contends that theories of the latter sort, which we find in the writings*

From Bernard Mayo, *Ethics and the Moral Life* (London: Macmillan, 1958). Reprinted by permission of Bernard Mayo.

of Plato and Aristotle, can provide us with what he calls a "unity of character."
Thus, instead of providing principles and rules telling us what to do, moral the-
ories such as Aristotle's tell us to be a person of a certain sort, and Mayo offers
the lives of such figures as St. Francis and Buddha as models.

The philosophy of moral principles, which is characteristic of Kant and the post-Kantian era, is something of which hardly a trace exists in Plato. . . . Plato says nothing about rules or principles or laws, except when he is talking politics. Instead he talks about virtues and vices, and about certain types of human character. The key word in Platonic ethics is Virtue; the key word in Kantian ethics is Duty. And modern ethics is a set of footnotes, not to Plato, but to Kant. . . .

Attention to the novelists can be a welcome correction to a tendency of philosophical ethics of the last generation or two to lose contact with the ordinary life of man which is just what the novelists, in their own way, are concerned with. Of course there are writers who can be called in to illustrate problems about Duty (Graham Greene is a good example). But there are more who perhaps never mention the words duty, obligation or principle. Yet they are all concerned—Jane Austen, for instance entirely and absolutely—with the moral qualities or defects of their heroes and heroines and other characters. This points to a radical one-sidedness and the philosophers' account of morality in terms of principles: it takes little or no account of qualities, of what people *are*. It is just here that the old-fashioned word Virtue used to have a place; and it is just here that the work of Plato and Aristotle can be instructive. Justice, for Plato, though it is closely connected with acting according to law, does not *mean* acting according to law; it is a quality of character, and a just action is one such as a just man would do. Telling the truth, for Aristotle, is not, as it was for Kant, fulfilling an obligation; again it is a quality of character, or, rather, a whole range of qualities of character, some of which may actually be defects, such as tactlessness, boastfulness, and so on—a point which can be brought out, in terms of principles, only with the greatest complexity and artificiality, but quite simply and naturally in terms of character.

If we wish to enquire about Aristotle's moral views, it is no use looking for a set of principles. Of course we can find *some* principles to which he must have subscribed—for instance that one ought not to commit adultery. But what we find much more prominently is a set of character-traits, a list of certain types of person—the courageous man, the niggardly man, the boaster, the lavish spender and so on. The basic moral question, for Aristotle, is not, What shall I do? but, What shall I be?

These contrasts between doing and being, negative and positive, and modern as against Greek morality were noted by John Stuart Mill; I quote from the *Essay on Liberty*:

Christian morality (so-called) has all the characters of a reaction; it is, in great part, a protest against Paganism. Its ideal is negative rather than positive, passive rather than active; Innocence rather than Nobleness; Abstinence from Evil, rather than energetic Pursuit of the Good; in its precepts (as has been well said) "Thou shalt not" predominates unduly over "Thou shalt . . ." Whatever exists of magnanimity, highmindedness, personal dignity, even the sense of honour, is derived from the purely human, not the religious part of our education, and never could have grown out of a standard of ethics in which the only worth, professedly recognised, is that of obedience.

Of course, there are connections between being and doing. It is obvious that a man cannot just *be;* he can only be what he is by doing what he does; his moral qualities are ascribed to him because of his actions, which are said to manifest those qualities. But the point is that an ethics of Being must include this obvious fact, that Being involves Doing; whereas an ethics of Doing, such as I have been examining, may easily overlook it. As I have suggested, a morality of principles is concerned only with what people do or fail to do, since that is what rules are for. And as far as this sort of ethics goes, people might well have no moral qualities at all except the possession of principles and the will (and capacity) to act accordingly.

When we speak of a moral quality such as courage, and say that a certain action was courageous, we are not merely saying something about the action. We are referring not so much to what is done, as to the kind of person by whom we take it to have been done. We connect, by means of imputed motives and intentions, with the character of the agent as courageous. This explains, incidentally, why both Kantians and Utilitarians encounter, in their different ways, such difficulties in dealing with motives, which their principles, on the face of it, have no room for. A Utilitarian, for example, can only praise a courageous action in some such way as this: the action is of a sort such as a person of courage is likely to perform, and courage is a quality of character the cultivation of which is likely to increase rather than diminish the sum total of human happiness. But Aristotelians have no need of such circumlocution. For them a courageous action just is one which proceeds from and manifests a certain type of character, and is praised because such a character trait is good, or better than others, or is a virtue. An evaluative criterion is sufficient: there is no need to look for an imperative criterion as well, or rather instead, according to which it is not the character which is good, but the cultivation of the character which is right. . . .

No doubt the fundamental moral question is just "What ought I to do?" And according to the philosophy of moral principles, the answer (which must be an imperative "Do this") must be derived from a conjunction of premises consisting (in the simplest case) firstly of a rule, or universal imperative, enjoining (or forbidding) all actions of a certain type in situations of a certain type, and secondly, a statement to the effect that this is a situation of that type, falling under that rule. In practice the emphasis may be on supplying only one of these premises, the other being assumed or taken for granted: one may answer the question "What ought I to do?" either by quoting a rule which I am to adopt, or by showing that my case is legislated for by a rule which I do adopt. To take a previous example of moral perplexity, if I am in doubt whether to tell the truth about his condition to a dying man, my doubt may be resolved by showing that the case comes under a rule about the avoidance of unnecessary suffering, which I am assumed to accept. But if the case is without precedent in my moral career, my problem may be soluble only by adopting a new principle about what I am to do now and in the future about cases of this kind.

This second possibility offers a connection with moral ideas. Suppose my perplexity is not merely an unprecedented situation which I could cope with by adopting a new rule. Suppose the new rule is thoroughly inconsistent with my existing moral code. This may happen, for instance, if the moral code is one to which I only pay lip-service; if . . . its authority is not yet internalised, or if it has ceased to be so; it is ready for rejection, but its final rejection awaits a moral crisis such as we are assuming to occur. What I now need is not a rule for deciding how to act in this situation and others of its kind. I need a whole set of rules, a complete morality, new principles to live by.

Now according to the philosophy of moral character, there is another way of answering the fundamental question "What ought I to do?" Instead of quoting a rule, we quote a quality of character, a virtue: we say "Be brave," or "Be patient" or "Be lenient." We may even say "Be a man": if I am in doubt, say, whether to take a risk, and someone says "Be a man," meaning a morally sound man, in this case a man of sufficient courage. (Compare the very different ideal invoked in "Be a gentleman." I shall not discuss whether this is a *moral* ideal.) Here, too, we have the extreme cases, where a man's moral perplexity extends not merely to a particular situation but to his whole way of living. And now the question "What ought I to do?" turns into the question "What ought I to be?"—as, indeed, it was treated in the first place. ("Be brave.") It is answered, not by quoting a rule or a set of rules, but by describing a quality of character or a type of person. And here the ethics of character gains a practical simplicity which offsets the greater logical simplicity of the ethics of principles. We do not have to give a list of characteristics or virtues, as we might list a set of principles. We can give a unity to our answer.

Of course we can in theory give a unity to our principles: this is implied by speaking of a *set* of principles. But if such a set is to be a system and not merely aggregate, the unity we are looking for is a logical one, namely the possibility that some principles are deductible from others, and ultimately from one. But the attempt to construct a deductive moral system is notoriously difficult, and in any case ill-founded. Why should we expect that all rules of conduct should be ultimately reducible to a few?

Saints and Heroes

But when we are asked "What shall I be?" we can readily give a unity to our answer, though not a logical unity. It is the unity of character. A person's character is not merely a list of dispositions; it has the organic unity of something that is more than the sum of its parts. And we can say, in answer to our morally perplexed questioner, not only "Be this" or "Be that," but also "Be like So-and-So"—where So-and-So is either an ideal type of character, or else an actual person taken as representative of the ideal, an exemplar. Examples of the first are Plato's "just man" in the Republic; Aristotle's man of practical wisdom, in the Nicomachean Ethics; Augustine's citizen of the City of God; the good Communist; the American way of life (which is a collective expression for a type of character). Examples of the second kind, the exemplar, are Socrates, Christ, Buddha, St. Francis, the heroes of epic writers and of novelists. Indeed the idea of the Hero, as well as the idea of the Saint, are very much the expression of this attitude to morality. Heroes and saints are not merely people who did things. They are people whom we are expected, and expect ourselves, to imitate. And imitating them means not merely doing what they did; it means being like them. Their status is not in the least like that of legislators whose laws we admire; for the character of a legislator is irrelevant to our judgment about his legislation. The heroes and saints did not merely give us principles to live by (though some of them did that as well): they gave us examples to follow.

Kant, as we should expect, emphatically rejects this attitude as "fatal to morality." According to him, examples serve only to render *visible* an instance of the moral principle, and thereby to demonstrate its practical feasibility. But every exemplar, such as Christ himself, must be judged by the independent criterion of the moral law, before we are entitled to recognize him as worthy of imitation. I am not suggesting that the subordination of exemplars to principles is incorrect, but that it is one-sided and fails to do justice to a large area of moral experience.

Imitation can be more or less successful. And this suggests another defect of the ethics of principles. It has no room for ideals, except the ideal of a perfect set of principles (which, as a matter of fact, is intelligible only in terms of an ideal character or way of life), and the ideal of perfect conscientiousness (which is itself a character-trait). This results, of course, from the "black-

or-white" nature of moral verdicts based on rules. There are no degrees by which we approach or recede from the attainment of a certain quality or virtue; if there were not, the word "ideal" would have no meaning. Heroes and saints are not people whom we try to be *just* like, since we know that is impossible. It is precisely because it is impossible for ordinary human beings to achieve the same qualities as the saints, and in the same degree, that we do set them apart from the rest of humanity. It is enough if we try to be a little like them. . . .

A DEFENSE OF PERFECTIONISM
Edmund L. Pincoffs

Edmund L. Pincoffs (1919–1991) was author of Quandaries and Virtues *(1986) and* Philosophy of Law: A Brief Introduction *(1991). Pincoffs defends a version of moral perfectionism, according to which the moral permissibility of an action depends on the extent to which the action accords with standards of excellence. On this theory, considerations of virtue serve as the standards of excellence governing the morality of an action. After presenting his theory, Pincoffs argues that it should be distinguished from various mistaken forms of perfectionism—what he calls Brittle Perfectionism, Arbitrary Perfectionism, and Spiritual Egotism.*

In what follows, I will defend a form of virtue-oriented ethics against criticisms that it is, in some damaging sense, a kind of perfectionism. The thesis I want to defend is that in talk and thought about what ought to be done, there is a certain kind of consideration that governs moral acceptability—a kind that has to do with the virtues and vices. Whether this thesis, more fully made out below, is one that is defensible, all things considered, I do not know and certainly do not try to show here. My objective is merely to show that, although it is perfectionistic in a sense that I will explain, it is a morally defensible form of perfectionism.

Ethical theorists have tended not to pay much attention to a range of considerations that often play a crucial role in reflection, debate, and justification. Quite often, a particular course of action or a policy is characterized as unkind, cowardly, cruel, dishonest, vindictive, unjust, disloyal, or selfish. These terms, plus a few more, and their positive counterparts—kind, honest, and so on—form a class, the size of which is indefinitely, but not very, large. Let us call this class the class of virtue and vice considerations. Each such consideration points to a particular quality of an act or policy, a quality that makes the doing of (or the agreeing to) it morally desirable or morally questionable. The introduction of a virtue consideration (for short) has a tendency to give shape to the subsequent discussion, since it introduces rules of relevance. Thus, to say of a proposal to sell sophisticated arms to Taiwan that it would be disloyal to Mainland China is to introduce a line of discussion that will focus on rather different, primarily historical, considerations than would have been relevant if the contention had been that the policy was dishonest. That discussion, in turn, would be a different one from the discussion of whether selling arms to Taiwan would be an unfair policy with respect to Mainland China or that it would be a cowardly policy or a merely selfish one. The discussion of whether an action or a policy is morally acceptable or unacceptable often turns on such considerations. These considerations have claim, at the least, to being weighty ones in moral discourse, as can be seen by reflecting on their relation to ones having to do with rights and duties.

Suppose it is contended that Mainland China has a right that we not sell arms to Taiwan. This contention appeals either to a supposed or to an actual network of rights and duties that result from agreed upon or understood rules or principles that govern relations between us and Mainland China or between nations generally. But in addition to the question of whether a right would be violated, there is the question of what the moral import would be of violating the right. This is a question that turns back on the agent, so to speak, and critically probes his motives. To violate the right of Mainland China might be morally more acceptable if at the same time the policy is what loyalty to Taiwan requires or if the policy is motivated by concern for the well-being of Taiwan, supposing that Taiwan is under a threat of invasion. To admit to violating a right is to concede that one has the burden of moral proof in adopting the course of action in question; but the admission does not dispose of the problem of what to do. It does not dispose of the problem because what is still at issue is what morally follows, if we do what it is proposed that we should do. We do not want to do what is cruel, unjust, cowardly, disloyal, and so forth. But if, on the other hand, none of this were to follow, if no virtue considerations could be brought to bear adversely on the course of action; then, even though a right is being violated, the course of action is morally permissible. Rights talk, in short, must be qualified by the sort of talk we engage in when we make use of virtue considerations.

It is possible, then, to hold a weak thesis to the effect that virtue considerations have weight, that they cannot be ignored, or that they qualify in some way the moral acceptability of a proposed action or policy. Or a stronger thesis can be maintained to the effect that they govern moral acceptability. I will defend the stronger thesis against "perfectionist" criticisms. To say that virtue considerations govern acceptability is to say that it is a necessary and sufficient condition of the moral acceptability of an action or a course of action that it not violate the requirements of the relevant set of virtue considerations. The "not violating" of those requirements is a relative matter. It may be that some balancing of the considerations must be done: some may have to give way, more or less, to others. In the happy circumstances when there is no conflict between virtue considerations with respect to a course of action, we may say that the course of action or the policy is the one that is fully acceptable. Thus, to show that it is morally fully acceptable that we sell sophisticated arms to Taiwan, we would have to show that there are no relevant virtue considerations that oppose it and that the relevant considerations approve it. Needless to say, it is difficult to show that a course of action is fully acceptable, and we may more typically have to settle for trying to show that it is acceptable—that, for example, even though the policy is arguably a bit unfair to the People's Republic of China, it is required by loyalty to Taiwan and by the sense that not to supply Taiwan with what would prevent its being invaded would be callous and, given the history of our relationships, ungrateful.

In what sense is the thesis that virtue considerations govern the moral acceptability of actions or policies ("the Thesis" for short) a perfectionistic one? Perfectionistic theories cover a very wide range. They differ on the criteria of perfection, on who or what is to be perfected, on who is to do the perfecting, and on how the perfecting is to be accomplished. Not only may the criteria of excellence in which perfection is thought to exist differ, but the height of the standards of excellence may vary. The legendary honesty of Lincoln may set a higher standard of honest behavior than that set by the average professor of philosophy. Perfectionistic doctrines may have primarily or exclusively to do with the perfection of the agent or of some group or of everyone in general. The agent of perfection may be a person or a group or everyone or God. And perfection may be brought about in a variety of ways.

I will take it that moral perfectionism, in its most general form, as it bears on actions and policies, is the doctrine that the overall acceptability or unacceptability of an action or policy is to be determined by the extent to which the action or policy accords with standards of excellence. That is a sufficiently general understanding to incorporate the differences in criteria, objects, agents, and means of perfection that I have mentioned. To say that virtue considerations govern moral acceptability is, then, a perfectionistic position. It may not be the most general perfectionistic position, since other criteria are imaginable; but it is very wide and open. It does not insist that any particular moral criterion—for example, justice—has sole claim to relevance when the question is what ought to be done. And it posits no hierarchical relations between the criteria, or considerations, whose relevance it maintains.

No ethical theory that I know of rules out virtue considerations as being relevant to moral decision or justification; but they may be systematically relegated to the periphery of moral thought. This may happen by making them conceptually vacuous, as deriving all of their force from "more fundamental" conceptions: rules, principles, rights, and duties. Or it may happen by promoting virtue considerations to the region of the supererogatory, a region that has to do, not with what is morally most significant, but with what is a kind of moral luxury: the admirable-if-it-occurs. A reason for relegating virtue considerations to the periphery may be the justified suspicion that they are perfectionistic, combined with the unjustified notion that perfectionistic considerations should not have a place at the center of moral concern. They should yield that place to sterner matters, matters that have to do, not with what would be more or less perfect, but with what is required of us, as morally mandatory. Achieving excellence, it might be thought, is fine enough, but we may pursue it with a clear conscience only after we have attended to our duties and met our obligations. What those are is the first and fundamental question. Let me sketch an alternative way of thinking about the weight of moral considerations.

As a preliminary, let me remark that in thinking about excellence, we must also think about the absence of excellence and the various ways in which we can be far from excellence. We can say that an act is a courageous or loyal thing to do only against a background understanding of what it is for an act to be cowardly or disloyal, so that we can think of courageous acts as having a preferred place on a continuum that leads all the way from "cowardly" to "indifferent" to "courageous." So we must not think that a consideration's being perfectionistic amounts only to its being concerned with the attainment of the high end of the scale. It may also have to do with the low end—with not doing what is morally to be avoided. Perfectionistic considerations should not, then, be regarded as being concerned only with moral luxuries, with pictures of ideal behavior, or with the emulation of ideal moral models. This is not at all to rule out the relevance to moral deliberation and justification of such notions; but it is to say that if the objection to perfectionism is that it is only concerned with this end of the continuum, then the objection is misconceived; it fails to find the mark.

One way to assess the weight of moral considerations is to think not so much in terms merely of what I ought to do simpliciter, what my rights and duties are, but of what I would be by doing or agreeing to a given thing. What has weight with me is what I think of myself as being. This is the side of moral deliberation that tends to be overlooked or underplayed by contemporary ethical theories. If I do not care what I am or am becoming, whether I am fair or unfair, cruel or kind, honest or dishonest, then moral talk will have little significance for me. To whatever extent I have moral standards or ideals, to whatever extent I have aversions to selves that I could become, I will find virtue considerations weighty.

Virtue considerations are sometimes thought of as moral principles. . . . But the way in which they function as principles must be set off rather carefully from the way in which some other sorts of principles operate. The point to notice is that these principles are substantive, in the sense that living by them is conceptually tied to being a certain sort of person, where the sort in question is morally significant. It will be helpful to contrast the principle that one should do what is required by a virtue consideration with the principle that one should so act as to maximize happiness and minimize misery. The latter principle can be adopted out of a variety of motives. A person may hope to gain glory by increasing the general happiness or power or the love of the populace. He will be nonetheless an effective advocate of the principle for any of that. The principle that one should act in this happiness-maximizing way should be distinguished from the principle that one should be benevolent toward others. Aside from the points that the happiness-maximizing principle is understood and advocated as the sole principle that ought to govern action and that the benevolence principle generally is not, there is the less-often-noted point that benevolence has to do with a particular kind of motive and happiness maximizing does not.

The argument has often been offered against utilitarianism that if the public happiness is taken as the sole end, a variety of morally questionable means could be used to achieve it: for example, the enslavement of a minority, the punishment of the innocent, or sub-rosa coercion. What should also be apparent is that being a good utilitarian is consistent with being a morally undesirable sort of person. It is not necessarily the case that the person who wants and strives for the general happiness is therefore benevolent. He could even be misanthropic and, in some Kafka-like scenario, think that by increasing the general average happiness, he will at the same time be contributing to the general decline of humanity and to its disappearance from the face of the earth.

A parallel point can be made about being a formalist, the sort of Kantian who insists on the first formulation of the categorical imperative and forgets the second. The first formulation, which has to do solely with the consistency of self-legislated universal rules, can be adhered to by a person of vile moral character who happens at the same time to be consistent—consistently vile. The second formulation, on the other hand, comes close to being a virtue consideration. It would be so if it told us to be respectful of other people, to be concerned about them. Perhaps that is what Kant means. I think that it is. But he says to treat everyone, including ourselves, as ends in themselves and never merely as means. While it may require a stretch of the imagination, it is still conceivable that even this principle could be obeyed for the wrong motives and by a person whose moral character is far from desirable. A person might treat others and himself as ends in themselves without any deeper concern for them or for himself than that he thought that was what was required of him by God (or perhaps by the ghost of Kant). He could even think that the treating of persons as ends in themselves was commanded by Satan, whom he worships and feels bound to obey, but who has malevolent intentions toward the human race. He could treat people as ends in themselves out of a sort of moral ennui in which he picks up that principle as no more tiring than the others that are offered to him.

But let us return to the question of whether the contention that virtue considerations govern moral acceptability (the Thesis) is a defensible form of moral perfectionism. In pursuing that question, I will take up three forms, or varieties, of perfectionism, corresponding to the chief objections to an undifferentiated "perfectionism": Brittle Perfectionism, Arbitrary Perfectionism, and Spiritual Egotism. These are, respectively, theories that require the attainment of an impossible ideal of perfection, theories that arbitrarily impose standards of perfection on persons who have a right to choose their own standards, and theories that emphasize a kind of psyche polishing that can rightly be regarded as a form of egotism. My conclusion will be not only that the Thesis has no necessary connection with theories of these kinds but also that it is a mistake to confuse the Thesis with any of these forms of perfectionism. The Thesis is, just the same, a perfectionistic one.

The advocate of the Thesis is not, of course, committed to the view that we must, on pain of some kind of moral failing, attain *perfect* honesty, justice, courage, or loyalty. It is nevertheless worth exploring Brittle Perfectionism a little so as to point up the ease with which one could come to think of the Thesis as a form of Brittle Perfectionism. To begin with, we should notice that it is not really clear what kind of impossibility is in question when it is said that it is impossible to attain perfect honesty or justice. Why is it *impossible* to attain perfect honesty, say? Is the impossibility in question an empirical one, a conceptual one, or some other kind? Is it so *difficult* to attain perfect honesty that we can never quite manage it, or is "perfect honesty" an incoherent notion, so that we don't know what it would mean to attain it? With respect to empirical impossibility, trying to be honest *does* seem to be like trying to overcome "real," not conceptual, difficulties. We can recognize that it is not enough to tell the truth in everyday contexts, not to filch from the cash register, or not to cheat at poker. We could pass these tests and still not be honest. But why is this so? Why is it hard, perhaps impossible, to be *completely* honest? It seems that no matter what we do or don't do, the question can still be asked whether we could not be more honest than we are.

The answer might be given that honesty is an open-textured concept: no formula will provide, in the end, all of the requirements for being honest. If we say that being honest is being open and undeceptive, then the problem descends to the question of what it is to be open and undeceptive. And if we offer formulae for those notions, the terms used in the formulae will be found to be open-textured too. We cannot find the end of that road. But is not our problem a general one? Very many of the terms in natural language are open-textured. Questions can be raised about what really is a mountain or a desk, as well as about what really is justice or honesty. If our problem is a special case of the general problem that many of the terms of natural language are open-textured, then it is not a problem that should disturb us. For just as we have no problem in deciding that the Rockies are mountains, we have no trouble in deciding that Lincoln was honest. Honest people are people who behave honestly, and we can "go on from there." By pointing to the open texture of virtue terms, we have not explained just why or in what sense it is very hard to fulfill the requirements of justice, honesty, or courage.

It is not a problem of open texture, but of "high redefinition" that makes perfect honesty impossible to attain. No matter what even an Abe Lincoln does in trying to be honest, he can still ask himself whether he is being truly honest. This is so because no matter what standards he attains, the standards can always be cranked up another notch, so that he can never reach *the* highest standard. Jones's maximal honesty—paying debts and telling the truth—may be Smith's minimal honesty, and Smith's minimal standard may fall below Green's minimal standard. The open question, then, is a question of the relative height of standards. If, in principle, the standard can always be set higher than "the top" standard, perfection can never be attained. Brittle Perfectionism thus requires the attainment of what it is impossible to attain. Since, however, the advocate of the Thesis need not also be engaged in the business of meeting the requirements of an ever-receding top standard, the Thesis is not a form of Brittle Perfectionism.

The second theory-defining objection, which defines Arbitrary Perfectionism, is that the standard of perfection is set by fiat, without regard for reasoned objections. Arbitrary Perfectionism would, presumably, attempt to regiment everyone under the banners of some improvement campaign to which people in a free society need not agree: a puritanical community, say, or a community of stoics or one of saints.

The question is whether the Thesis, by insisting that virtue considerations govern, becomes or in some way invites Arbitrary Perfectionism. This raises, in turn, the question of whether appeals to honesty, justice, and so forth, invoke arbitrary standards, standards that can then only be imposed on everyone by fiat. In approaching the issue, it is useful to bear in mind a distinction. The Thesis does not hold that any particular act or policy is morally acceptable or unacceptable. It holds, rather, that to justify choice or rejection, one must show that the choice or rejection accords with the requirements of the virtue considerations. Therefore the Thesis is perfectionistic at the level of criteria of justification, rather than at the level of choice or decision. It is, thus, not an objection to the Thesis that it would or would not approve of this or that choice. . . .

An example of Arbitrary Perfectionism is the theory that speaks of the "real nature" of human beings as something that we must strive toward. This is to introduce a supposed standard under which it is possible to list just those qualities that the writer or speaker approves as virtues. The notion may be, as in Saint Thomas, that we have a God-given nature that we must do our best to attain. It may be that we are urged, as by Epictetus, to "follow our natures." Or it may be that, in some inverted sense of moral perfection, following our natures becomes, as for Freud, the attainment of an ideal of mental health. Self-realizational ethics, too, may provide us with examples of Arbitrary Perfectionism, since the choice between possible selves to be realized may be an arbitrary one.

It could be argued that arbitrariness is inevitable in insisting that virtue considerations govern the acceptability of actions and policies, since that insistence amounts to saying that the action or policy that is worthy of choice is the one that approximates most closely to a certain arbitrarily chosen *ideal*. The ideal is, so it might be thought, a certain pattern of virtues in action or policy. It must be an arbitrarily chosen pattern, since there is no general agreement on which pattern is most desirable. Whichever pattern we choose is, thus, chosen arbitrarily and becomes the ideal against which we measure the moral acceptability or unacceptability of the act or policy. However, this argument presupposes, falsely, that to say of an action or policy that it is the alternative most favored by the virtue considerations is to appeal tacitly to some ideal pattern of virtues. It does not follow from the admission of multiple criteria of assessment—the virtue considerations—that there is some preferred pattern, an ideal, that must be exemplified by that which is chosen. It is possible to honor virtue in the absence of a picture of some ideal model of action toward which we must move. One need not have any such ideal in order to assess actions and policies along the different parameters of justice, loyalty, noncruelty, and so on.

I turn now to the third theory-defining objection to perfectionism: that it is what John Dewey calls "spiritual egotism." "Some," Dewey says, "are preoccupied with the state of their character, concerned for the purity of their motives and the goodness of their souls. The exultation of conceit which sometimes accompanies this absorption can produce a corrosive inhumanity which exceeds the possibilities of any other known form of selfishness."[1]

One kind of spiritual egotist, Dewey might agree, is the "moral athlete" approved by James Walker, Francis Wayland, and other nineteenth-century textbook writers. Some of these earnest men convey a picture of the world as an arena in which people are engaged in the testing of virtue, like athletes striving for the greatest distance or the fastest time. Another sort of spiritual egotist is the perfectionist who regards detachment from political affairs as a necessary condition of the attainment of his ideal. . . .

The charge of "spiritual egotism," if well founded, converts an apparent advantage of the Thesis into a disadvantage. An apparent advantage of the Thesis over other conceptions of what it is to justify a moral conclusion is that it bridges the supposed gap between the description of an act or policy and the conclusion that it ought to be done or adopted. It performs this feat, supposedly, by describing the feat in such a way—for example, as dishonest—that if I do it, I am to that extent dishonest. But since I ought not to do what is dishonest, I ought not do this act. It also bridges a supposed gap between "cognition" and motivation, since in coming to know that the act would be dishonest, I come to know that it is something I do not want to do, given that I do not want to be a person of bad character, that is, a person who is not worthy of preference by others. But this double gap-bridging feat can be looked at in another way, the way in which the Deweyan critic might look at it. For he can say that the gaps may be bridged only because my whole moral orientation is askew. In thinking about whether what I am doing is truly honest or kind, I could be concerned just with the perfecting of my own image. I could be a narcissistic moral preener whose motivation is thus morally questionable. The virtue considerations bridge the gap, if they do, because they supposedly look both ways at once. They apply both to me and to the act that I propose to do. If the act has a certain characteristic, then, thus far, I have that characteristic if I do it: if it is kind, I am thus far kind. What, then, is my motivation? Is it to have that characteristic, or is it to do an act that has that characteristic? If it is to have that characteristic—kindness, say—then what is the source of that motive, the motive to do what is kind? Is it a morally defensible motive, or is it pride in the portrait of perfection that I am thereby touching up?

Another way to pose the issue is by drawing a contrast between "self-regarding" and "other-regarding" considerations. Is the point that what I propose to do is dishonest a remark about what I would be if I were to do it or about the effect that it would have on other people if I did it? To whatever extent it is self-regarding, Dewey could hold, it presents a morally suspect, because possibly "spiritually egotistic," reason for doing the act.

What defense of the Thesis can be offered, then, against the charge that it is a form of "spiritual egotism"? The answer is reasonably clear, once the charge is understood. For the charge amounts to this: that whoever holds that the virtue considerations govern moral acceptability of what we ought to do runs a certain *danger*. He can come to make the virtue considerations the accomplices of a morally repugnant way of thinking. Instead of thinking simply what is the honest or kind or just thing to do, he can think whether by doing the proposed act, he will embellish his character in this or that way. He is concerned to polish up his attainments of justice, honesty, or kindness so that he can be satisfied with the image of self that he then sees. He will *do* what is honest, and so forth, but his motives will be narcissistic ones.

The answer is that the seen danger is a real danger, that we should be on our guard against it, that we should be continually aware of it. It is, however, far from a necessary consequence of accepting the Thesis that one must fall victim to "spiritual egotism." Even though the virtue considerations may *seem* to be inherently self-regarding, even though arguing that if I did this or that, I would be being cruel may *seem* to be taking too much interest in my own moral image, there is no necessary narcissistic self-regarding interpretation, no necessity for image burnishing. A more straightforward interpretation is that what is wrong is not that the act would put blotches and smears on the escutcheon of my character, thus ruining the picture of perfection, but that what I propose to do is wrong because it would be cruel to someone. The reflection that a given act would be cruel is no more inherently self-regarding than it is other-regarding. The interesting thing about the virtue considerations is that it is both.

Have I, in this sketch of possible objections to the Thesis as a form of perfectionism, overlooked some underlying source of uncomfortableness with the Thesis's perfectionistic tendency? Perhaps I have. But I think that the chief source of uncomfortableness with perfectionism as an ethical theory is with the amorphousness of the theory, the sense that it can take shapes that we would do well to shy away from. And I have tried to show that Thesis perfectionism does not necessarily have the most repugnant of those shapes. Yet it is a perfectionistic theory. It insists that the moral acceptability of actions or policies turns entirely on the extent to which they approximate the requirements of a set of standards: the closer the approximation, the more preferable the act or policy. The standards set by a perfectionistic theory need not be impossible of attainment, arbitrarily imposed, or made use of in morally questionable ways. These are simply dangers that must be avoided by those who believe, as I suspect, that the virtue considerations constitute the set of standards that govern moral acceptability.

Note

1.   John Dewey, *Human Nature and Conduct* (George Allen & Unwin, 1922), p. 7.

ON SOME VICES OF VIRTUE ETHICS
Robert B. Louden

Robert B. Louden is professor of philosophy at the University of Southern Maine. In the following excerpt, he raises a number of objections to virtue-based moral theories. For example, in emphasizing character over conduct, Louden notes, virtue-based views have difficulty dealing with moral quandaries in which we need clear guidance in deciding what to do.

It is common knowledge by now that recent philosophical and theological writing about ethics reveals a marked revival of interest in the virtues. But what exactly are the distinctive features of a so-called virtue ethics? Does it have a special contribution to make to our understanding of moral experience? Is there a price to be paid for its different perspective, and if so, is the price worth paying?

Contemporary textbook typologies of ethics still tend to divide the terrain of normative ethical theory into the teleological and deontological. Both types of theory, despite their well-defined differences, have a common focus on acts as opposed to qualities of agents. The fundamental question that both types of theory are designed to answer is: What ought I to do? What is the correct analysis and resolution of morally problematic situations? A second feature shared by teleological and deontological theories is conceptual reductionism. Both types of theory start with a primary irreducible element and then proceed to introduce secondary derivative concepts which are defined in terms of their relations to the beginning element. Modern teleologists (the majority of whom are utilitarians) begin with a concept of the good—here defined with reference to states of affairs rather than persons. After this criterion of the good is established, the remaining ethical categories are defined in terms of this starting point. Thus, according to the classic maxim, one ought always to promote the greatest good for the greatest number. Duty, in other words, is defined in terms of the element of ends—one ought always to maximize utility. The concepts of virtue and rights are also treated as derivative categories of secondary importance, definable in terms of utility. For the classic utilitarian, a right is upheld "so long as it is upon the whole advantageous to the society that it should be maintained," while virtue is construed as a "tendency to give a net increase to the aggregate quantity of happiness in all its shapes taken together."[1]

From Robert B. Louden, "On Some Vices of Virtue Ethics," *American Philosophical Quarterly* 21(3) (1984): pp. 227-236. Reprinted by permission of American Philosophical Quarterly.

For the deonotologist, on the other hand, the concept of duty is the irreducible starting point, and any attempt to define this root notion of being morally bound to do something in terms of the good to be achieved is rejected from the start. The deontologist is committed to the notion that certain acts are simply inherently right. Here the notion of the good is only a derivative category, definable in terms of the right. The good that we are to promote is right action for its own sake—duty for duty's sake. Similarly, the virtues tend to be defined in terms of pro-attitudes toward one's duties. Virtue is important, but only because it helps us do our duty.

But what about virtue ethics? What are the hallmarks of this approach to normative ethics? One problem confronting anyone who sets out to analyze the new virtue ethics in any detail is that we presently lack fully developed examples of it in the contemporary literature. Most of the work done in this genre has a negative rather than positive thrust—its primary aim is more to criticize the traditions and research programs to which it is opposed rather than to state positively and precisely what its own alternative is. A second hindrance is that the literature often has a somewhat misty antiquarian air. It is frequently said, for instance, that the Greeks advocated a virtue ethics, though what precisely it is that they were advocating is not always spelled out. In describing contemporary virtue ethics, it is therefore necessary, in my opinion, to do some detective work concerning its conceptual shape, making inferences based on the unfortunately small number of remarks that are available.

For purposes of illustration, I propose to briefly examine and expand on some key remarks made by two contemporary philosophers—Elizabeth Anscombe and Philippa Foot—whose names have often been associated with the revival of virtue movement. Anscombe, in her frequently cited article, "Modern Moral Philosophy," writes: "you can do ethics without it [viz., the notion of 'obligation' or 'morally ought'], as is shown by the example of Aristotle. It would be a great improvement if, instead of 'morally wrong,' one always named a genus such as 'untruthful,' 'unchaste,' 'unjust.'"[2] Here we find an early rallying cry for an ethics of virtue program, to be based on contemporary efforts in philosophical psychology and action theory. On the Anscombe model, strong, irreducible duty and obligation notions drop out of the picture, and are to be replaced by vices such as unchasteness and untruthfulness. But are we to take the assertion literally, and actually attempt to do moral theory without any concept of duty whatsoever? On my reading, Anscombe is not really proposing that we entirely dispose of moral oughts. Suppose one follows her advice, and replaces "morally wrong" with "untruthful," "unchaste," etc. Isn't this merely shorthand for saying that agents *ought* to be truthful and chaste, and that untruthful and unchaste acts are *morally wrong* because good agents don't perform such acts? The concept of the moral ought, in other words, seems now to be explicated in terms of what the good person would do.[3]

A similar strategy is at work in some of Foot's articles. In the Introduction to her recent collection of essays, *Virtues and Vices and Other Essays in Moral Philosophy,* she announces that one of the two major themes running throughout her work is "the thought that a sound moral philosophy should start from a theory of virtues and vices."[4] When this thought is considered in conjunction with the central argument in her article, "Morality as a System of Hypothetical Imperatives," the indication is that another virtue-based moral theory is in the making. For in this essay Foot envisions a moral community composed of an "army of volunteers," composed, that is, of agents who voluntarily commit themselves to such moral ideas as truth, justice, generosity, and kindness.[5] In a moral community of this sort, all moral imperatives become hypothetical rather than categorical: there are things an agent morally ought to do if he or she wants truth, justice, generosity, or kindness, but no things an agent morally ought to do if he or she isn't first committed to these (or other) moral ideals. On the Foot model (as presented in "Morality as a System"), what distinguishes an ethics of virtue from its competitors is that it construes the ideal moral agent as acting from a direct desire, without first believing that he or she morally ought to perform that action or have that desire. However, in a more recent paper, Foot has expressed doubts about her earlier attempts to articulate the relationship between oughts and desires. In "William Frankena's Carus Lectures" (1981), she states that "*thoughts* [my emphasis] about what is despicable or contemptible, or low, or again admirable, glorious or honourable may give us the key to the problem of rational moral action."[6] But regardless of whether she begins with desires or with thoughts, it seems clear her strategy too is not to dispense with oughts entirely, but rather to employ softer, derivative oughts.

In other words, conceptual reductionism is at work in virtue ethics too. Just as its utilitarian and deontological competitors begin with primitive concepts of the good state of affairs and the intrinsically right action respectively and then derive secondary concepts out of their starting points, so virtue ethics, beginning with a root conception of the morally good person, proceeds to introduce a different set of secondary concepts which are defined in terms of their relationship to the primitive element. Though the ordering of primitive and derivatives differs in each case, the overall strategy remains the same. Viewed from this perspective, virtue ethics is not unique at all. It has adopted the traditional mononomic strategy of normative ethics. What sets it apart from other approaches, again, is its strong agent orientation.

So for virtue ethics, the primary object of moral evaluation is not the act or its consequences, but rather the agent. And the respective conceptual starting points of agent and act-centered ethics result in other basic differences as well, which may be briefly summarized as follows. First of all, the two camps are likely to employ different models of practical reasoning. Act theorists, because they focus on discrete acts and moral quandaries, are naturally very interested in formulating decision procedures for making practical choices. The agent, in their conceptual scheme, needs a guide—hopefully a determinate decision procedure—for finding a way out of the quandary. Agent-centered ethics, on the other hand, focuses on long-term characteristic patterns of action, intentionally downplaying atomic acts and particular choice situations in the process. They are not as concerned with portraying practical reason as a rule-governed enterprise which can be applied on a case-by-case basis.

Secondly, their views on moral motivation differ. For the deontological act theorist, the preferred motive for moral action is the concept of duty itself; for the utilitarian act theorist, it is the disposition to seek the happiness of all sentient creatures. But for the virtue theorist, the preferred motivation factor is the virtues themselves (here understood nonreductionistically). The agent who correctly acts from the disposition of charity does so (according to the virtue theorist) not because it maximizes utility or because it is one's duty to do so, but rather out of a commitment to the value of charity for its own sake.

While I am sympathetic to recent efforts to recover virtue from its long-standing neglect, my purpose in this essay is not to contribute further to the campaign for virtue. Instead, I wish to take a more critical look at the phenomenon, and to ask whether there are certain important features of morality which a virtue-based ethics either handles poorly or ignores entirely. In the remainder of this essay, I shall sketch some objections which (I believe) point to genuine shortcomings of the virtue approach to ethics. My object here is not to offer an exhaustive or even thoroughly systematic critique of virtue ethics, but rather to look at certain mundane regions of the moral field and to ask first what an ethics of virtue might say about them, and second whether what it says about them seems satisfactory.

Agents vs. Acts

As noted earlier, it is a commonplace that virtue theorists focus on good and bad agents rather than on right and wrong acts. In focusing on good and bad agents, virtue theorists are thus forced to deemphasize discrete acts in favor of long-term, characteristic patterns of behavior. Several related problems arise for virtue ethics as a result of this particular conceptual commitment.

CASUISTRY AND APPLIED ETHICS

It has often been said that for virtue ethics the central question is not "what ought I to *do*?" but rather "What sort of person ought I to *be*?" However, people have always expected ethical theory to tell them something about what they ought to do, and it seems to me that virtue ethics is structurally unable to say much of anything about this issue. If I'm right, one consequence of this is that a virtue-based ethics will be particularly weak in the areas of casuistry and applied ethics. A recent reviewer of Foot's *Virtues and Vices,* for instance, notes that "one must do some shifting to gather her view on the virtues." "Surprisingly," he adds, "the studies of abortion and euthanasia are not of much use."[7] And this is odd, when one considers Foot's demonstrated interest in applied ethics in conjunction with her earlier cited prefatory remark that a "sound moral theory should start from a theory of virtues and vices." But what can a virtues and vices approach say about specific moral dilemmas? As virtue theorists from Aristotle onward have rightly emphasized, virtues are not simply dispositions to behave in specified ways, for which rules and principles can always be cited. In addition, they involve skills of perception and articulation, situation-specific "know-how," all of which are developed only through recognizing and acting on what is relevant in concrete moral contexts as they arise. These skills of moral perception and practical reason are not completely routinizable, and so cannot be transferred from agent to agent as any sort of decision procedure "package deal." Due to the very nature of the moral virtues, there is thus a very limited amount of advice on moral quandaries that one can reasonably expect from the virtue-oriented approach. We ought, of course, to do what the virtuous person would do, but it is not always easy to fathom what the hypothetical moral exemplar would do were he in our shoes, and sometimes even he will act out of character. Furthermore, if one asks him why he did what he did, or how he knew what to do, the answer—if one is offered—might not be very enlightening. One would not necessarily expect him to appeal to any rules or principles which might be of use to others.

We can say, á la Aristotle, that the virtuous agent acts for the sake of the noble (*tou kalou heneka*), that he will not do what is base or depraved, etc. But it seems to me that we cannot intelligently say things like: "The virtuous person (who acts for the sake of the noble) is also one who recognizes that all mentally deficient eight-month-old fetuses should (or should not) be aborted, that the doctor/patient principle of confidentiality must always (or not always) be respected, etc." The latter simply sounds too strange, and their strangeness stems from the fact that motives of virtue and honor cannot be fully routinized.

Virtue theory is not a problem-oriented or quandary approach to ethics: it speaks of rules and principles of action only in a derivative manner. And its derivative oughts are frequently too vague and unhelpful for persons who have not yet acquired the requisite moral insight and sensitivity. Consequently, we cannot expect it to be of great use in applied ethics and casuistry. The increasing importance of these two subfields of ethics in contemporary society is thus a strike against the move to revive virtue ethics.

TRAGIC HUMANS

Another reason for making sure that our ethical theory allows us to talk about features of acts and their results in abstraction from the agent and his conception of what he is doing is that sometimes even the best person can make the wrong choices. There are cases in which a man's choice is grounded in the best possible information, his motives honorable and his action not at all out of character. And yet his best laid plans may go sour. Aristotle, in his *Poetics,* suggests that here lies the source of tragedy: we are confronted with an eminent and respected man, "whose misfortune, however, is brought upon him not by vice *(kakia)* and depravity *(moktheira)* but by some error of judgment *(amartia)*" (1453a8–9). But every human being is morally fallible, for there is a little Oedipus in each of us. So Aristotle's point is that *regardless of character,* anyone can fall into the sort of mistake of which tragedies are made. Virtue ethics, however, since its conceptual scheme is rooted in the notion of the good person, is unable to assess correctly the occasional (inevitable) tragic outcomes of human action. . . .

INTOLERABLE ACTIONS

A third reason for insisting that our moral theory enable us to assess acts in abstraction from agents is that we need to be able to identify certain types of action which produce harms of such magnitude that they destroy the bonds of community and render (at least temporarily) the achievement of moral goods impossible. In every traditional moral community one encounters prohibitions or "barriers to action" which mark off clear boundaries in such areas as the taking of innocent life, sexual relations, and the administration of justice according to local laws and customs. Such rules are needed to teach citizens what kinds of actions are to be regarded not simply as bad (a table of vices can handle this) but as intolerable. Theorists must resort to specific lists of offenses to emphasize the fact that there are some acts which are absolutely prohibited. We cannot articulate this sense of absolute prohibition by referring merely to characteristic patterns of behavior.

In rebuttal here, the virtue theorist may reply by saying: "Virtue ethics does not need to articulate these prohibitions—let the law do it, with its list of do's and don't's." But the sense of requirement and prohibition referred to above seems to me to be at bottom inescapably moral rather than legal. Morality can (and frequently does) invoke the aid of law in such cases, but when we ask *why* there is a law against, e.g., rape or murder, the proper answer is that it is morally intolerable. To point merely to a legal convention when asked why an act is prohibited or intolerable raises more questions than it answers.

CHARACTER CHANGE

A fourth reason for insisting that a moral theory be able to assess acts in abstraction from agents and their conception of what they're doing is that people's moral characters may sometimes change. Xenophon, toward the beginning of his *Memorabilia* (I.II.21), cites an unknown poet who says: "Ah, but a good man is at one time noble (*esthlos*), at another wicked (*kakos*)." Xenophon himself agrees with the poet ". . . many alleged (*phaskonton*) philosophers may say: A just (*dikaios*) man can never become unjust; a self-controlled (*sophron*) man can never become wanton (*hubristes*); in fact no one having learned any kind of knowledge (*mathesis*) can become ignorant of it. I do not hold this view. . . . For I see that, just as poetry is forgotten unless it is often repeated, so instruction, when no longer heeded, fades from the mind."

Xenophon was a practical man who was not often given to speculation, but he arrived at his position on character change in the course of his defense of Socrates. One of the reasons Socrates got into trouble, Xenophon believed, was due to his contact with Critias and Alcibiades during their youth. For of all Athenians, "none wrought so many evils to the *polis*." However, Xenophon reached the conclusion that Socrates should not be blamed for the disappearance of his good influence once these two had ceased their close contact with him.

If skills can become rusty, it seems to me that virtues can too. Unless we stay in practice we run the risk of losing relative proficiency. We probably can't forget them completely (in part because the opportunities for exercising virtues are so pervasive in everyday life), but we can lose a certain sensitivity. People do become morally insensitive, relatively speaking—missing opportunities they once would have noticed, although perhaps when confronted with a failure they might recognize that they had failed, showing at least that they hadn't literally "forgotten the difference between right and wrong." If the moral virtues are acquired habits rather than innate gifts, it is always possible that one can lose relative proficiency in these habits. Also, just as one's interests and skills sometimes change over the course of a life as new perceptions and influences take hold, it seems too that aspects of our moral characters can likewise alter. (Consider religious conversion experiences.) Once we grant the possibility of such changes in moral character, the need for a more "character free" way of assessing action becomes evident. Character is not a permanent fixture, but rather plastic. A more reliable yardstick is sometimes needed.

MORAL BACKSLIDING

Finally, the focus on good and bad agents rather than on right and wrong actions may lead to a peculiar sort of moral backsliding. Because the emphasis in agent ethics is on long-term, characteristic patterns of behavior, its advocates run the risk of overlooking occasional lies or acts of selfishness on the ground that such performances are mere temporary aberrations— acts out of character. Even the just man may on occasion act unjustly, so why haggle over specifics? It is unbecoming to a virtue theorist to engage in such pharisaic calculations. But once he commits himself to the view that assessments of moral worth are not simply a matter of whether we have done the right thing, backsliding may result.

I have argued that there is a common source behind each of these vices. The virtue theorist is committed to the claim that the primary object of moral evaluation is not the act or its consequences but rather the agent— specifically, those character traits of the agent which are judged morally relevant. This is not to say that virtue ethics does not ever address the issue of right and wrong actions, but rather that it can only do so in a derivative manner. Sometimes, however, it is clearly acts rather than agents which ought to be the primary focus of moral evaluation. . . .

Notes

1. The rights definition is from Bentham's "Anarchical Fallacies," reprinted in A. I. Melden (ed.), *Human Rights* (Belmont, CA: Wadsworth, 1970), p 32. The virtue definition is from Bentham's "The Nature of Virtue," reprinted in Bhiku Parekh (ed.), *Bentham's Political Thought* (New York: Barnes and Noble, 1973), p. 89.
2. G. E. M. Anscombe, "Modern Moral Philosophy," *Philosophy,* Vol. 33 (1958), pp. 1–19; reprinted in J. J. Thomson and G. Dworkin (eds.), *Ethics* (New York: Harper & Row, 1968), p. 196.
3. Anscombe appears to believe also that moral oughts and obligations only make sense in a divine law context, which would mean that only divine command theories of ethics employ valid concepts of obligation. I see no reason to accept such a narrow definition of duty. See pp. 192, 202 of "Modern Moral Philosophy." For one argument against her restrictive divine law approach to moral obligation, see Alan Donagan, *The Theory of Morality* (Chicago: University of Chicago Press, 1977), p. 3.
4. Philippa Foot, *Virtues and Vices and Other Essays in Moral Philosophy* (Berkeley and Los Angeles: University of California Press, 1978), p. xi.
5. Foot, "Morality as a System of Hypothetical Imperatives," *The Philosophical Review,* Vol. 81 (1972), pp. 305–16; reprinted in *Virtues and Vices,* pp. 157–73. See especially the long concluding footnote, added in 1977.
6. Foot, "William Frankena's Carus Lectures," *The Monist,* Vol. 64 (1981), p. 31.
7. Arthur Flemming, "Reviving the Virtues." Review of Foot's *Virtues and Vices* and James Wallace's *Virtues and Vices, Ethics,* Vol. 90 (1980), p. 588.